THE NEO-VYGOTSKIAN APPROACH TO CHILD DEVELOPMENT

For the first time, the neo-Vygotskian approach to child development is introduced to English-speaking readers. Russian followers of Vygotsky have elaborated his ideas into a theory that integrates cognitive, motivational, and social aspects of child development with an emphasis on the role of children's activity as mediated by adults in their development. This theory has become the basis for an innovative analysis of periods in child development and of the mechanism of children's transitions from one period to the next. In this book, the discussion of the neo-Vygotskians' approach to child development is supported by a review of their empirical data, much of which have never before been available to English-speaking readers. The discussion is also supported by a review of recent empirical findings of Western researchers, which are highly consistent with the neo-Vygotskian analysis of child development.

Yuriy V. Karpov is Professor and Associate Dean at the Graduate School of Education and Psychology of Touro College. He did his undergraduate and graduate studies and then worked as a faculty member at the School of Psychology of Moscow State University, the center of Vygotsky-based studies in the former Soviet Union. His studies on the implementation of Vygotsky's ideas in education, psychological assessment, and the analysis of child development have been published as books, chapters, and journal articles in Russian, English, and Spanish.

THE NEO-VYGOTSKIAN APPROACH TO CHILD DEVELOPMENT

YURIY V. KARPOV

Touro College

CAMBRIDGE
UNIVERSITY PRESS

CAMBRIDGE UNIVERSITY PRESS
Cambridge, New York, Melbourne, Madrid, Cape Town, Singapore, São Paulo, Delhi

Cambridge University Press
32 Avenue of the Americas, New York, NY 10013-2473, USA

www.cambridge.org
Information on this title: www.cambridge.org/9780521696135

First published 2005
Reprinted 2006
First paperback edition 2006
Reprinted 2007, 2008 (twice), 2009

Printed in the United States of America

A catalog record for this publication is available from the British Library.

Library of Congress Cataloging in Publication Data
Karpov, Yuriy V. 1957–
The neo-Vygotskian approach to child development / Yuriy V. Karpov.
p. cm.
Includes bibliographical references and index.
ISBN 0-521-83012-5
I. Vygotskii, L. S. (Lev Semenovitch), 1896–1934. 2. Child development. I. Title.
HQ767.9.K363 2006
305.231 – dc22   2005006331

ISBN 978-0-521-83012-6 hardback
ISBN 978-0-521-69613-5 paperback

The book is dedicated to my parents, Viktor Ioffe and Sofya Karpova.

Contents

CONTENTS

Figures

Acknowledgments

My interest in, and knowledge of, the neo-Vygotskian approach to child development formed during my 17-year affiliation with the School of Psychology of Moscow State University, which was the center of Vygotsky-based research in the former Soviet Union. I am deeply indebted to my former teachers, especially to Daniel Elkonin, Piotr Galperin, Alexey Leontiev, Alexander Luria, and Nina Talyzina, whose writings, lectures, and generous sharing of their ideas with students and younger colleagues have shaped my entire professional life.

I have a special debt to John Borkowski, Steven Warren, and Carl Haywood, whose help and support made it possible for me to restart my scientific career after my immigration to the United States in 1991.

My efforts to produce this book have benefited from all kinds of support from my colleagues and Dean Anthony Polemeni at the Graduate School of Education and Psychology of Touro College. My deepest gratitude must be reserved for my friend and colleague Ronald Lehrer, who provided extremely useful scholarly consultations, commentary, and suggestions on my analysis and presentation of the material.

ACKNOWLEDGMENTS

I am also grateful to anonymous reviewers, who reviewed an early draft of the manuscript for Cambridge University Press and provided very helpful feedback.

I express my gratitude to Mikhail Akopyan for the design of figures that illustrate the book.

The work for this book could not have been completed without the understanding and moral support of my wife Lora.

Finally, I want to thank Philip Laughlin, the book editor; Nicole M. McClenic, the project manager; Elizabeth Budd, the copy editor; and other staff at Cambridge University Press and TechBooks who dedicated their expertise, time, and effort to the preparation of this book for publication.

Introduction The Problem of Determinants and Mechanisms of Child Development; The Structure and Content of the Book

Having reviewed studies in the field of developmental psychology, Hetherington and McIntyre (1975) came to a sad conclusion:

> Perhaps the most marked feature in the field of developmental psychology is the lack of satisfactory theories of child development. Many investigators seem to have coped with this problem by doing completely atheoretical research; others are busy patching, mending, and modifying old theories; and some are building mini-theories that deal with very restricted areas of behavior. Although some modest theoretical convergence between areas is occurring, notably in the increased awareness of the role of cognitive factors in a variety of behaviors, one comes away from a review of the literature feeling that developmental psychologists working in different areas don't talk to each other.... The literature is replete with highly redundant, often trivial research or "single shot" studies that add little to our understanding of developmental processes. It seems to be an inefficient approach to the study of children's behavior.... The current need is for a careful analysis, synthesis, and evaluation of the information we now have and an attempt to evolve theories which will result in more systematic and fruitful strategies of research. (pp. 125–126)

This comment on the absence of a satisfactory theory of child development in Western developmental psychology of the 1970s is also

1

applicable to the current state of developmental psychology in the West. In contemporary Western psychology, there are detailed studies of the development of perception, memory, cognition, and other mental processes in each period of the child's life. What is missing, however, is a powerful theory of child development. Dissatisfaction with existing theories among contemporary developmental and child psychologists reveals itself in the advocacy by some of reductionist approaches in which, for example, developmental biology is suggested as a "metatheory for cognitive development" (Bjorklund, 1997, p. 144).

What are the reasons for this broad disappointment with existing theories of child development? The kernel of any theory of child development is the description of *the determinant of development* (that is, the major factor that leads to development) and the explanation of *the mechanism of development* (that is, the analysis of how the suggested determinant of development leads to development). What follows is a discussion of how determinants and mechanisms of child development are presented and explained in the most popular Western theories of child development.

Approaches to Determinants and Mechanisms of Child Development in Western Psychology

Theories of child development in Western psychology can be classified into three general approaches based on the suggested determinants of child development (Cole, 1992).

THE NATIVIST (MATURATIONAL) APPROACH
TO CHILD DEVELOPMENT

Early nativists (Bühler, 1918/1930; Gesell, 1933; Hall, 1904) saw genetically predetermined maturation as the major (if not only) determinant of children's development. According to Bühler (1918/1930), for example, even criminal behavior is the result of "bad" heredity. Although most contemporary nativists would not take such an extreme stand as to attribute criminal behavior to inherited criminal predispositions, their explanations of the determinants of child development are still not far from those of early nativists. Scarr (1992), for example, although not denying the role of environment in child development, claims that *how* the environment influences children's development depends on children's genotypes rather than on the characteristics and quality of their environment:

> Ordinary differences between families have little effect on children's development...Children's outcomes do not depend on whether parents take children to the ball game or to a museum so much as they depend on genetic transmission, on plentiful opportunities, and on having a good enough environment that *supports children's development to become themselves.* (p. 15, emphasis mine)

Similar positions have been taken by those nativists who derive their models of development from the principles of evolutionary natural selection (Cosmides & Tooby, 1987, 1994; Geary, 1995). Geary (1995), for example, holds that "the biologically primary cognitive abilities," which have been selected for in evolution, "appear to orient the child to relevant features of the environment and guide the processing of those features" (p. 27).

The major problem with the nativists' views is that, when discussing neo-formations in the development of children's cognition, personality, and so forth, they do not "answer the question: Where do these wonderful things *really* come from?" (Richardson, 1998, p. 79). This shortcoming of nativist explanations becomes especially clear in the case of nativist stage-by-stage theories of development. Why, for example, does a child transit from the oral to anal stage of development in Freud's (1920/1955) developmental model, or from the "trust versus mistrust" to "autonomy versus shame and doubt" stage in Erikson's (1963, 1968) model? The statement that these transitions primarily have been the result of maturation can hardly be accepted as a satisfactory explanation of the mechanism of development. In fact, "invoking the concept of innateness amounts to abdicating responsibility for explaining development" (Johnston, 1994, p. 721).

THE BEHAVIORIST (ENVIRONMENTAL) APPROACH TO CHILD DEVELOPMENT

The behaviorists' view (Skinner, 1953; Thorndike, 1914; Watson, 1925) of the determinant of child development is just the opposite of the nativist position in this respect. For early behaviorists, Scarr's (1992) statement that children develop "to become themselves" (p. 15) would not make any sense because they considered a newborn child to be a tabula rasa, a blank slate, and attributed all the child's developmental accomplishments to the child's environment. A classic quote from Watson (1925) is revealing in this respect: "Give me a dozen healthy infants, well-formed, and my own specified world to bring them up in and I'll guarantee to take any one at random and train him to become any type of specialist I might select" (p. 82). Although later behaviorists would avoid making such provocative statements, their position in regard to the determinant of child development is very similar to the position of early behaviorists (see, for example, Bijou, 1976, 1992).

In contrast to nativists, behaviorists not only describe the determinant of development but also explain the mechanism of children's development. For them, the development of new responses in children is the result of conditioning, that is, the creation of new associations between stimuli and responses as the result of practice and reinforcement. It turned out, however, that the mechanism of conditioning could not explain the development of new behavioral patterns, even in animals (Köhler, 1930; Tolman & Honzik, 1930), not to mention children. Therefore, since the 1960s, behaviorist theories of development have lost their popularity among American psychologists (for one of a few exceptions, see Bijou, 1976, 1992).

As Gesell (1933), with a touch of sarcasm, characterized the behaviorist approach to child development, it suggests "that the individual is fabricated out of the conditioning pattern" (p. 230). This characteristic of behaviorism accentuates one of the major shortcomings of this approach: Behaviorists consider children to be passive recipients of environmental influences rather then active contributors to their development. Similar criticism, however, can be applied to the nativist views of child development, including the view of Gesell himself. Whereas behaviorists tend to view children as "fabricated" by the environment, nativists tend to view them as "fabricated" out of genetically predetermined maturation. An important accomplishment of the constructivist approach to child development is that it overcomes the nativists' and behaviorists' view of the child as a passive object of internal or external development-generating forces.

THE CONSTRUCTIVIST (INTERACTIONAL) APPROACH
TO CHILD DEVELOPMENT

The major representative of this approach is the theory of Piaget (1936/1952, 1955, 1923/1959). Piaget holds that the major determinant of children's development is their activity aimed at the exploration of the external world. In the course of this activity, children come across new environmental phenomena and try to "assimilate" them into their mental schemas (that is, into their existing ways of thinking). These new environmental phenomena, however, often do not fit exactly into children's mental schemas, which creates "disequilibrium" between children's mental schemas and the external world. Therefore, children need to "accommodate" their mental schemas to

5

the new environmental phenomena, which leads to the development of these schemas and their integration into new cognitive structures. As a result, temporary "equilibrium" between children's mental schemas and the external world is achieved, which lasts until children come across new environmental phenomena that create a new state of disequilibrium. Thus, Piaget views children as active "constructors" of their cognition.

Although Piaget's idea of equilibration (that is, the reaching of equilibrium between children's mental schemas and the external world) as the mechanism of development explains the development of mental schemas in children, this explanation has a weak point. Indeed, what makes children, according to Piaget, leave their comfortable state of equilibrium (that is, the state of adaptation to their environment) and explore the external world, which will inevitably lead to the state of disequilibrium? Piaget (1936/1952) answers this question by assuming that children's exploratory activity is driven by their curiosity, a quality with which children are born and that is similar to the "curiosity" of research scientists. In chapter 3, the limitations of such an explanation for children's exploratory activity are discussed in some detail. At this point, I merely note that not all the children have been shown to demonstrate such innate "curiosity" toward the external world (Bowlby, 1951; Kistyakovskaya, 1970; Rozengard-Pupko, 1948; Spitz, 1945, 1946).

Even more problematic is Piaget's explanation of the mechanism of children's stage-by-stage cognitive development. Indeed, Piaget holds that microdevelopmental changes in children's cognition (that is, the development of mental schemas) eventually results in a major qualitative shift in their cognitive development (that is, in their transition to a new stage of cognitive development). Discussing the mechanism of such transitions, however, he could not give a more satisfactory explanation of this mechanism than stating that these transitions "become necessary with development" (Piaget, 1971b, p. 9). Piaget

(1971b) himself formulated the weakness of such an explanation: "This solution is difficult to prove. It is even difficult to express or to explain" (p. 9). Everybody would probably agree that a solution that is difficult to prove, express, and explain can hardly be accepted as a satisfactory solution.

Attempts to explain children's stage-by-stage transitions have been made within neo-Piagetian theories of child development. These explanations, however, typically refer to genetically predetermined maturational processes as the mechanism of such transitions. For Pascual-Leone (1970) and Case (1985), for example, stage-by-stage transitions are the result of maturation of an innate information-processing capacity. For Karmiloff-Smith (1993), these transitions occur because of innately predetermined "redescriptions" of children's representations. Thus, in their attempts to support Piaget's theory of stage-by-stage development by suggesting the genetically predetermined maturational processes as the mechanism of such development, the neo-Piagetians take the stand of "nativist predeterminism that Piaget was striving to overcome" (Richardson, 1998, p. 168).

THE LACK OF A SATISFACTORY EXPLANATION OF THE MECHANISM OF CHILD DEVELOPMENT AS THE MAJOR SHORTCOMING OF NATIVISM, BEHAVIORISM, AND CONSTRUCTIVISM

I suggest that there are two major reasons for the lack of a satisfactory explanation of the mechanism of child development in nativism, behaviorism, and constructivism. The first is that these approaches are built around inadequate understanding of the determinants of child development. Indeed, despite substantial differences between the discussed approaches, they have an important point in common: Their founders and advocates do not see a *principal* difference between the development of animals and humans. To be sure, they are far from claiming that the outcomes and accomplishments of child development are comparable to those of animal development. The determinants of child development as they describe them, however, can easily be applied to the explanations of animal development. In nativism, animal development would be attributed to genetically predetermined maturation, in behaviorism to environmental influences, and in constructivism to animals' activity aimed at the exploration of the external world. If we assume (as is elaborated in this book) that the determinants of development are principally different in animals and humans, this may explain to a large extent the failure of nativists, behaviorists, and constructivists to give a satisfactory answer to the question of the mechanism of child development.

The second suggested reason for the failure of these approaches to give a satisfactory explanation of the mechanism of child development is that the proposed theories address, as a rule, just one of the aspects of such development without considering the development of the whole child. For example, psychoanalytic theories (Freud, 1954; Erikson, 1963) address the development of children's personality, whereas Piaget (1936/1952, 1955, 1923/1959) and neo-Piagetian theorists (Case, 1985; Karmiloff-Smith, 1993) emphasize children's cognitive development. Several attempts have been made to "expand" existing theories of child development to explain certain aspects of child development other than those addressed in these theories. Kohlberg (1984), for example, used Piaget's theory of cognitive development as the foundation for his model of moral development in children. Similarly, Clayton and Birren (1980) used Erikson's (1963, 1968) theory of personality to explain certain aspects of cognitive development. These "expanded" developmental models, however, have not resulted in a holistic view of child development because they do not describe interrelationships of different aspects of child development. Rather, a "secondary" aspect of development is derived in these models from the expansion of the "central" developmental aspect.

The Neo-Vygotskian Approach to Child Development as an Alternative to the Nativist, Behaviorist, and Constructivist Approaches

The goal of this book is to introduce to English-speaking readers the neo-Vygotskian approach to child development, which was founded by Vygotsky and elaborated by his Russian followers.[1] I see two major differences between this approach and the approaches discussed earlier in this Introduction. The first pertains to an innovative view of Vygotsky and his followers on the determinant of child development. As I discussed, nativists, behaviorists, and constructivists do not see a principal difference between the determinants of animal and human development. In contrast, Vygotsky and his followers argue that these determinants are principally different because of the dominant role of the social environment in human development. This statement needs a more detailed discussion to avoid possible misunderstanding.

To be sure, none of the prominent scholars whose theories I discussed would disregard the role of social environment in child development. Nevertheless, although nativists, behaviorists, and constructivists "implicitly or explicitly suggest that the environment side of the equation can be partitioned into culture or social factors versus the physical environment, these distinctions are not well developed in their writings" (Cole, 1992, p. 735). In fact, they consider social

---

[1] Russian followers of Vygotsky were not the only ones who elaborated his ideas in their research and writings. In particular, a number of American scholars (Berk, Cole, Rogoff, Valsiner, and Wertsch, to name just a few) contributed much to further elaboration of some of Vygotsky's notions. It has been Russian neo-Vygotskians, however, who have elaborated Vygotsky's contentions into a theory that describes and explains the stage-by-stage development from birth through adolescence of children in industrialized societies. Therefore, the definition of this theory as *the* neo-Vygotskian approach to child development, from my point of view, is legitimate.

phenomena and physical phenomena to be two components of environment, which are more or less equally important for children's development and which facilitate their development in similar ways. This statement will probably evoke objections from those Piagetians who would argue against Bruner's (1985) characterization of Piaget's approach as that in which "a lone child struggles single-handed to strike some equilibrium between assimilating the world to himself or himself to the world" (p. 25). Doise (1988), for example, emphasized Piaget's idea that cognitive conflict arising between peers in the course of their interaction results in disequilibrium, which turns on equilibration as the mechanism of development. From this perspective, Piaget does admit an important role of social interactions in cognitive development. The point is, however, that the Piagetian mechanism of equilibration in the case of peer interaction is not any different from the equilibration in which the child gets involved when dealing with a new physical object. In other words, in Piaget's developmental model, interactions with peers contribute to the child's state of disequilibrium, but not to the child's construction of a new, more advanced mental schema. Thus, to reach a new state of equilibrium, the Piagetian child does struggle, using Bruner's words, as "a lone" and "single-handed" child.

According to Vygotsky and his Russian followers, social environment is not just a context in which children develop and to which they struggle to adapt. Rather than that, adults, as representatives of children's social environment, supply them with so-called psychological tools, which, being acquired and internalized, come to mediate children's mental processes. From this perspective, human mental processes are not independently "constructed" by children (as constructivists would say), nor do they "unfold" as a result of children's maturation (as nativists would hold), nor are they inculcated into children by adults (as behaviorists would hold). Rather than that, the development of mental processes is *mediated*[2] by adults in the context of social interactions with children. Thus, Vygotsky and his followers consider mediation in the context of social interactions to be the major determinant of children's development.

The second important difference between the neo-Vygotskian approach to child development and the alternative approaches by nativists, behaviorists, and constructivists is that Vygotsky and his followers view the development of the child as a whole person. Rather than considering the development of children's cognition, personality, and their social development as separate processes, they have integrated these processes into a holistic model of child development. The innovative view of the neo-Vygotskians on the determinant of child development and their holistic approach to the developmental process made it possible for them to suggest a new explanation for the mechanism of child stage-by-stage development and to describe the stage-by-stage development from birth through adolescence of children in industrialized societies.

The Structure and Content of the Book

The structure and content of the book reflect my desire to present the neo-Vygotskian approach to child development in a comprehensible and coherent fashion so that the book will be useful and interesting to both experts and novices in the field of Vygotsky-based research.

Chapter 1 is devoted to the analysis of the classic theory of Vygotsky. Despite the translation of practically all of Vygotsky's works into English, as well as the availability of numerous reviews of his theory by Western psychologists, Western readers often misunderstand

---

[2] The notion of mediation is discussed in detail in chapters 1 and 2.

his theory. An obvious reason for these misunderstandings (some of which are discussed in the first and second chapters) is that Vygotsky did not sufficiently elaborate many of his ideas. There is, however, another reason for these misunderstandings. Many reviewers present Vygotsky's theory as a set of separate ideas (such as the ideas of mediation, psychological tools, higher mental processes, zone of proximal development, scientific concepts, etc.) without showing (or even understanding) that these ideas are interrelated as basic components of Vygotsky's holistic theory. Therefore, one cannot subscribe, for example, to Vygotsky's idea of the zone of proximal development while disregarding his ideas of mediation and psychological tools (which often occurs in Vygotsky-based approaches to instruction developed by American educational psychologists). Explication of the holistic nature of Vygotsky's theory is the major goal of the first chapter.

Chapter 2 is devoted to the analysis of the elaboration of Vygotsky's theory by his Russian colleagues and followers (Elkonin, Galperin, Leontiev, Zaporozhets, and others) into the so-called activity theory of child development. Despite the translation of the major works of the founders of activity theory into English, as well as reviews of the theory by Western scholars, this theory remains poorly understood by the majority of English-speaking readers. One of the major reasons for this is the complexity of activity theory, which has a solid philosophical foundation and includes different levels of scientific analysis from meta-psychological to methodological. Even among the Western reviewers of this theory, one can find opposing views of the relationships between activity theory and the classical theory of Vygotsky. For example, Gauvain (2001) holds that activity theory was founded by Vygotsky (p. 48), whereas Kozulin (1986) insists that the succession from Vygotsky's approach to activity theory is just a "myth" (p. 264).

In discussing activity theory, I have set two major goals for myself. First, I have tried to introduce this theory in a "reader-friendly" manner, doing my best to avoid overly complex philosophical and meta-theoretical discussions without reducing the quality of the analysis. I want to mention in this respect that A. Leontiev, the major founder of activity theory, when presenting this theory to students at Moscow State University, did it in "simple words," with the use of both scientific and everyday-life examples to illustrate his presentation. The second goal I have had in mind when presenting activity theory has been to explain this theory as a logical and internally consistent elaboration of Vygotsky's approach, that is, as the *neo-Vygotskian approach*. Thus, I disagree with both those who do not see important differences between the views of Vygotsky and his Russian followers and those who erect a wall between these views.

Chapters 3–7 are devoted to the neo-Vygotskian analysis of periods in development of children in industrialized societies. When discussing children's development in each of the periods, I have paid special attention to the analysis of how children's development in one period prepares them for the transition to the next period (that is, to the analysis of *the mechanism* of child development). In these chapters, readers will find much empirical data collected by Russian researchers about children's development in each of the periods, much of which has never been available to English-speaking readers. The discussion is also supported by a review of recent empirical findings of Western researchers, which turn out to be highly consistent with the neo-Vygotskian analysis of child development in different periods.

The neo-Vygotskian approach to child development was developed and elaborated by Vygotsky's colleagues and students. Most of them worked as a team at the School of Psychology of Moscow State University, where I spent 17 years as an undergraduate and graduate student and as a faculty member. During my study and work there, I became a devoted follower of the neo-Vygotskian approach. In writing this book, however, I have attempted to present the approach in a nonbiased fashion, pointing out those of the neo-Vygotskians' contentions that still remain at the level of theoretical speculation or that can even be disputed. The most disputable contention of the neo-Vygotskians is their thesis of the minimal, if any, role of heredity in child development. Special analysis of this neo-Vygotskian contention is provided in the **Conclusion**.

1 Vygotsky's Approach to Child Development

The basic idea of Vygotsky that underlies his approach to child development is that its determinants are principally different from the determinants of animals' development. Vygotsky holds that the role of mental processes in both animals and humans is to serve their practical activity (Vygotsky & Luria, 1930/1993). The practical activity of humans, however, is principally different from the practical activity of animals. Animals live in a natural environment, and the goal of their activity is adaptation to that environment. In the course of evolution and natural selection, each species of animal has developed adaptive mechanisms (instincts) that are genetically transmitted from one generation to the next. The behavior of lower animals (invertebrates) is predominantly of an instinctive nature. Vertebrate animals, in addition to instinctive forms of behavior, demonstrate many learned behavioral patterns, which are called conditioned reflexes. In contrast to instincts, which are "the means of adaptation to such environmental conditions that are more or less permanent and stable," conditioned reflexes are "a much more flexible, delicate, and perfected mechanism of adaptation to the environment, which deals with the accommodation of inherited instincts to the animal's individual, specific

15

environmental conditions" (Vygotsky & Luria, 1930/1993, pp. 24–25). The formation of conditioned reflexes in the course of individual learning represents "a new step" (Vygotsky & Luria, 1930/1993, p. 24) in the development of mechanisms of animals' adaptive behavior. Vygotsky, however, indicates that, rather than creating new reactions in animals, their learning

> just combines inherited reactions and creates new conditioned connections between inherited reactions and environmental stimuli. Thus, this new step in the development of behavior is built upon the previous step [instincts]. Any conditioned reflex is nothing else but inherited reaction changed by the environmental conditions. (Vygotsky & Luria, 1930/1993, p. 24)

The highest level of the development of mechanisms of animals' adaptive behavior is associated with their use of tools. Although the use of tools can sometimes be observed in various vertebrate animals, this type of behavior is most typical of apes. Vygotsky (1930) was highly impressed by Köhler's (1930) study demonstrating that chimpanzees frequently use and even create tools to solve everyday life problems. For example, in one of Köhler's observations, an ape was trying to reach a fruit that was placed outside his cage. Initially, the ape would try to grasp the fruit or to reach it with one of the reeds, which were inside the cage, but these attempts turned out to be unsuccessful because the fruit was too far from the cage. After a while, the ape "gave up" and resorted to playing with the reeds. In the course of the play, he happened to pose two reeds end to end. Immediately, he put the end of the thinner reed into the end of the thicker reed, ran to the cage bars, and used this composed long reed to obtain the fruit.

This example illustrates a qualitative difference between tool-mediated animal behavior on the one hand and their instincts and conditioned reflexes on the other. In contrast to instincts, tool-mediated behavior is not inherited, and, in contrast to conditioned reflexes, this behavior is not learned via trial-and-error procedure. As Vygotsky wrote, "When solving a problem, an ape either makes 100% of mistakes, that is, cannot solve the problem at all, or, having found the correct solution, he solves the problem promptly and surely with no mistakes at all" (Vygotsky & Luria, 1930/1993, p. 52). Thus, an ape seems to come to the right solution as a result of "mental trials" (Vygotsky & Luria, 1930/1993, p. 51), which indicates that the level of development of apes' mental processes is qualitatively different from that of lower animals.

Köhler's (1930) study with the apes was especially important for Vygotsky because he, after C. Darwin, F. Engels, B. Franklin, K. Marx, G. Plekhanov, and other scholars and philosophers, considered the use of tools to be the major characteristic of human activity. Therefore, he viewed the creation and use of tools by apes as "a precondition for historical development of humans [which] can be found as far back as in the animal period of development of our ancestors" (Vygotsky, 1930, p. VI). In contrast to C. Darwin, however, Vygotsky (1930) emphasized that there is a principal difference between the use of tools by the apes and humans: "The use of tools by the apes...does not play any significant role in their adaptation to the environment" (p. X). As opposed to this, the entire practical (labor) activity of humans is mediated by tools: "The use of tools, which is the basis of human labor, as is generally known, is the distinctive feature of humans' adaptation to the environment, which makes them different from other animals" (Vygotsky, 1930, p. V).

Tools as Mediators of Human Mental Processes

As just discussed, even episodic use of tools by apes is associated with a new level of mental processes, which are qualitatively different from the mental processes of lower animals. Vygotsky's basic assumption is that the *systematic* use of tools, which mediate the entire range of human activity, requires a principally new level of mental processes that serve this activity. To describe this new level of human mental processes, Vygotsky draws an analogy between practical and mental activities of humans. The major characteristic of human mental processes is that they, just like human labor, are mediated by tools. These, however, are special, psychological tools such as language, concepts, signs, and symbols. Human babies are not born with tools of labor (hammers, spades, etc.) in their hands. These tools are invented by human society, and children acquire and master them. The same is true of psychological tools, which reflect the accumulated experience of humankind. Rather than being born with such tools, children acquire and master them. Having been mastered by children, these psychological tools come to mediate their mental processes. Specifically human mental processes, which are mediated by tools, were called higher mental processes by Vygotsky to distinguish them from lower mental processes, with which children are born and which are specific to both young children and animals.

Thus, according to Vygotsky, not only are mental processes of animals and humans qualitatively different but, more important, the laws of their development are different. The development of lower mental processes of any animal is predetermined by the mechanisms of adaptation that the species to which this animal belongs has developed as a result of evolution and natural selection. A wolf cub will always grow into a wolf. The development of higher mental processes of a human child, rather than being predetermined, is the result of his or her mastery of psychological tools that represent the history of human culture into which the child is born. As Vygotsky wrote,

> the use and "invention" of tools by humanlike apes crowns the organic development of behavior in evolution and paves the way for the transition of all development to take place along new paths, creating the basic psychological prerequisite for the historical development of behavior.... In child development, along with the

processes of organic growth and maturation, the second path of development is clearly distinguished. This is the cultural development
of behavior, which is based on the mastery of tools of cultural behavior and thinking. (Vygotsky & Luria, 1930/1993, p. 19)

Children's mastery of psychological tools, which leads to the development of their higher mental processes, is a process that has two
components. The first deals with an adult's handing over a new psychological tool to the child and mediating the child's mastery of it. In contrast to Piaget (1970), who believed that children develop new mental
processes as a result of independent exploration of the environment,
Vygotsky held that, being products of human culture, psychological
tools should be taught to children by representatives of this culture.
Indeed, social progress, in general, comes about when every new generation receives, ready-made, the essence of knowledge accumulated
by previous generations. Nobody would expect a new generation to
reinvent tools of labor that were invented by previous generations. The
same is true of psychological tools that serve as mediators of human
mental processes. Therefore, the starting point in the development
of a new higher mental process in children can be found in the
situation of their interpersonal communication with adults. Vygotsky
(1981a) wrote:

> Any function [mental process] in the child's cultural development
> appears twice, or on two planes. First it appears on the social plane,
> and then on the psychological plane. First it appears between people
> as an interpsychological category, and then within the child as an
> intrapsychological category. This is equally true with regard to vol-
> untary attention, logical memory, the formation of concepts, and the
> development of volition. (p. 163)

The second component of the process of the child's mastery of psychological tools deals with the internalization of these tools. When
adults are presenting a new psychological tool to the child, they

inevitably "exteriorize" this tool and present it to the child in the form of an external device. The child appropriates this tool and uses it initially in the same form of an external device as it was presented. As the child increasingly masters the tool, it gets internalized and turns into an internal mediator of the child's mental processes. As Vygotsky (1981a) indicated,

> any higher mental function [process] necessarily goes through an external stage in its development because it is a social function.... When we speak of a process, "external" means "social." Any higher mental function was external because it was social at some point before becoming an internal, truly mental function. (p. 162)

Vygotsky's Notion of Mediation as the Determinant of Child Development

The analysis in the previous section of Vygotsky's ideas of the development of higher mental processes leads to the conclusion that he considered mediation to be the major determinant of child development, with mediation being a two-component process: Adults *mediate* the child's acquisition and mastery of new psychological tools, which get internalized and come to *mediate* the child's mental processes. These two components of the process of mediation are interconnected, and the process of development of a child's new, higher mental process can be presented as follows. In the course of interpersonal communication, an adult presents to the child a new psychological tool in the form of an external device and mediates the child's appropriation and mastery of this tool. As the child masters the tool, it gets internalized and turns into an internal mediator of the child's mental process. Simultaneously, the adult is less and less involved in mediating the child's mastery of this tool. As a result, the child transits from the use of the external psychological tool as mediated by the adult to the independent use of

20

the internal psychological tool, which indicates the completion of the development of a new higher mental process.

Vygotsky used his notion of mediation to describe the development of such higher mental processes as categorized perception, intentional (or mediated) memory, verbal thinking, self-regulation, and others. Vygotsky himself did not classify into broader classes different mental processes and types of mediation that lead to the development of these processes. The use of the terminology of cognitive science (Borkowski & Kurtz, 1987; Brown, 1987; Brown, Bransford, Ferrara, & Campione, 1983; Brown & DeLoache, 1978; Flavell, 1976; Kluwe, 1987), however, makes it possible to distinguish two major types of mental processes (and, accordingly, two types of mediation) described in Vygotsky's works. The first type comprises so-called cognitive processes (the processes of perception, memory, thinking, and so on). Vygotsky's ideas in regard to mediation of the development of these processes into higher mental processes can be defined as *cognitive mediation*. The second type of mental processes comprises those that are responsible for control and regulation of cognitive processes. In contemporary cognitive psychology, these processes have been called metacognitive (executive) processes. Therefore, Vygotsky's ideas in regard to mediation of the development of these processes can be defined as *metacognitive mediation*. What follows are two examples that illustrate Vygotsky's ideas of cognitive and metacognitive mediation as the determinant of the development of higher mental processes.[1]

---

[1] I am aware of the relativity of the distinction between metacognitive and cognitive mediation in Vygotsky's works. This relativity is partially due to the fact that cognitive and metacognitive processes are not clearly differentiated in cognitive science (Brown, 1987; Kluwe, 1987) and also because a sharp separation of these processes may not be justifiable (Kluwe, 1987). As indicated, Vygotsky himself did not differentiate explicitly between what I call cognitive and metacognitive mediation. Thus, discussing the acquisition of scientific concepts (the major type of cognitive mediation of pupils that I analyze in chapter 6), Vygotsky also pointed out "metacognitive" outcomes of such acquisition: "Reflective consciousness comes to the child through the portals of scientific concepts" (Vygotsky, 1934/1986, p. 171).

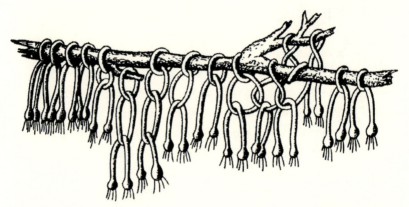

Figure 1.1. A quipu. Reprinted from Leontiev, 1959, p. 325. Originally printed in R. Thurnwald (1922). *Psychologie des primitiven Menschen. Handbuch der vergleichenden Psychologie.* Munich.

COGNITIVE MEDIATION

The example of cognitive mediation that I discuss here deals with the development of memory. A child is born with so-called natural memory, which is similar to memory in animals and which "is characterized by the nonmediated impression of materials, by the retention of actual experiences as the basis of mnemonic (memory) traces. . . . This kind of memory is very close to perception, because it arises out of the direct influence of external stimuli upon human beings" (Vygotsky, 1978, pp. 38–39). Thus, using the terminology of contemporary cognitive science, natural memory does not involve deep information processing or, in other words, a restructuring of incoming information with the use of prior knowledge.

The historical development of human kind led to the invention of external aids (symbols and signs) that were used as mediators of memory. Examples of such a mediator were quipus, which were invented and used in the ancient Incan empire, China, and some other countries (Vygotsky & Luria, 1930/1993). Each quipu was a set of ropes with knots tied in the ropes (Fig. 1.1). The types of knots, their placement, and the interweaving of the ropes within a quipu represented a message that a runner had to convey from one part of the country to another. When the runner came to the official to whom he was sent, he retold the message looking at the quipu. It is important to note that quipus were not a kind of written language because a quipu did not represent a stable meaning and had to be interpreted by the runner rather than being read by the addressee. Thus, the purpose of a quipu was to remind the runner of the major aspects of the message, which is similar to the use of a string around one's finger in order not to forget to mail a letter or to buy bread on the way home. Discussing the invention and use of memory aids such as quipus, Vygotsky (1978) noted that they "demonstrate that even at early stages of historical development humans went beyond the limits of the psychological functions given to them by nature and proceeded to a new culturally-elaborated organization of their behavior" (Vygotsky, 1978, p. 39).

As discussed earlier, the development of any higher mental process passes through the stage in which children use external devices, presented to them by adults, as psychological tools to mediate their mental processes. Therefore, according to Vygotsky, in the course of ontogenetic development of memory, children should inevitably pass through the stage of the use of external memory aids (similar to quipus used by our ancestors) that they appropriate and master in the context of communication with adults. As a result of children's experience in the use of external memory aids, they later develop internal psychological tools (mnemonics) that come to mediate their memory. Children use these psychological tools to restructure the information to be memorized, to search for links between new information and their current knowledge, or, in terms of cognitive science, to process the incoming information. Contemporary cognitive psychologists often define information processing as the process of thinking, which is consistent with what Vygotsky said in the 1930s: "For the young child, to think means to recall; for the adolescent, to recall means to think" (Vygotsky, 1978, p. 51).

The Vygotskian view on the development of memory as higher mental process was tested in studies by his closest friends and colleagues, A. Leontiev and A. Luria. Leontiev's (1931) study was aimed at testing the Vygotskian idea of the stages in the development of human memory. The study was performed with subjects of different ages, from 4-year-old children to 28-year-old students, and it included two series. In the first series, the subjects were read aloud 15 words (for example, a theater, a spade, a wish, happiness, etc.) to be memorized and recalled. In the second series, they were read aloud another list of 15 words to be memorized and recalled. This time, however, the subjects were also offered cards with different pictures (for example, a plane in the sky, a crab on the beach, etc.) that could be used as external memory aids. The subjects were encouraged to choose a picture for each of the pronounced words so that the picture would help them to recall the word.

The results of the study were as follows. Four- to five-year-old children demonstrated poor recall (between two and three words) in the first and second series of study. The use of the cards in the second series resulted in a 33% increase in the children's recall in comparison with their recall in the first series. In general, however, they failed to use these cards as external memory aids because they could hardly find a link between a word to be memorized and a picture. Thus, those children's memory was still nonmediated, or, using the Vygotskian term, natural.

One may see as a paradox that adults in the study demonstrated a recall pattern that was similar to the results of the preschoolers. Of course, in both series, the adults' recall was much better than that of preschoolers. The use of the cards in the second series, however, resulted in just a moderate increase in their recall compared with their recall in the first series (the adults recalled about 10 words in the first series with a 42% increase in the number of recalled words in the second series). These results are very consistent with the Vygotskian understanding of memory development: Because the adults already possessed internal psychological tools (mnemonics), the use of external memory aids did not make a substantial difference in their recall.

The recall pattern of 7- to 12-year-old children was very different in comparison with both young children and adults. The use of the cards in the second series resulted in a 93% increase in their recall compared with their recall in the first series (their average recall in the first series was 6.75 words, and in the second series it was 12.03 words). These children were able to choose a picture for each word to be memorized and to create a meaningful link between the word and the picture. For example, to memorize the word *theater*, a child chose the picture of a crab on the beach and said, "The crab is sitting on the beach and is looking at the beautiful stones under the water. To him, this is like a theater." Thus, although the children of this age did not yet possess efficient internal psychological tools to mediate their memory, they could successfully use external memory aids that adults presented to them.

The described results confirmed Vygotsky's idea that the development of memory does proceed from nonmediated ("natural") memory, through memory as mediated by external memory aids ("externally mediated memory"), to memory as mediated by internal psychological tools ("internally mediated memory"). An additional confirmation of this idea was obtained in the course of a teaching session with those young children whose memory was defined as natural based on the results of the discussed experiments. These children were taught to use external memory aids (the cards) to memorize words. After that, their memory was evaluated again with the use of memory tasks similar to those described earlier. It turned out that not only the children's externally mediated memory significantly improved, but, more important, their internally mediated memory improved as well.

Because mediated memory is based on processing of incoming information, it would be reasonable to assume that subaverage cognitive functioning, which is one of the attributes of mental retardation, would result in problems with mediated memory. This assumption was investigated in another two-series study of Leontiev's (1931) with 10- to 12-year-old nonretarded children and 9- to 14-year-old children with mild mental retardation. In the first series, children were read aloud 10 words to be memorized and recalled. In the second series, they were read aloud another list of 10 words to be memorized and recalled with the use of external memory aids (cards with different pictures).

The results of the study were as follows. The recalls of the nonretarded children and the children with mental retardation in the first series were very similar: The nonretarded children recalled 4.8 words, and the children with mental retardation recalled 4.2. In the second series, however, the recalls of the two groups were drastically different. The nonretarded children recalled all 10 words, demonstrating a more than 100% increase in their recall compared with their recall in the first series. In contrast, the use of the cards in the second series by the children with mental retardation resulted in a decrease, rather than an increase, in their performance: They managed to recall only 3.8 words. The reason for this was that the children with mental retardation could not create a logical link between a word to be memorized and a card. Therefore, rather than serving as memory aids, the cards, as irrelevant stimuli, just interfered with these children's memorization. Thus, proceeding from the results of the study, mild mental retardation did not lead to a deficiency of the children's natural (nonmediated) memory, but it resulted in serious deficiencies in their mediated memory.

Leontiev's data confirmed Vygotsky's idea that natural memory and memory as a higher mental process have different origins, involve different mechanisms, and develop in accordance with different laws. Another confirmation of this Vygotskian idea was obtained in Luria's (1936) study with twins who belonged to two age groups: 5- to

7-year-olds and 11- to 13-year-olds. Within each of these groups, there was the same number of identical (monozygotic) and fraternal (heterozygotic) twins. All the children were given two memory tasks.

In the first task, the children were shown 9 geometric shapes and were asked later to recognize these shapes among 34 geometric shapes presented to them. The analysis of the children's performance showed that the completion of this visual recognition task did not involve the use of any memory aids, and, therefore, the children's recall reflected the capacity of their natural memory. The comparison of the children's recalls within each twin pair showed that, in both age groups, identical twins performed 3 times more similarly than the fraternal twins. The reasonable conclusion was made that the capacity of the children's natural memory was determined in large part by heredity, which was the same in identical twins but not the same in fraternal twins.

In the second task, the children were read aloud a list of 15 words to be memorized and recalled. They were also offered cards with different pictures, which they could use as external memory aids (see Leontiev's study described earlier). In contrast to the children's performance in the first task, which was very similar for both age groups, in this task, the performance of 5- to 7-year-old children was very different from the performance of 11- to 13-year-old children.

Most of the 5- to 7-year-old children were unable to systematically use the cards with pictures as external memory aids, although some of them managed to benefit from the presence of the cards. Thus, their recall mostly reflected the capacity of their natural memory. The comparison of the children's recalls within each twin pair showed that identical twins performed 2.3 times more similarly than the fraternal twins. These results were another confirmation of the idea that the capacity of the children's natural memory was greatly determined by heredity.

In contrast to the performance of the younger children, the 11- to 13-year-old children, when performing in the second task, tried to find logical links between the words to be memorized and the pictures, and they used these links later when asked to recall the words. Thus, their recall reflected their ability to use external memory aids as mediators of their memory. The comparison of the children's recalls within each twin pair showed that the difference between scores of identical twins was the same as the difference between scores of fraternal twins. Thus, the capacity of the children's mediated memory was shown not to be determined by heredity.

The importance of Luria's (1936) study goes far beyond the confirmation of Vygotsky's idea that, in contrast to natural memory, memory as a higher mental process is not determined by heredity but rather is the result of mediation. The results of this study contributed to the general underestimation by Vygotsky's Russian followers of the role of genetically predetermined maturation in children's development. This issue is discussed in detail in the concluding chapter.

METACOGNITIVE MEDIATION

The studies on the development of memory as a higher mental process were presented to illustrate Vygotsky's ideas in regard to so-called cognitive mediation. The next example to be discussed illustrates his ideas in regard to metacognitive mediation, which leads to the development of children's ability to control and regulate their cognitive processes and their behavior in general. This example deals with the development of self-regulation in children.

According to Vygotsky (1984), a young child is "a slave of his visual field" (p. 103) whose behavior is involuntary and regulated by stimuli. A new or interesting stimulus automatically draws the child's attention, and the child remains involved in the stimulus-directed activity until this stimulus loses its attractiveness. This type of regulation belongs to the class of natural or lower mental processes with which children are born and which are specific for both young children and animals. Just like the development of any higher mental process, the development of self-regulation is the result of mediation, that is, children's mastery of psychological tools in the course of interpersonal communication with adults. This mediation is a long process, which includes several steps.

The starting point in the development of self-regulation, according to Vygotsky, is the infant's use of the so-called indicatory or pointing gesture to direct the behavior of a caregiver. Discussing the origins of the indicatory gesture, Vygotsky (1983/1997) finds them in the situation in which an infant is trying to grasp an object and fails because the object is too far away. The mother gives the object to the infant. The importance of the mother's action, however, goes far beyond her intention to help the child get the object. She, in fact, gives the indicatory meaning to the infant's grasping movement, that is, supplies the infant with the ontogenetically earliest nonverbal social tool to direct another person's behavior. As a result, the infant's grasping movement transforms and reduces, turning into a truly indicatory gesture, which the infant starts to use to direct the mother's behavior.[2]

Later, nonverbal means of mother–infant communication are replaced by the use of language (Vygotsky, 1934/1986). The mother uses language to label different objects in the child's environment and, especially important, to regulate the child's behavior. For example, she may say "look" to draw the child's attention to a certain object, or she may say "no" to prevent the child from doing something dangerous or undesirable. When doing this, however, she is not only regulating the child's behavior but is also supplying the child with verbal tools of self-regulation. The child acquires these tools and starts to use them by talking aloud to himself or herself (for example, the child says "no"

---

[2] Alternative interpretations of the origins of the indicatory gesture are discussed in chapter 3.

to himself to overcome a temptation to do something inappropriate). Such self-addressed child's speech has been called egocentric (or private) speech.

Egocentric speech is interesting not only as a phenomenon in children's development but also as a phenomenon that was interpreted in diametrically opposite ways by Piaget and Vygotsky. Piaget (1923/1959) interpreted the preschoolers' self-talk as a manifestation of the major shortcoming of their cognition and personality, that is, their egocentrism (therefore, he called this self-talk "egocentric speech"). According to Piaget, egocentric children, on the one hand, are not social creatures yet and are still involved in autistic thought but, on the other hand, they have already mastered language as a social means of communication. Egocentric speech reflects this "intermediate" state of development of children's cognition and personality in which they often use language not as the means of communication but as a verbal accompaniment to their autistic thoughts. Accordingly, this speech just accompanies children's activity without playing any role in this activity. As children grow into society, egocentric speech declines more and more, and at age 7 or 8 years, it almost completely disappears.

For Vygotsky (1934/1986), as indicated earlier, egocentric speech reflects the child's appropriation of verbal tools that adults use to regulate his or her behavior and the use of these tools for self-regulation. Rather than being just a useless accompaniment to the child's activity, as Piaget believed, egocentric speech "serves mental orientation, conscious understanding; it helps in overcoming difficulties" (Vygotsky, 1934/1986, p. 228). The decline of egocentric speech and its final disappearance, according to Vygotsky, means that external verbal tools, just like all the other psychological tools, become internalized (turn into inner speech) and come to mediate children's self-regulation as their new higher mental process.

To test Vygotsky's interpretation of the role of egocentric speech in children's activity, he and his colleagues performed several studies.

What follows is the description of one of them:

> In order to determine what causes egocentric talk...we organized the children's activities in much the same way Piaget did, but we added a series of frustrations and difficulties. For instance, when a child was getting ready to draw, he would suddenly find that there was no paper, or no pencil of the color he needed. In other words, by obstructing his free activity we made him face problems.
>
> We found that in these difficult situations the coefficient of egocentric speech almost doubled, in comparison with Piaget's normal figure for the same age and also in comparison with our figure for children not facing these problems. The child would try to grasp and to remedy the situation in talking to himself: "Where's the pencil? I need a blue pencil. Never mind, I'll draw with the red one and wet it with water; it will become dark and look like blue." (Vygotsky, 1934/1986, p. 30)

Thus, the study demonstrated that egocentric speech does play an important role in children's activity as an external tool of self-regulation.

Vygotsky's ideas in regard to the origins of egocentric speech, its role in children's activity, and its eventual turning into inner speech have been confirmed in many studies and observations. Luria (1961) observed that, when using egocentric speech, children not only repeated the exact words that their caregivers used to direct and regulate the children's behavior, but they sometimes even imitated the caregivers' voice. Jamieson's (1995) observations of deaf children revealed a fascinating fact: When involved in a demanding activity, these children used self-directed sign language. It could be reasonably assumed that self-directed sign language plays the same self-regulatory role in their activity as egocentric speech plays in the activity of hearing children. Vygotsky's idea of children's transition from egocentric speech as the external tool of self-regulation to inner speech as the internal tool of self-regulation has been tested and confirmed in several studies (Berk & Landau, 1993; Berk & Spuhl, 1995; Bivens & Berk, 1990; Frauenglass & Diaz, 1985; and others).

As Berk and Winsler (1995) indicate, "today, Vygotsky's perspective on children's private speech is preferred over Piaget's, and practically all contemporary studies of the phenomenon are conducted within the Vygotskian framework" (p. 37). As one can conclude from this quotation, this preference of contemporary researchers is even reflected in their terminology: They use the term "private speech" rather than "egocentric speech" when referring to children's self-talk.

Although the use of egocentric (private) speech as an external tool of self-regulation determines children's transition to self-regulation as mediated by inner speech, this is not the only determinant of such a transition. An important point that is often overlooked in reviews of Vygotsky's theory is that another determinant of children's transition to internally mediated self-regulation is their use of semiotic tools for regulating the behavior of others. This proposition of Vygotsky (1981a) is a logical elaboration of his general theoretical statement that "a sign is always originally a means used for social purposes, a means of influencing others, and only later becomes a means of influencing oneself" (p. 157). Therefore, "regulation of others' behavior by means of the word gradually leads to the development of verbalized behavior of the people themselves" (Vygotsky, 1981a, p. 159). As I discuss in chapter 5, Russian neo-Vygotskians consider sociodramatic play to be crucially important for the development of preschoolers' self-regulation because this play is a natural context for play peers' mutual regulation.

Thus, Vygotsky's ideas on the development of self-regulation in children may be summarized as follows. Primary caregivers regulate children's behavior by the use of verbal tools. Children appropriate these verbal tools and start to use them in the form of egocentric (private) speech to regulate their own behavior. Also, they use these tools in the form of external speech to regulate others' behavior. As a result, children master the verbal tools, and these tools get internalized and come to mediate children's self-regulation as their new higher mental process. Thus, "the specifically human capacity for language

enables children to provide for auxiliary tools in the solution of difficult tasks, to overcome impulsive action, to plan a solution to a problem prior to its execution, and to master their own behavior" (Vygotsky,
1978, p. 28).

Mediation as Instrumental in the Creation of the Zone of Proximal Development of Mental Processes

The examples just provided of the development of new higher mental
processes illustrate Vygotsky's general idea of mediation as the major determinant of child development. As discussed, in the course of
mediation, the child transits from the use of an external psychological tool for solving new problems under an adult's supervision to the
independent use of the internal psychological tool for solving these
problems. Therefore, at each point of mediation, the development of
a new higher mental process in the child can be characterized by two
criteria. The first is the child's success in independent use of a new psychological tool for solving the relevant class of problems. This criterion
characterizes, as Vygotsky (1978) called it, "*the actual developmental
level*, that is, the level of development of a child's mental functions
[processes] that has been established as a result of certain *completed* developmental cycles" (p. 85). The second criterion for the development
of a new higher mental process is the child's success in an adult-assisted
use of a new psychological tool for solving the relevant class of problems. This criterion characterizes the "level of potential development"
of this mental process (Vygotsky, 1978, p. 86) because "what the child
can do today in cooperation and with guidance, tomorrow [figuratively
speaking] he will be able to do independently" (Vygotsky, 1984/1998,
p. 202).

Until the final point of mediation (that is, the moment when the development of a new higher mental process is successfully completed),

there must be a distance between the levels of actual and potential development of this mental process. Vygotsky (1978) called this distance the "zone of proximal development" (ZPD; p. 86). In these terms, mediation deals with involving the child in performing at the level of potential development of a certain mental process, which will create the zone of proximal development of this process.

As Chaiklin (2003) correctly indicated, although "the term *zone of proximal development* is probably one of the most widely recognized and well-known ideas associated with Vygotsky's scientific production" (p. 40), it remains poorly understood, wrongly interpreted, and inadequately used by many Western scholars. Striking examples of the wrong interpretation and use of this term can be found, for example, in the works of such famous proponents of the Guided Discovery in a Community of Learners approach as Brown and Campione (1994):

> A zone of proximal development can include people, adults, and children with varying expertise, but it can also include artifacts such as books, videos, wall displays, scientific equipment, and a computer environment intended to support intentional learning. . . . In our classroom, teachers and students create zones of proximal development by *seeding* the environment with ideas and concepts that they value and by harvesting those which "take" in the community. Ideas seeded by community members *migrate* to other participants and persist over time. Participants in the classroom are free to *appropriate* vocabulary, ideas, methods, etc., that appear initially as part of the shared discourse, and by appropriation, transform these ideas via personal interpretation. (pp. 236–237)

As one can see, the position of these scholars has little in common with Vygotsky's concept of the ZPD. They seriously undermine the role of adults as mediators of children's learning, and they do not even mention the mastery and internalization of psychological tools as the major content of learning that leads to the development of new higher mental processes in children. No wonder the instructional methods that the proponents of the Guided Discovery in a Community of

Learners approach advocate are not consistent with Vygotsky's views on school instruction (see chapter 6 for a more detailed discussion).

The importance of Vygotsky's concept of the ZPD is that it contains in a condensed form his solution to such fundamental problems of developmental and educational psychology as the problem of assessment of children's mental development and the problem of the interrelationships between instruction and development. In regard to the problem of assessment of children's mental development, the concept of ZPD implies that it is important to assess not only the child's level of actual development but his or her ZPD as well. Vygotsky (1934/1986) wrote:

> Most of the psychological investigations concerned with school learning measured the level of mental development of the child by making him solve certain standardized problems. The problems he was able to solve by himself were supposed to indicate the level of his mental development at the particular time. But in this way, only the completed part of the child's development can be measured, which is far from the whole story. We tried a different approach. Having found that the mental age of two children was, let us say, eight, we gave each of them harder problems than he could manage on his own and provided some slight assistance: the first step in a solution, a leading question, or some other form of help. We discovered that one child could, in cooperation, solve problems designed for twelve-year-olds, while the other could not go beyond problems intended for nine-year-olds. The discrepancy between a child's actual mental age and the level he reaches in solving problems with assistance indicates the zone of his proximal development; in our example, this zone is four for the first child and one for the second. Can we truly say that their mental development is the same? Experience has shown that the child with the larger zone of proximal development will do much better in school. *This measure gives a more helpful clue than mental age does to the dynamics of intellectual progress.* (pp. 186–187)

Vygotsky's concept of ZPD has become one of the theoretical foundations of an innovative approach to the assessment of children's mental development, the so-called Dynamic Assessment approach (for a description of this approach, see Haywood & Tzuriel, 1992; Lidz & Elliott,

2000). For our discussion, however, much more important is the analysis of this concept in relation to the problem of the interrelationships between instruction and development.

To introduce his solution to the problem of the interrelationships between instruction and development, Vygotsky contrasted it to the alternative solutions to this problem suggested by other researchers at that time. The first such solution was presented in early writings of Piaget (1923/1959). In Piaget's approach, "development is seen as a process of maturation subject to natural laws, and instruction as the utilization of the opportunities created by development" (Vygotsky, 1934/1986, p. 174). Thus, according to Piaget, instruction "hobbles behind development" (Vygotsky, 1934/1986, p. 175); it can refine the already developed cognitive structures, but it cannot result in developing new structures. Vygotsky's analysis of early writings of Piaget is applicable to Piaget's later views on the interrelationships between instruction and development as well. In one of his later works, Piaget clearly indicated that a child can learn new ideas "only if he is capable of assimilating them, and he can do this only if he already possesses the adequate instruments or structures" (Piaget, Gellerier, & Langer, 1970/1988, p. 14). As Siegler (1991) summarized:

> Piaget's views concerning the possibility of accelerating cognitive development through training are among his most controversial. Some of his comments appear to rule out the possibility of any training being successful. Others suggest that training might at times be effective, but only if the child already possesses some understanding of the concept and if the training procedure involves active interaction with materials. (p. 53)

Although the influence of Piaget's ideas on the research of contemporary American psychologists is not as great as it was in the 1970s, his view on the interrelationships between instruction and development is still dominant in American psychology. Ormrod (1995), for example, summarized the views of American cognitive psychologists on this topic as follows:

> A student's level of cognitive development affects the kinds of learning and behavior that are possible. Teachers must consider their students' levels of cognitive development (perhaps in terms of Piaget's stage characteristics) when planning topics and methods of instruction. For example, explanations based on concrete operational logic may be ineffective ways of presenting ideas to kindergartners not yet capable of such logic. (p. 190)

Another reason for a broad acceptance by American psychologists of the view that instruction should follow development may be the influence of nativist theories of child development. As I briefly discussed in the Introduction, nativists have seen genetically predetermined maturation as the major determinant of children's development and the reason for individual differences in development. Therefore, instruction, from their point of view, just realizes the potentials created by development without determining development. As Scarr (1992) wrote, "Feeding a well-nourished but short child more and more will not give him the stature of a basketball player. Feeding a below-average intellect more and more information will not make her brilliant" (p. 16).

Vygotsky (1934/1986) considered instruction to be the major avenue for mediation in the period of middle childhood. Sometimes he even used the term instruction in the broadest meaning of the word as a synonym for mediation: "Instruction and development do not meet for the first time at school age; in fact, they are interrelated from the child's very first day of life" (Vygotsky, 1956, p. 445). Therefore, he strongly disagreed with the view that instruction should "hobble" behind development. Of course, Vygotsky was far from claiming that instruction should be organized without taking into consideration the actual level of the child's development. He indicated that "it remains necessary to determine the lowest threshold at which instruction in, say, arithmetic may begin, since a certain minimal ripeness of functions [mental processes] is required" (Vygotsky, 1934/1986, pp. 188–189). Correctly organized instruction, however, should not target the actual level of development of these mental processes. Rather, like any other type of mediation, instruction "marches ahead of development and leads it; it must be aimed not so much at the ripe as at the ripening functions [mental processes]" (Vygotsky, 1934/1986, p. 188).

The second alternative solution to the problem of the interrelationships between instruction and development that Vygotsky analyzed was introduced, in particular, by Thorndike (1914), who was an antecedent of behaviorism. Thorndike "sees the intellectual development of the child as a gradual accumulation of conditional reflexes; and learning is viewed in exactly the same way" (Vygotsky, 1934/1986, p. 176). Therefore, students' learning in the course of instruction and the process of their development are viewed within this theoretical perspective as identical. Similar views were formulated by such behaviorists as Watson (1925) and Skinner (1953). Because behaviorists' ideas have lost their popularity among American psychologists since the 1960s, their solution to the problem of the interrelationships between instruction and development does not have many supporters these days (for one of a few exceptions, see Bijou, 1976, 1992).

Although behaviorists seem to emphasize the leading role of instruction in children's development, Vygotsky indicated that their approach has an important shortcoming. For behaviorists, any learned knowledge and skills contribute to the child's development, and this contribution is equal to the amount of learned knowledge. For Vygotsky, first, learning does not lead to students' development if instruction targets the level of actual rather than potential development of their mental processes. Second, under properly organized instruction, students' development is not reduced to the amount of acquired knowledge. As Vygotsky (1956) indicated, "one step in learning may mean a hundred steps in development" (p. 256). For example, as discussed earlier, children's acquisition of language leads to the development of their self-regulation.

Thus, according to Vygotsky, instruction should be organized in accordance with general principles of mediation. It should lead development through targeting the level of potential development of the child's mental processes. Such instruction "awakens and rouses to life those processes that are ready to develop, that are in the zone of proximal development" (Vygotsky, 1956, p. 278).

Motivational Factors in Child Development

The theoretical ideas of Vygotsky just described are mostly related to the analysis of children's cognitive and metacognitive development as the outcome of social mediation, but not to the analysis of the role of children as active contributors to their development. Because the familiarity of Western psychologists with Vygotsky's theory is often limited to these ideas, they sometimes criticize Vygotsky for viewing children as passive recipients of social influences. Kuhn (1992), for example, wrote: "In emphasizing the external influences stemming from social interaction, [Vygotsky] neglects the complementary part of the individual–environment interaction, that is, the role of the individual" (p. 259). Although some of Vygotsky's writings may lead to this impression (this issue is discussed in more detail in the next chapter), such an interpretation of Vygotsky's general theoretical position is simply wrong. Discussing children's development, Vygotsky (1984/1998) emphasized that "not just the child's habits and psychological functions (attention, memory, thinking, etc.) are developing – at the base of mental development lies, first of all, an evolution of the child's behavior and *interests* [emphasis mine], a change in the structure of the direction of his behavior" (p. 4). This is the development of new interests (that is, motives) in children that, according to Vygotsky, results in their active participation in social interactions, in the context of which mediation takes place. Discussing, for example, instruction, which he viewed as the major avenue for mediation during the period of middle childhood, Vygotsky (1984) wrote: "The problem of interest in instruction is not whether or not children learn with interest; they never learn without interest" (p. 35). Thus, the development of new motives in children is a necessary prerequisite for the development of their mental processes. Moreover, Vygotsky (1966/1976) clearly indicated that children's transition from one stage to the next could not be explained without taking into consideration the development of new motives in children:

> I think that the mistake of a large number of accepted theories is their disregard for the child's needs . . . the disregard of everything that can come under the category of incentives and motives for action. We often describe a child's development as the development of his intellectual functions, i.e. every child stands before us as a theoretical being who, according to the higher or lower level of his intellectual development, moves from one stage to another. Without a consideration of the child's needs, inclinations, incentives, and motives to act – as research has demonstrated – there will never be any advance from one stage to the next. . . . It seems that every advance from one stage to another is connected with an abrupt change in motives and incentives to act. (pp. 537–538)

What factors are responsible for the development of new motives in children? When answering this question, Vygotsky equally disagreed with those who viewed this development as the outcome of physiological maturation, and those who viewed this development as the result of instilling new motives into the child by society. Discussing, for example, the development of new motives in adolescents, Vygotsky (1984/1998) wrote:

> Authors-biologizers lose sight of the fact that the human adolescent is not only a biological and natural, but also a historical and social being and of the fact that together with social maturation and a growing of the adolescent into the life of the community that surrounds

> him, his interests are not poured into him mechanically like a liquid into an empty vessel, into the biological forms of his tendencies, but, in the process of internal development and reconstruction of the personality, themselves reconstruct the very forms of the tendencies, carrying them to a higher level and converting them into human interests, and themselves become internal component factors in the personality. (p. 23)

Thus, according to Vygotsky (1984/1998), new motives "are not acquired, but *develop*" (p. 9) from the child's existing motives as a product of complex relationships between the processes of maturation and social interaction. At the same time, discussing the comparative importance of physiological and social factors in the development of children's motives, Vygotsky (1984/1998) emphasized that the development of new motives "is the content of the social-cultural development of the child to a much greater degree than of his biological formation" (p. 11). He never elaborated this contention. Because, however, Vygotsky viewed the sociocultural development of the child as the result of mediation, it is logical to assume that he considered mediation to be mainly responsible for the development of new motives in children.

Vygotsky's Model of Child Stage-by-Stage Development

Viewing child development as "a single process of self-development" (p. 189), Vygotsky (1984/1998) presented a holistic model of stage-by-stage development that integrated the development of children's motives, cognition, and their social development. Unfortunately, he presented this model in an abbreviated and schematic fashion, which makes it difficult to understand. In particular, when describing his model, Vygotsky introduced new terms without defining them in an explicit manner. If, however, we analyze Vygotsky's model in the

41

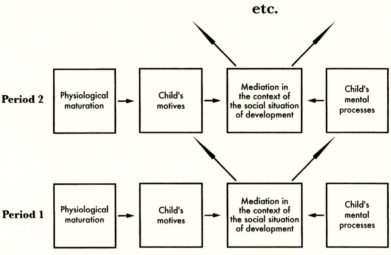

Figure 1.2. Vygotsky's model of child development.

context of his theoretical ideas discussed earlier, this model becomes much more meaningful (see Fig. 1.2).

According to Vygotsky (1984/1998), each age period is character-ized by "the structure of the child's consciousness" (p. 199), which includes as its components the child's motives and mental processes at the present level of their development. The age-specific structure of the child's consciousness determines a "unique relation, specific to the given age, between the child and reality, mainly the social reality, that surrounds him" (p. 198). Vygotsky (1984/1998) called this relation *"the social situation of development* at the given age" (p. 198). It is in the context of the present social situation of development that adults in-volve children in age-specific mediational interactions. Therefore,

> the social situation of development represents the initial moment for all dynamic changes that occur in development during the given pe-riod. It determines wholly and completely the forms and the path along which the child will acquire ever new personality characteris-tics, drawing them from the social reality as from the basic source of

development, the path along which the social becomes the individual. (Vygotsky, 1984/1998, p. 198)

As the result of adults' mediation in the context of the present social situation of development, the child develops new mental processes and new motives (the development of which is also influenced by physiological maturation). These "neoformations that arise toward the end of a given age lead to a reconstruction of the whole structure of the child's consciousness and in this way change the whole system of relations to external reality and to himself... [which]... means that the social situation of development... must also change" (Vygotsky, 1984/1998, p. 199). The change of the social situation of development manifests the child's transition to the next period of development. In Vygotsky's (1984/1998) words,

> the forces moving the child's development at one age or another inevitably lead to rejection and disruption of the base of development of the whole age, with internal necessity determining the annulment of the social situation of development, the termination of the given period of development, and a transition to the following, or higher age level. (p. 199)

Thus, the innovative view of Vygotsky on the determinant of child development and his holistic approach to the developmental process made it possible for him to present a new explanation of the mechanism of children's stage-by-stage development. This explanation, however, as well as Vygotsky's general theoretical ideas that underlie his model of child development, had shortcomings and were not elaborated well enough. The credit for overcoming these shortcomings and the elaboration of Vygotsky's approach into an internally consistent theory of child development should be granted to his Russian followers, whose ideas are discussed in the next chapter.

2 The Neo-Vygotskian Elaboration of Vygotsky's Approach to Child Development

Although Vygotsky's approach became the general theoretical foundation of the scientific research and discourse of his Russian colleagues and followers (Elkonin, Galperin, Leontiev, Luria, Zaporozhets, and others), they were far from considering this approach a dogma. For many years after Vygotsky's death, their scientific effort was aimed at overcoming the shortcomings of his approach and elaborating those of his ideas that he had merely sketched.

The starting point of the neo-Vygotskians' analysis was the same as the starting point of Vygotsky's discourse, that is, the difference between the practical activity of humans and animals that results in the difference in their mental processes. Vygotsky (1930) saw the difference between the practical activity of humans and animals in the fact that humans systematically use tools in the course of their activity, whereas animals either do not use such tools or, in the case of apes, use these tools episodically. This view, however, reduced the difference between the use of tools by humans and animals to *quantitative* differences (systematic vs. episodic use of tools), and it did not explain *why* the use of tools by humans requires a qualitatively new level of mental processes.[1] In contrast, the neo-Vygotskians have shown *qualitative* differences between both the use of tools by humans and animals and the structures of animals' and humans' activities and have analyzed as well how these differences lead to differences between mental processes of humans and animals.

The Use of Tools by Humans and Animals

The major difference between the use of tools by humans on one hand and by animals and young children on the other was revealed in Galperin's (1937) study. The study has shown that both animals and young children use a tool as an extension of their hand. For example, an ape uses a stick to get a fruit in the same way as it would use its hand if the fruit were closer to the cage. Similarly, an infant uses a spoon as a cupped hand, that is, as if he were lifting to his mouth his fist rather than the spoon. In both cases, the tool enters into the composition of the manual operation without changing its structure, and it is used in accordance with the "logic" of this manual operation.

The neo-Vygotskians do not deny that, sometimes, apes do try to imitate human tool-mediated operations. As a rule, however, these attempts are not successful. Ladygina-Kohts (1935), for example, described an ape's multiple attempts to imitate the operation of hammering in nails. The ape, however, turned out to be unable to follow the "logic" of the tools that he was using (for example, he would not hold the nail perpendicularly to the wall). As a result, "despite his intensive

---

[1] Discussing the difference between the use of tools by apes and by human children, Vygotsky (1978) indicated that, in contrast to apes, the use of tools by children is accompanied by speech, which regulates and directs their tool-mediated operations: "Children solve practical tasks with the help of their speech, as well as their eyes and hands" (p. 26). This analysis, however, does not answer the question of what the characteristics of children's tool-mediated operations are that require children to use speech when performing these operations.

practicing, [he] has never hammered in a single nail" (Ladygina-Kohts, 1935, p. 226).

As a result of acquisition of cultural experience, children learn to use tools in accordance with the social meanings of these tools; for example, when using a spoon to eat, a child holds the spoon horizontally at the end of the handle while lifting it from dish to mouth. Thus, the use of the spoon as a cultural tool has changed the whole structure of the child's manual operation, which has come to follow the "logic" of the spoon. The child's adjustment of his manual operation to the "logic" of the cultural tool being mastered requires a special regulation of the tool-mediated operation, which involves, in particular, the child's attending to an adult demonstration of how the tool should be used, self-monitoring his or her own movements, and comparing them with the socially appropriate way to use the tool demonstrated by the adult. Thus, Galperin's (1937) study confirmed Vygotsky's notion that, in contrast to the use of tools by animals, the specifically human use of tools requires a qualitatively new level of mental processes.

Galperin's (1937) analysis of the difference between the use of tools by humans and animals has been supported and enriched by many studies and observations of the behavior of great apes, most often chimpanzees (for reviews and selected studies and observations, see Boesch & Tomasello, 1998; Boysen & Himes, 1999; Goodall, 1986; Inoue-Nakamura & Matsuzawa, 1997; Matsuzawa et al., 2001; Nagell, Olguin, & Tomasello, 1993; McGrew, 1992; Sumita, Kitahara-Frisch, & Norikoshi, 1985; Takeshita & van Hoof, 2001; Tomasello, 1999; Tomasello, Davis-Dasilva, Camak, & Bard, 1987). Their findings may be summarized by noting that wild and mother-reared captive apes often have been shown to use (and even manufacture) physical tools efficiently in their everyday lives: They use a pair of stones as hammer and anvil to crack nuts, a stick to push food out of a transparent tube, a stick for fishing for termites by probing termite mounds, a stick to rake in food, and so on. Researchers have also reported that young apes imitate adult tool use. Some studies, however, documented that young apes, although successfully imitating adults' single operations with a tool, could not imitate the whole tool-use strategy (Boesch & Tomasello, 1998; Inoue-Nakamura & Matsuzawa, 1997; Nagell et al., 1993; Sumita et al., 1985; Tomasello et al., 1987). For example, although successfully imitating single operations of nut cracking, young chimpanzees did not combine these operations in the right sequence but rather learned this sequence through personal experience by trial and error (Inoue-Nakamura & Matsuzawa, 1997; Sumita et al., 1985).

As Tomasello (1999) concluded in his review of the studies of tool use by chimpanzees, "chimpanzees are very good at learning about the dynamic affordances of objects that they discover through watching others manipulate them, but they are not skillful at learning from others a new behavioral strategy per se" (p. 29).[2] In contrast, human 2-year-olds have been shown to imitate successfully a new behavioral tool-use strategy that was modeled for them by an adult (Nagell et al., 1993). What is the reason for this difference between apes' and children's imitation? Tomasello (1999) wrote:

> Chimpanzees . . . do not seem to understand the instrumental behavior of conspecifics in the same way as do humans. For humans the goal or intention of the demonstrator . . . is understood as something separate from the various behavioral means that may be used to accomplish the goal. Observers' ability to separate goal and means serves to

[2] This conclusion seems to be challenged by the finding of Whiten (1998) that chimpanzees were able to imitate a novel behavioral sequence. It is important to note, however, that in Whiten's study chimpanzees did not imitate a tool-use strategy. Rather, they imitated the strategy of opening a box with several locks and food inside, which was "an analogy of food processing, a common activity among primates, who have to peel, tear, poke, twist, or otherwise manipulate defenses to get at an edible core" (Whiten, 1998, p. 272). Also, the subjects were chimpanzees who "had experienced a rich social life, including interactions with conspecifics and humans" (Whiten, 1998, p. 274). As will be discussed further, Tomasello (1999) holds that "encultured" apes, to which category some of Whiten's (1998) subjects belonged, do show a better ability to imitate.

> highlight for them the demonstrator's method or strategy of tool use
> as an independent entity – the behavior she is using in an attempt to
> accomplish the goal.... In the absence of this ability to understand
> goal and behavioral means as separate in the actions of others, chim-
> panzee observers focus on the changes of state (including changes of
> spatial position) of the objects involved during the demonstration,
> with the actions of the demonstrator being, in effect, just other phys-
> ical motions. (p. 30)

The analysis by Tomasello (1999) confirms and elaborates the neo-
Vygotskian contention of differences between both the use of tools by
humans and animals and the mental processes that serve their use of
tools. Indeed, as discussed, even in the case of learning how to use
physical tools, the process of learning is promoted by the observer's attending to a demonstrator's strategy of tool use, which wild or mother-
reared captive apes seem not to be able to do. In this case, however,
apes' inability to attend to a demonstrator's strategy of tool use can
be compensated for by their independent discovery of this strategy
through trial and error. In contrast, in the case of learning how to use
tools invented by human culture, observer's attending to a demonstrator's tool-use strategy is a must for successful learning of the strategy.
Indeed, as opposed to physical characteristics of objects, their social
meanings are not "written" (Elkonin, 1989, p. 48) on objects and therefore cannot be discovered in the course of independent explorations.
For example, one can discover by him- or herself that banging a spoon
on the table will produce a sound but cannot discover by independent
exploration how to use a spoon for eating.[3] Thus, apes' inability to
attend to a demonstrator's tool-use strategy prevents them from learning how to use tools invented by human culture. Indeed, there are no

---

[3] Proceeding from their empirical findings, Connolly and Dalgleish (1993) have argued
that maternal mediation is not required by the infant for the mastery of the use of
a spoon as a cultural tool. A persuasive critical analysis of such an interpretation of
these empirical findings has been provided by Vauclair (1993).

scientific observations of imitation by wild or mother-reared captive apes of the use of cultural tools.

One of the reasons for the difference between the ability of apes and children to attend to a demonstrator's tool-use strategy can be attributed to the difference between adult–infant interactions in apes and humans. Vauclair (1993) writes:

> Our results indicated that adult apes rarely acted on objects with the apparent intent of engaging the infant's attention. In contrast, adult humans manipulated objects primarily with the intent of stimulating, sustaining or enhancing an infant's actions on those objects. (p. 207)[4]

In this respect, of great interest are findings that have been provided by studies of so-called enculturated apes, that is, the apes "raised like human beings in a human-like cultural environment" (Tomasello, 1999, p. 35). In particular, it has been documented that enculturated apes demonstrate a better ability to imitate tool-use strategies than their mother-reared captive conspecifics (Tomasello, Savage-Rumbaugh, & Kruger, 1993). As a possible explanation of these findings, Tomasello (1999) suggested that "in human-like cultural environments apes receive a kind of 'socialization of attention,'" (p. 35) that is, their attending to a demonstrator's performance is encouraged and promoted.

It is important to stress, however, that even enculturated apes demonstrate much better performance when imitating strategies of the use of physical rather then cultural tools. Indeed, although there are anecdotal reports of somewhat successful imitation by enculturated apes of the use of cultural tools (Byrne & Russon, 1998; Russon, 1999; for an overview, see also Whiten & Ham, 1992),[5] scientific studies

---

[4] This observation is highly consistent with the neo-Vygotskian findings on the role of adult mediation in the development of infant object-centered actions that are discussed in chapter 4.

[5] It is worthy of note that the most impressive examples of successful imitation by enculturated apes of the use of cultural tools, as reported by Byrne and Russon (1998)

have documented that such imitation is very difficult for the apes. For example, in the study by Bering, Bjorklund, and Ragan (2000), enculturated chimpanzees and orangutans imitated a strategy that involved placing a large plastic nail in a hole in the wooden board and then striking its head once with the striking surface of the plastic hammer. This task by itself was much simpler than the cultural task of hammering in nails: It did not require that the performer follow the logic of the tools used, that is, coordinate the positions of a nail and the hammer (hold the nail perpendicularly to the wall while striking its head with the hammer). Rather, it consisted of two simple consecutive operations: placing a nail in a ready-made hole (which is not a "cultural" operation) and then striking the nail with the hammer. Moreover, the performance of the task did not even require that the apes imitate precisely the hammering-in strategy (striking the *head* of the nail with *the striking surface* of the hammer): Even striking the nail on its side once with the head of the hammer was counted as a "good" performance. Accordingly, the performance of the task did not require that the performer accomplish the goal of hammering in (to hammer in a nail). Thus, the only "cultural" operation that the apes had to imitate to perform the task successfully was striking the nail (but not

and Russon (1999), do not meet Beck's (1980) definition of tool use: "the external employment of an unattached, environmental object to alter more efficiently the form, position, or condition of another object, another organism, or the user itself" (quoted in Russon, 1999, p. 118), to which Russon seems to have subscribed herself. For example, Russon (1999) describes the imitation by an orangutan of sharpening an axe blade. The ape performed several operations that resembled those of blade-sharpening such as wetting the stone by dipping it in the water and then rubbing the stone three to four times on the face (but not *along the edge*) of the axe blade (although she also performed such irrelevant operations as sucking the blade and trying to chew the stone). There is no indication, however, that the ape performed these operations "to alter more efficiently the form, position, or condition of another object," that is, to sharpen the blade. It is possible that the operations that the ape performed were aimed at something else – for example, at producing an interesting sound. If that was the case, however, the ape's operations had nothing to do with the imitation of the use of cultural tools.

necessarily *the head* of the nail) with the head of the hammer (but not necessarily with *the striking surface* of the hammer). It turned out, however, that even such a "culturally impoverished" operation was successfully imitated by only one of the four enculturated apes.

In conclusion, recent data and observations have confirmed and elaborated Galperin's (1937) analysis of the difference between animal and human use of tools. Of special interest are the findings that apes' tool use may benefit from human cultural environment, although the level of enculturated apes' tool use still remains qualitatively different from that of human children.

The Structures of Animal and Human Activities

Whereas Galperin's (1937) study was aimed at the analysis of difference between the use of tools by animals and humans, Leontiev (1959/1964, 1975/1978, 1972/1981) investigated the difference between animal and human activities. According to Leontiev (1972/1981), any activity

> answers to a specific need of the active agent. It moves toward the object of this need, and it terminates when it satisfies it. . . . It is precisely an activity's object that gives it a specific direction. In accordance with the terminology I have proposed, an activity's object is its real motive. . . . There can be no activity without a motive. "Unmotivated" activity is not activity devoid of a motive: It is activity with a motive that is subjectively and objectively concealed. (p. 59)

At this level of analysis, there is no difference between the activities of animals and humans, but if we analyze the structures of animals' and humans' activities, the difference between them becomes obvious.

Any animal's activity is always directed toward the immediate gratification of its physiological need, that is, toward its motive. Even if this activity has several steps, each of them brings the animal nearer to the motive. For example, a wolf's pursuing, catching, killing, and

52

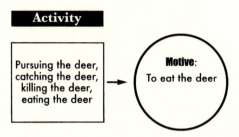

Figure 2.1. Example of the structure of animal activity.

eating a deer are the consecutive steps in the wolf's activity that bring it nearer and nearer to the motive of this activity (Fig. 2.1).

Sometimes an animal's activity may look like an exception to this rule. For example, a spider spins a web although a fly is not near by, which does not result in the immediate gratification of the spider's physiological need. Spinning a web, however, is an instinct that has been developed by the species in the course of evolution and natural selection and that is transmitted genetically from one generation to the next. Another example of an animal's activity that is not directed toward the immediate gratification of its physiological need, that is, toward its motive, is the activity of a rat in the Skinner box who pushes down a metal bar to get food. This activity, however, is the result of operant conditioning, which has made it possible to develop an artificial connection between pushing down the bar and getting food. Finally, as was already discussed, apes are able to use and even create tools to solve everyday life problems (for example, an ape attaches two short reeds and uses the composed longer reed to obtain a fruit that is placed outside his cage). The creation of a tool, to be sure, is not directed toward the immediate gratification of the ape's physiological need. As Köhler (1930) noticed, however, this type of behavior could be observed in apes only in the situation in which both the fruit and the reeds together were in the ape's visual field. Therefore, there was a perceptual connection between the reeds as a potential tool and getting the fruit as the motive of the ape's activity, which made the ape's tool-making operation a natural part of his fruit-directed activity. Thus, in all the discussed examples, those steps in animals' activity that seem not to be directed to the motive of this activity are still tied to this motive genetically, by conditioning, or by a perceptual connection between a potential tool and the motive.

Humans' use of tools changes the whole structure of their activity. In contrast to animals' activity, human activity consists of a set of steps (Leontiev called them "actions"), each being directed to its goal rather than toward the motive of the activity. Leontiev (1972/1981) wrote:

> The isolation of goals and the formation of actions subordinated to them lead to a division of functions that were formerly interwoven in the motive. Of course, the motive fully retains its energizing function, but the directive function is another matter. The actions that constitute activity are energized by its motive, but are directed toward a goal. Let us take the case of a human being's activity that is motivated by food. The food is the motive. However, in order to satisfy his/her need for food, he/she must carry out actions that are not *immediately* directed toward obtaining food. For example, his/her goal may be to make a tool for hunting. (p. 60)

Thus, the structure of the human activity in Leontiev's example can be presented as shown in Figure 2.2. It is not only that all the actions within this activity except for the last one are not directed toward its motive, but some of them even interfere with this motive. Instead of looking for food, the man is looking for the materials to make a hunting tool and is making the tool, *consciously* postponing the gratification of his physiological need in the hope of getting his reward later. Thus, the goals of the actions that constitute his activity are consciously formulated and used by him as intermediate objectives to be accomplished in the course of the activity.[6] It is easy to see that

---

[6] Leontiev (1959/1964, 1975/1978, 1972/1981) specially emphasized that the goals of *any* human actions are always conscious. Later in this chapter, I discuss the problems associated with this Leontiev's contention.

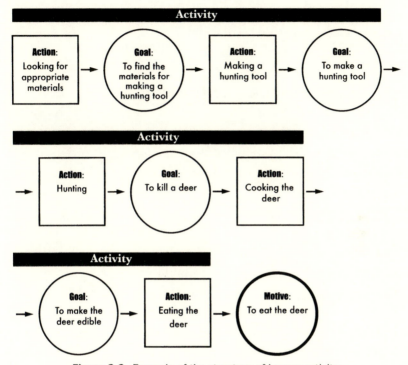

Figure 2.2. Example of the structure of human activity.

the performance of this activity requires planning and self-regulatory processes that are not required by any animal's activity.

Humans' use of tools leads to the division of labor in society, which makes human activity even more complicated and demanding in terms of its requirements for the development of mental processes that serve this activity. Imagine that the member of a hunting tribe from the example of Leontiev is making a hunting tool not for himself but to trade it with a hunter for a part of the hunter's prospective catch. In this case, when making the tool, the man should proceed from the hunter's requirements to, for example, the dimensions of the tool, rather than following his own preferences. The ability to take into consideration the interests and requirements of another person, according to

Piaget (1923/1959), is associated with a rather high level of the development of human cognitive structures.

Psychological Tools as Procedures

Thus, Galperin (1937) and Leontiev (1959/1964, 1975/1978, 1972/1981) have elaborated Vygotsky's idea that qualitative differences between practical activities of animals and humans lead to qualitative differences in their mental processes. To characterize these differences, the Russian followers of Vygotsky used the analogy that he drew between practical and mental activities of humans: Just as human labor is mediated by technical tools, human mental processes are mediated by so-called psychological tools. Vygotsky's followers, however, have considerably elaborated on his notion of psychological tools.

As discussed in chapter 1, Vygotsky emphasized the role of semiotic tools (language, concepts, signs, and symbols) as mediators of human higher mental processes. Vygotsky, to be sure, would agree that a child's learning a new word, concept, sign, or symbol does not automatically make this word, concept, sign, or symbol a psychological tool that comes to mediate this child's mental processes. Discussing, for example, scientific concepts as psychological tools that come to mediate mental processes of school-age children, Vygotsky (1934/1986) noted that "the difficulty with scientific concepts lies in their *verbalism*" (p. 148). He also pointed out that "scientific concepts . . . just start their development, rather than finish it, at a moment when the child learns the term or word-meaning denoting the new concept" (Vygotsky, 1934/1986, p. 159). Vygotsky, however, never elaborated these reservations. Therefore, his theory is traditionally (and, in general, correctly) associated with the notion of semiotic tools as mediators of human mental processes (see, e.g., Kozulin, 1986).

Could, however, words, concepts, signs, or symbols by themselves serve as psychological tools mediating human mental processes? To answer this question, let us use the analogy that Vygotsky and his followers draw between practical and psychological tools. From Vygotsky's (1981b) perspective, a sign "alters the entire flow and structure of mental functions. It does this by determining the structure of a new instrumental act, just as a technical tool alters the process of a natural adaptation by determining the form of labor operations" (p. 137).[7] The point is, however, that a practical (or technical) tool by itself does not determine the form or structure of a human operation because the possession of a tool does not lead automatically to the mastery of the procedure for the use of this tool. Everybody can probably remember his or her first unsuccessful experience with the use of chopsticks: The tool was given, but the procedure for the use of this tool as a tool for eating was missing. Similarly, as Galperin's (1937) study demonstrated, giving a spoon to an infant did not change the structure of her manual operation, and it was not sufficient for her use of this tool in the right way. To use the spoon as a tool for eating, the infant should master the procedure for the use of this tool. Therefore, "the mastery of a tool does not simply mean the possession of the tool, but it means the mastery of the procedure for the use of this tool" (Leontiev, 1959, p. 213).

The same is true of psychological tools. The mastery of a psychological tool requires that the child has mastered the procedure for the use of this tool (Elkonin, 1956; Galperin, 1957, 1966, 1969; Leontiev, 1959/1964; Zaporozhets, 1986b). To illustrate this point, let us return to Leontiev's (1931) memory study that was described in chapter 1. The study demonstrated that, in contrast to young children, 7- to

---

[7] This idea of Vygotsky has been supported by some of his American followers. Wertsch (1998), for example, wrote: "The major point . . . is that mediated action can undergo a fundamental transformation with the introduction of a new mediational means" (p. 45). And further: "Skills [needed to use new mediational means] emerge through the use of mediational means" (p. 46).

12-year-old children were able to use external memory aids (cards with different pictures) to memorize and recall the list of words that was presented to them. When interpreting these results, Vygotsky would emphasize the role of the cards as external psychological tools that came to mediate the children's memory. Although the following quotation from Vygotsky (1978) refers to another Leontiev memory study, it is quite applicable to the definition of his position in regard to the study discussed and to the problem of psychological tools in general:

> The introduction of cards as a system of auxiliary, external stimuli raises the effectiveness of the child's activity considerably. At this stage, the external sign predominates. The auxiliary stimulus [the card] is a psychological instrument acting from the outside. (p. 45)

Vygotsky, of course, would never deny that to use a card for memorizing and recall the child had to know *how* to use this card so that it would serve its role as an external memory tool, but this issue was not in the focus of his attention. In contrast, from the point of view of the neo-Vygotskians, it was the procedure for the use of the cards that mediated the children's memorizing and recall: The children had to find or develop a logical link between the word to be memorized and the chosen card. The procedure for the use of the cards, but not the cards themselves, served the role of the psychological tool that mediated the 7- to 12-year-old children's performance of the memory task. This explains why the young children who participated in the study could not use the cards given to them to memorize and recall: They simply did not possess this procedure.

In accordance with their new understanding of psychological tools as procedures that mediate children's mental processes, the neo-Vygotskians have reformulated Vygotsky's notion of internalization of psychological tools (Galperin, 1957, 1966, 1969; Leontiev, 1959/1964). Let us return again to Leontiev's (1931) memory studies, which demonstrated, in particular, that the use of external memory aids (the cards with pictures) by adults did not substantially increase their recall. Interpreting these data, Vygotsky (1978) wrote: "What takes place is what we have called internalization; the external sign [a card] that school children require has been transformed into an internal sign produced by the adult as a means of remembering" (p. 45).

From the neo-Vygotskian perspective, the primary difference between the performance of the school children and the adults in Leontiev's (1931) memory studies was not that, in order to memorize and recall, the children were using external signs and adults were using internal signs. Rather, the difference was in the level of internalization of their mnemonic procedures. The mnemonic procedures of the school children were partially exteriorized and therefore could not be performed without a visual support in the form of the cards, whereas the adults' mnemonics were internalized and did not require such a visual support. Thus, internalization for neo-Vygotskians is the internalization of procedures rather than the internalization of signs. As Leontiev (1959) wrote, "The mastery of mental procedures, which *underlies the acquisition by an individual of knowledge and concepts* [emphasis mine] accumulated by human kind, necessarily requires the transition from the performance of external procedures to...gradual internalization of the procedures, which results in their transformation into abridged mental procedures" (p. 305).

As Kozulin (1986) correctly indicates, "the role of a sign as the chief mediator has been played down [by the neo-Vygotskians]" (p. 270). In contrast, however, to Kozulin's (1986) criticism of this "revisionist position" (p. 264) of the neo-Vygotskians, I consider this position to be a fruitful elaboration of Vygotsky's notion of psychological tools. The neo-Vygotskians' notions of procedures as mediators of mental processes, and of internalization as internalization of procedures rather than signs, were especially important for their development of an innovative approach to school instruction, which is discussed in detail in chapter 6.

Mediation in the Context of Child–Adult Joint Activity as the Determinant of Mental Development

As mentioned in chapter 1, Vygotsky considered mediation to be a two-component process: Adults *mediate* the child's acquisition and mastery of new psychological tools, which become internalized and come to *mediate* the child's mental processes. Vygotsky's view on psychological tools as semiotic tools influenced his understanding of the process of adults' mediation of the acquisition and mastery by children of new psychological tools.

Indeed, a natural context for a child's acquisition of a new word, concept, sign, or symbol is the situation of child–adult verbal communication. To be sure, Vygotsky was far from viewing children as passive recipients of semiotic tools presented by adults in the course of interpersonal communication. As Wertsch and Tulviste (1992) correctly indicated, the "assumptions about human action . . . underlie the entire framework of Vygotsky's approach" (p. 554). However, when turning his discussion from general theoretical issues to children's development at different stages, Vygotsky often limited this discussion to the analysis of children's acquisition of semiotic tools in the course of interpersonal communication with adults (see, for example, Vygotsky's [1934/1986] doctrine of acquisition of scientific concepts as instrumental in the development of school-age children). This analysis by itself leads to the position that "whatever is of major importance for the development of individual consciousness, is introduced into it through social consciousness" (Leontiev & Luria, 1968, p. 353).

Such interpretation of Vygotsky's position in regard to the process of acquisition of psychological tools can often be found in the works of American psychologists. The most striking examples in this respect are the programs of so-called self-instructional training, which have been designed to promote the development of self-regulation in children with attention-deficit/hyperactivity disorder (ADHD; Meichenbaum & Goodman, 1971; Palkes, Stewart, & Kahana, 1968). The designers of the self-instructional training proceeded from Vygotsky's (1934/1986) idea that children's self-regulation develops as a result of internalization of their egocentric (private) speech (see chapter 1 for a discussion of this idea). Therefore, they assumed that if children with ADHD were taught to use private speech to regulate their performance and were then encouraged to internalize their private speech, the children's impulsivity would be reduced, and their self-regulation would be promoted. The self-instructional training starts with the therapist's modeling the use of private speech, talking aloud to himself or herself when performing a task. After that, the child is given the same task to perform, and the therapist is repeating the self-instructions while the child is performing the task. Then, the child performs the task, with the therapist encouraging the child to talk to himself or herself, imitating the statements that were used by the therapist. At the next step of the self-instructional training, the internalization of the child's private speech starts: The child is encouraged to use soundless, self-addressed speech accompanied with lip movements when performing the task. Finally, the child is supposed to use inner speech to regulate the task performance.

As evaluation studies have demonstrated, the benefits of self-instructional training are limited (Dush, Hirt, & Schroeder, 1989; Ervin, Bankert, & DuPaul, 1996). This training has sometimes resulted in better children's performance on the same type of tasks that were used in the course of training. There is little evidence, however, to suggest that maintenance and transfer of these positive outcomes of self-instructional training do take place. From the neo-Vygotskian perspective, these results are anything but surprising: Making children repeat, like parrots, the self-addressed verbal statements of the therapist does not teach them *how* to use these statements to regulate their performance. In other words, the situation of self-instructional training is analogous to the situation in which one is given chopsticks but is not taught the procedure for their use as a tool for eating.

From the point of view of the neo-Vygotskians, children can master the procedures for the use of psychological tools only in the context of their joint activity with adults aimed at performing a task rather than in context of their verbal communication (Elkonin, 1956; Galperin, 1957, 1966, 1969; Leontiev, 1959/1964; Zaporozhets, 1986b). In the context of such activity, the adult mediates the child's acquisition, mastery, and internalization of the procedure. The mediation starts with the adult's "exteriorizing" (modeling and explaining) the procedure for the use of the new psychological tool, which is necessary to perform the task. Then the adult involves the child in joint performance of this procedure, creating the zone of proximal development of a new mental process, and guides the child's mastery and internalization of this procedure. As the child becomes more and more proficient in the use of the procedure, the adult withdraws from the situation of joint performance, passing more and more responsibility for performing the task to the child. As a result, the mastered and internalized procedure comes to mediate the child's mental processes.

Some of the instructional programs developed by the neo-Vygotskians on the basis of their notion of mediation in the course of joint child–adult activity are described in the following chapters. In American educational psychology, a good example of an instructional program that is consistent with the neo-Vygotskian notion of mediation is "reciprocal teaching," which was developed to improve students' reading comprehension (Palincsar & Brown, 1984; Palincsar, Brown, & Campione, 1993). Reciprocal teaching is built around the joint activity of a teacher and students aimed at the analysis and understanding of a written text. At the beginning, the teacher models and explains four reading comprehension strategies: questioning, summarizing, clarifying, and predicting. The teacher uses these strategies to lead the group analysis of the text. Gradually, the role of the discussion leader is passed to the children, who take turns using the reading comprehension strategies that the teacher modeled, with the teacher providing the students with feedback and assistance. As the students become more proficient in the use of the reading comprehension strategies, the teacher withdraws from the group activity, passing more and more responsibility for performing the task to the students.

As one can see, reciprocal teaching, although inspired by Vygotsky's classical notion of mediation rather than the ideas of his Russian followers, perfectly meets the neo-Vygotskian requirement for mediation. The students' impressive success in independent reading comprehension, which has been shown to be the outcome of reciprocal teaching (Palincsar et al., 1993), confirms both the effectiveness of this instructional program and the fruitfulness of the neo-Vygotskian notion of mediation.

Mediation in the Context of Child–Adult Joint Activity as the Determinant of Development of New Activities

In addition to the development of the child's mental processes, systematic mediation by adults of the child's acquisition of new psychological tools in the course of their joint activity results in another important outcome: The child becomes engaged in a new activity. To discuss the mechanism of this shift from one activity to another, let us return to Leontiev's (1959/1964, 1975/1978, 1972/1981) analysis of human activity.

As discussed earlier, in contrast to an animal's activity, which is always directed toward its motive, human activity consists of separate actions, each directed toward its goal rather then toward the motive of the activity. This difference in the structures of animal and human activities leads to different prospects in terms of the development of these activities.

The development of an animal's activity is limited to changes within this activity. For example, through the use of conditioning, we can add new steps to an animal's original activity. This enriched activity, however, will still be "energized" by, and directed toward, the same biological motive. In other words, an enrichment and transformation of an animal's activity will never lead to the development of a new motive in the animal.

This general law has found much support in behaviorist studies of animal behavior. In classical studies by Wolfe (1936) and Cowles (1937), chimpanzees were taught to use poker chips to get food from vending machines. Then the situation was made more complicated: The chimpanzees had to collect 20 chips to get food. After that, the chips were used as rewards in the chimpanzees' learning new skills. Their successful learning with the use of chips as the reinforcement indicated that the chips acquired the reinforcing power: The chimpanzees worked the whole day to collect 20 chips, which could be exchanged for food only at the end of the day. It turned out, however, that if the chips became ineffective in getting food, they quickly lost their reinforcing power. Therefore, the conclusion can be made that the chimpanzees' successful learning with the chips as the reinforcement was still energized by, and directed toward, getting food, rather than getting the chips, as the motive of their activity.

Because animals can never develop new motives and because activities in Leontiev's theoretical model are distinguished on the basis of their motives, according to Leontiev, animals can never develop new activities. Therefore, a certain step within an animal's activity can never be converted into a new activity. Using as an example the studies with chimpanzees, learning new skills could never become their new activity.

In contrast, the development of a human activity may result in originating a new motive and, accordingly, a new activity. This happens as a result of the conversion of the goal of an action, which initially was a component of a human activity, into a new motive, and the conversion of this action into a new activity. In Leontiev's (1959) words,

> a human, under the influence of a certain motive, starts to perform some action, and ends with performing this action for its own sake because the goal [of the action] has converted into the motive. That means that the action has converted into the activity. (p. 234)

The phenomenon of the conversion of goals into motives and actions into activities can be illustrated with many examples from everyday life, works of fiction, and scientific observations. One such example can be found in the novel *Gobsek* by the famous French writer Honoré de Balzac. Gobsek, a moneylender, lived on the line of poverty. You can imagine everybody's surprise when, after his death, tremendous wealth was found hidden in his poor apartment. Let us analyze this case in Leontiev's terms. For the majority of people, saving up money is an action directed toward the goal of accumulating enough money to buy something, to ensure financial well-being after retirement, or, in general, simply to use it. For them, accumulation of money is not an end in itself, or a motive. Probably that was also true for Gobsek at the beginning of his moneylending career. At a certain point in his life, however, the accumulation of money converted from the goal of the action of saving up money into the motive of his new activity, with converting the action of saving up money into this new activity.

Another example of this kind deals with the eating disorder anorexia nervosa. For those suffering from this disorder, losing weight is their dominant motive, and starvation is the activity directed toward this motive. The famous Russian clinical psychologist Zeigarnik (1986) interpreted the origins of anorexia in terms of the conversion of goals into motives and actions into activities. According to her observations, the majority of girls and young women suffering from this disorder were plump at the age of puberty. At school, the peers would tease them, calling them "fat slobs" and "fatso," which not only made them feel bad but also was an obstacle in their interactions with peers (as discussed in chapter 7, interactions with peers is the leading activity of adolescents). The girls went on a diet, which resulted in their losing weight and in encouragement from their peers. At that point, starvation was an action directed toward the goal of losing weight within their activity of interactions with peers. At a certain point, however, losing weight turned into an end in itself: The girls switched to much more exhausting diets and would make themselves vomit if their concerned parents had made them eat something. Their extreme emaciation and all the associated unhealthy symptoms would make them pleased as indicators that they were not gaining weight. Thus, losing weight, which was initially a goal of their action of starvation, turned into the motive of their activity of starvation. This activity came to dominate the girls' lives with their sacrificing all the other activities (learning at school, interactions with peers, and others) to this dominant activity of starvation.

A similar interpretation can probably be given to the phenomenon of alcoholism. Drinking spirits never starts as an activity directed toward the motive of getting intoxicated. Initially, drinking spirits is an action within another activity (such as socializing or interaction with peers), and it is "energized" by the motive of this activity. Sometimes, however, to get intoxicated becomes an end in itself, or the motive of a person's drinking spirits, which makes drinking spirits an activity (often the dominant activity) of this person.

To be sure, the phenomenon of the conversion of goals into motives and actions into activities should not be associated only with the development of pathological motives and activities, although this is the case in the previous examples. What follows is a more optimistic

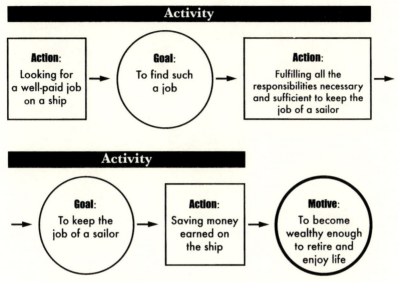

Figure 2.3. Initial activity of a character from Leontiev's story.

illustration of this phenomenon, which Leontiev often used when explaining it to his students.

A young man decided to spend several years working as a sailor and saving money to become wealthy enough to retire and enjoy life. He successfully implemented the first part of his plan: He found a well-paid job on a ship, spent several years working as a sailor, and saved enough money to retire. But at that point, he realized he had come to love the life of a sailor and gave up the idea of retirement. Instead, he enrolled in a navigation school to advance in the profession of a sailor, and after graduation, he continued to work on a ship for many years.

How does one interpret this story in terms of Leontiev's notion of the conversion of goals into motives and actions into activities? In the initial activity of the story's character (Fig. 2.3), the fulfillment of all the responsibilities necessary and sufficient to keep the job of a sailor was an action directed toward the goal to keep the job of a sailor. This

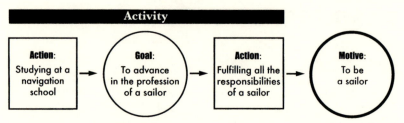

Figure 2.4. New activity of the character from Leontiev's story that developed from his initial activity (see Fig. 2.3) attributable to the phenomenon of the conversion of goals into motives and actions into activities.

goal turned into an end in itself for the character, that is, converted into the motive of his new activity (Fig. 2.4), which replaced his initial activity. Accordingly, what used to be an action in the character's initial activity became enriched and converted into his new activity.

These examples could hardly be explained within the behaviorist approach, in which the laws of humans' development are not considered any different from the laws of animals' development. As Baldwin (1967) indicates,

> there are objects and people whose value does not seem to depend – at least not any longer – on their usefulness in providing more basic rewards. The values attached to mother, country, virtuous behavior, and high achievement, for example, are apparently acquired in such a way that they become autonomous; they need not be reinforced. They pose a puzzling problem for a learning [behaviorist] theory of child development. (p. 404)

Thus, Leontiev's theoretical model makes it possible to interpret phenomena in human development that do not fit the behaviorist theory.

All the previous examples of the development of new activities in humans dealt with situations in which a new activity *happened* to ripen within an initial activity of the person. To be sure, in each of those cases, there were certain factors (physiological, psychological, or social) that led to the conversion of the person's goal into the motive and the action into the activity. Those outcomes, however, were not predetermined by the person's engaging in the initial activity. After all, not all the people who drink spirits are going to become alcoholics, and not all the people who choose a certain profession for pragmatic reasons come to love their profession for its own sake. In contrast, mediation, from the point of view of the neo-Vygotskians, is the optimal and direct way to lead children to the development of new activities through the conversion of their goals into motives and actions into activities (Elkonin, 1971/1972, 1989; Leontiev, 1959/1964, 1975/1978, 1972/1981; Zaporozhets, 1978/1997; Zaporozhets & Elkonin, 1964/1971). As an example, let us discuss infants' transition from the activity of emotional interactions with caregivers to their joint object-centered activity (discussed in detail in the next chapter).

According to the neo-Vygotskians, although young infants are actively engaged in object-centered manipulations, these manipulations are just actions within their activity of emotional interactions with caregivers (Elkonin, 1989; Lisina, 1974, 1986; Zaporozhets & Lisina, 1974). Initially, these are caregivers who involve infants into joint object-centered actions and mediate these actions in the context of their activity of emotional interactions. As a result of such mediation, by the end of the first year of life, joint object-centered actions become ends in themselves for children, that is, these actions turn into child–caregiver joint object-centered activity.

How does mediation lead to the development of this new joint object-centered activity? Although not differentiated explicitly by the neo-Vygotskians, the following two outcomes of mediation that lead to the development of this (or any other) new activity of children can be pointed out.

First, in the course of mediation, adults encourage the shift of the child's interests from the motive of the present activity to the goal of one of its actions. Discussing the development in infants of the motive of object-centered activity in the course of their activity of emotional interactions with caregivers, Lisina (1974) wrote: "Through manipulations of objects and drawing the child's attention to these manipulations, an adult can shift the child's interests and positive emotions from herself to these objects" (p. 67). This leads to the conversion of the goals of object-centered actions into the motive of the child's new object-centered activity.[8]

Second, in the course of mediation, children acquire and master new psychological tools, which results in the development of their new mental processes. These mental processes outgrow children's current activity, which creates the basis for their switching to a new activity. For example, caregivers' mediation of infants' object-centered actions in the context of their emotional interactions results in the mastery by infants of object-centered means of gestural communication. The infants' mastery of these means leads, as discussed in the next chapter, to major transformations of their mental processes, which will come

---

[8] As discussed earlier, Leontiev (1959/1964, 1975/1978, 1972/1981) held that the goals of any human actions are always conscious. As applied to his theoretical analysis of adults' activity, this contention seems logical. Indeed, actions are not directed toward the motive of the person's activity. Therefore, to substantiate for him- or herself the necessity of carrying out certain actions, the person should consciously formulate the goals of these actions in relation to the motive of the activity to be performed. When applied to the analysis of children's activity, however, the contention that the goals of human actions are always conscious is highly disputable. Indeed, to use the discussed example, nobody would seriously claim that infants consciously formulate for themselves the goals of object-centered actions to be performed. Surprisingly enough, neither Leontiev nor his followers have ever addressed this inconsistency when applying Leontiev's theoretical model to explain the development of new activities in young children. Proceeding from the neo-Vygotskians' writings (Elkonin, 1989; Lisina, 1974, 1986; Zaporozhets & Lisina, 1974), however, the following solution of this problem can be suggested. Because the major activities of young children are joint activities with adults, it is sufficient that *adults* have conscious goals of the actions in which they engage children. As discussed later, soon after the birth, children become extremely susceptible to all the influences from caregivers. Therefore, infants become engaged in new actions (such as object-centered actions) because these actions have been introduced by *adults* and because these actions are joint actions with *adults*.

to serve their object-centered joint activity with adults by the end of the first year of life.

This analysis shows that, from the neo-Vygotskian perspective, mediation not only creates zones of proximal development of new mental processes, but it also creates zones of proximal development of new activities of children through the conversion of their goals into motives and actions into activities. Adults come to mediate these new children's activities, which results again in developing new motives and new mental processes in children and thus creates zones of proximal development of new children's activities.

Activity Theory of Child Development

Stressing the role of children's activity as mediated by adults in their development, Leontiev (1959/1964), at the same time, emphasized that in each age period, children are involved in different activities, which play different roles in their development. He suggested that among all these activities there is one so-called *leading activity* that plays the major role in children's development in the given age period and prepares the children for the transition to the next age period. What activity is leading in the given age period is crucially determined by the society in which children find themselves. For example, in industrialized societies, in which children are required to learn in educational settings during the period of middle childhood, the leading activity of preschoolers would be the one that results by the end of the preschool period in children's school readiness. Sociodramatic play, according to Leontiev (1959/1964), meets this requirement the best. Therefore, he defined sociodramatic play as the leading activity of preschool children in industrialized societies.

It is worthy of note that the term *leading activity* in reference to preschoolers' play was initially introduced by Vygotsky (1966/1976,

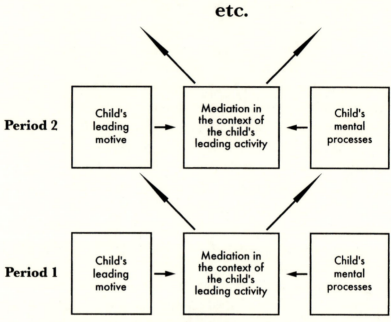

Figure 2.5. The neo-Vygotskian model of child development.

p. 537). For Vygotsky, however, the term was a figure of speech rather than a well-defined concept. On the same page on which he applied this term to children's play, Vygotsky (1966/1976) referred to play as "the leading source of development in pre-school years" (p. 537). In contrast, for Leontiev (1959/1964, 1975/1978) and other neo-Vygotskians (Elkonin, 1971/1972, 1989; Zaporozhets, 1978/1997; Zaporozhets & Elkonin, 1964/1971), the concept of leading activity became the cornerstone of their *activity theory* of child development. They analyzed and described the periods of children's development in industrialized societies in terms of their leading activities, and they explained children's transitions from one period to the next as their transitions from one leading activity to the next.

The model of child development elaborated within activity theory can be presented as follows (Fig. 2.5). In each period of development, children are engaged in the leading activity, which is specific to this age period in the given culture. This activity is driven by the children's *leading motive*, that is, the most important one in the hierarchy of the children's motives in this age period. The children's present *mental processes* serve this activity, but they are not sufficient for the children's independent performance of this activity. Therefore, this activity should inevitably be performed as joint child–adult activity with adults serving the role of mediators. As an outcome of mediation in the context of children's leading activity, the goal of one of the actions within this activity converts into a motive, which becomes the children's new leading motive. Another outcome of mediation is the children's acquisition and mastery of new psychological tools, which results in the development of new mental processes. Not only does the mastery of these mental processes make it possible for the children to perform this activity independently, but these processes also outgrow the children's current leading activity. The outcomes of mediation in the context of the children's leading activity create the basis for their transition to the new leading activity, which is specific to their next age period.

The analysis of activity theory makes it possible to present it as an elaboration of the strong notions of Vygotsky's theory of child development while successfully overcoming his theory's shortcomings. The strongest notion of Vygotsky's (1978, 1981a, 1934/1986) theory was his emphasis on the role of the social environment in child development. In his theory, adults' mediation (that is, supplying children with new psychological tools and the organization of the process of the acquisition, mastery, and internalization of these tools) is considered the major determinant of child development. Vygotsky, however, defined psychological tools as semiotic means rather than as mental procedures. Also, he was not consistent in his views on the role of children's activity in their development, which interfered with his notion of child development as "a single process of *self-development*"

(Vygotsky, 1984/1988, p. 189, emphasis mine). Sometimes, he described mediation as the process of children's assimilation of semiotic tools presented to them by adults in the course of interpersonal communication (Vygotsky, 1934/1986). In his writings, one can even find such expressions as "the forces moving the child's development" (Vygotsky, 1984/1998, p. 199), which are hardly compatible with the view of children as active contributors to their development.

Similar to Vygotsky, his Russian followers (Elkonin, 1971/1972, 1989; Leontiev, 1959/1964, 1975/1978; Zaporozhets, 1978/1997; Zaporozhets & Elkonin, 1964/1971) hold that mediation is the major determinant of child development. In their approach, however, mediation takes place within a specially organized children's activity rather than in the context of child–adult interpersonal communication, and it involves children's acquisition, mastery, and internalization of new mental procedures rather than of semiotic means. This synthesis of the notions of children's activity and mediation in activity theory of child development is an important accomplishment of the neo-Vygotskians. Their innovative view on the determinants of child development made it possible for them to give a much more thorough explanation of the mechanism of stage-by-stage development than the explanation one can find in Vygotsky's works.

As was discussed earlier, Vygotsky (1984/1998) was first to attempt to explain the mechanism of child development by integrating the development of children's cognition, motives, and their social development into a holistic model of stage-by-stage development. In his model, children's present motives and mental processes determine their "social situation of development" (that is, their relationships with the external world) in the given age period. The social situation of development is the context within which adults involve the children in the age-specific mediational interactions. As a result of such mediation, children develop new mental processes and new motives (the development of which is also influenced by physiological maturation). These neo-formations lead to change of the social situation of development and children's transition to the next period of development.

The mechanism of child development suggested by Vygotsky (1984/1998) is not free from shortcomings, however. First, Vygotsky never elaborated the notion of the social situation of development. In his writings, this notion is presented as a vague theoretical construct rather than as a well-defined unit of analysis of the periods in child development. In particular, Vygotsky did not explicitly differentiate between the contributions of children's motives and mental processes to the formation of the age-specific social situation of development. Second, the reasons for children's transition from one period to the next were declared rather than explained by Vygotsky. In other words, his theoretical model does not explain how changes in children's motives and mental processes lead to the change of their social situation of development and their transition to the next period of development.

In activity theory, Vygotsky's vague notion of the social situation of development as the characteristic of developmental periods has been replaced by the notion of leading activity. The neo-Vygotskians do not argue against Vygotsky's idea that each period of development is associated with children's relationships with the external world that are specific to this period (or, in Vygotsky's terms, with their social situation of development). They stress, however, that children's age-specific relationships with the external world manifest themselves in children's activity (so-called leading activity) aimed at the exploration of those aspects of the world that are related to these children's relationships with the world. Children do not have all the required means for such exploration, however. Therefore, adults' mediation of children's leading activity is a necessary component of such an activity.

The notion of leading activity as the characteristic of developmental periods has important advantages in comparison with Vygotsky's notion of the social situation of development. First, it stresses the role of children's activity in their development. Second, it integrates in a meaningful way motivational, cognitive, and social factors as contributors to children's age-specific leading activity. The leading motive drives children's leading activity, which is served by the children's present mental processes, and social mediation supplies children with the psychological tools they are missing to perform this activity. Finally, the notion of leading activity explains the reasons for children's transition from one period to the next. As an outcome of mediation in the context of children's leading activity, the goal of one of the actions within this activity converts into a motive, which becomes the children's new leading motive. Another outcome of this mediation is the development in children of new mental processes, which outgrow the children's current leading activity. These outcomes of mediation in the context of children's leading activity create the basis for their transition to the new leading activity, which is specific to their next age period. Thus, activity theory presents a much more elaborated explanation of the mechanism of child development than Vygotsky's explanation.

As the previous discussion has shown, the elaboration of Vygotsky's theory of child development into activity theory has made it possible for his Russian followers to accomplish the goal formulated by Vygotsky (1984/1998): to present and analyze the process of child development as "a single process of self-development" (p. 189). The neo-Vygotskians, however, refused to accept Vygotsky's (1984/1998) idea of the role of physiological maturation in the development of new motives in children. This, as will be shown, has sometimes weakened their analysis of child development. The neo-Vygotskian analysis of different periods of children's development in industrialized societies is presented in the following chapters.

3 First Year of Life: Emotional Interactions With Caregivers as the Leading Activity of Infants

Child psychologists working within different theoretical perspectives (except, maybe, for those working within the Piagetian framework) would agree that *attachment* (the establishment of infants' emotional ties to primary caregivers) is one of the important, if not the most important, neo-formations of infancy. In this respect, the neo-Vygotskian perspective is not different, for example, from Freud's (1940/1964), Erikson's (1963), and Bowlby's (1969/1982) views of the period of infancy. The neo-Vygotskians, however, have given an innovative explanation of the roots of attachment, the mechanism of its development, and the role of attachment in children's further development.

The Roots of Attachment: Alternative Perspectives

Discussing the first year of life, Vygotsky (1984/1998) emphasized infants' helplessness, their inability to satisfy vital physiological needs by themselves. Indeed, in contrast to animal offspring, human babies are born with only a few reflexes serving survival purposes, which, to make it worse, are not fully developed. For example, even a basic reflex such as sucking is so imperfect in newborn babies that they must learn how to suck. Therefore,

> the infant cannot himself satisfy even one vital need. The most elementary and basic vital needs of the infant can be satisfied in no other way than with the help of the adults who take care of him. Feeding and changing the infant and even turning him from side to side is done only with cooperation of adults. (Vygotsky, 1984/1998, p. 215)

At first glance, this "biological helplessness" (Vygotsky, 1984/1998, p. 215) of human infants is their great disadvantage – especially in comparison with animal offspring, who are born much better equipped to meet the demands and challenges of the environment. This "disadvantage" of infants that results in their dependence on adults, however, becomes the basis for the development of infants' emotional ties to primary caregivers: "With complete confidence, we can say that a positive interest in people is elicited by the fact that all the needs of the child are met by adults" (Vygotsky, 1984/1998, p. 230).

Vygotsky's explanation of the roots of attachment is surprisingly close to the explanations suggested within the psychoanalytic (Freud, 1940/1964) and the behaviorist (Sears, Maccoby, & Levin, 1957) theoretical frameworks, which dominated American psychology until the 1960s. In these theories, attachment is attributed primarily to the mother's gratification of the infant's need for nourishment. Empirical findings and observations that have been accumulated by psychologists since the 1960s have revealed the limitations of such "pragmatic" explanations of the roots of attachment. For example, infants were shown to develop attachment to those caregivers who do not gratify their physiological needs (Schaffer & Emerson, 1964). Even infant rhesus monkeys who had a choice of two "surrogate mothers" (one made of wire with a feeding bottle attached, and the other made of soft terry cloth) turned out to prefer to cling to the useless (in terms of feeding) but soft "mother" (Harlow, 1959, 1961; Harlow & Harlow, 1966).

These and similar data led most American psychologists to reject the explanations of attachment as the result of the gratification of infants' physiological needs in favor of the explanation suggested in Bowlby's (1969/1982) "ethological" theory.

Bowlby (1969/1982), like Vygotsky, stressed the helplessness of human infants, which makes their survival crucially dependent on the gratification of their physiological needs by caregivers. Rather than explaining attachment as an outcome of caregivers' gratification of infants' physiological needs, however, Bowlby found the roots of attachment in the evolutionary history of humankind. As a result of evolution and natural selection, human babies, like offspring of some animal species, are born with certain innate behaviors (such as crying, smiling, and following). These innate behaviors increase infants' chances of survival through evoking parenting responses. The caregiver (most likely the mother) who is the "target" of these behaviors is "genetically programmed" to respond to them by providing the infant with feeding and care and, most important, by protecting the infant from danger. As a result, the infant becomes more and more discriminative in his or her responses to the mother as opposed to other adults and over time develops attachment to her.

As discussed in the Introduction, "invoking the concept of innateness amounts to abdicating responsibility for explaining development" (Johnston, 1994, p. 721). The convenience of Bowlby's explanation of attachment is that it gives simple answers to difficult questions. Why do infants start smiling at adults? Because this is innate behavior aimed at evoking parenting! Why, as Spitz (1945, 1946) observed, do infants in orphanages not smile at adults? Because maternal deprivation has suppressed this innate behavior! Why do primary caregivers respond to infants' parenting-evoking behaviors by providing them with care, protection, and feeding? Because they are genetically programmed this way! In conclusion, Spitz's (1960) evaluation of Bowlby's early ideas about attachment as ones that "becloud the observational facts, are oversimplified, and make no contribution to the better understanding of observed phenomena" (quoted in Meins, 1997, p. 13) seems to be quite applicable to Bowlby's (1969/1982) later attachment theory as well.

Russian neo-Vygotskians (Elkonin, 1989; Lisina, 1986; Zaporozhets & Lisina, 1974) have suggested an explanation of the roots of attachment that, I believe, has overcome the shortcoming of the alternative explanations. As discussed, the neo-Vygotskians hold that the determinants of development are principally different in animals and humans. They emphasize the dominant role of social environment in children's development. Therefore, in their view, attachment as an important developmental neo-formation of the first year of life is not rooted in the evolutionary history of humankind, as Bowlby (1969/1982) believed.[1] Rather, the roots of attachment should be sought in the history of early interactions of infants with primary caregivers.

The infant–caregiver early interactions deal with the gratification of the infant's physiological needs by the caregiver. This does not mean, however, that attachment is the direct and necessary outcome of the gratification of infants' physiological needs, as Vygotsky (1984/1998), Freud (1940/1964), and behaviorists (Sears et al., 1957) believed. Rather, primary caregivers use the situations of gratification of infants' physiological needs to involve them in emotional interactions. The development of attachment is viewed by the neo-Vygotskians as the direct outcome of these infant–caregiver emotional interactions. Thus, attachment "is not innately predetermined, as it is in some

---

[1] Proceeding from this general theoretical position, Russian neo-Vygotskians would deny the validity of the use of animal studies, including Harlow's (Harlow, 1959, 1961; Harlow & Harlow, 1966), to explain attachment (as well as human development in general). Possible surface similarities between animal and human behavior, from their point of view, do not mean that their behavior is similar by nature. Therefore, "bodily contact and the immediate comfort it supplies" (Harlow, 1959, p. 70), which underlies the development of attachment in baby monkeys, cannot be used as an explanation of the development of attachment in human infants.

animal species, but it should be built up by adults" (Elkonin, 1989, pp. 95–96). What follows is the neo-Vygotskian analysis of how infant–caregiver emotional interactions develop and lead to the development of attachment.

The Development of Infant–Caregiver Emotional Interactions

Observations and studies of Russian researchers have shown that the development of infant–caregiver emotional interactions proceeds through several stages (Figurin & Denisova, 1949; Lisina, 1986; Zaporozhets & Lisina, 1974; Rozengard-Pupko, 1948).

THE FIRST STAGE: BIRTH TO 1 MONTH[2]

During the first month of life, infants do not demonstrate any positive emotional reaction toward either caregivers or the external world in general. Their emotional reactions (cry, facial expressions, and body gestures) are mostly negative, and they are triggered by physiological needs. Caregivers respond to infants' emotional reactions by determining the reason for their discomfort (whether the infant is wet, cold, or hungry) and gratifying their physiological needs. However, the gratification of infants' physiological needs by itself does not result in their positive emotional reactions toward caregivers; rather, infants just relax or fall asleep. Infants' behavior during this period can hardly provide any evidence in favor of Bowlby's (1969/1982) idea that they are innately preprogrammed to develop attachment to caregivers. The opposite is true, for "it is extremely difficult to develop a contact and communicate with infants during the first month of life" (Rozengard-Pupko, 1948, p. 15). If caregivers limit their interactions with infants to

---

[2] Here and further, all the time frames are approximate.

mere gratification of their physiological needs (which is often the case in orphanages), children will not develop any positive attitude toward them later on (Kistyakovskaya, 1970).[3] Normally, however, caregivers use the situations of feeding and changing the infants for talking to them, fondling them, and smiling at them, that is, *they take the initiative in establishing emotional contacts with infants.* As the outcome of these caregivers' initiatives, infants start responding to caregivers' emotional actions, which indicates the beginning of the second stage in the development of infant–caregiver emotional interactions.

THE SECOND STAGE: 1 TO 2.5 MONTHS

The infant's first positive emotional reaction toward caregivers can be observed at the beginning of the second month, when infants start smiling as a response to caregivers' talking to them, fondling them, and smiling at them in the context of feeding or changing. Russian researchers emphasize that the infant's first smiles are *evoked* through caregivers' substantial effort: "Initially, it is difficult to evoke the [infant's] smile: You should protractedly talk to the infant and make him or her concentrate on your face" (Figurin & Denisova, 1949, p. 14). By the middle of the second month, infants' smiles can be evoked outside of the context of gratification of their physiological needs, although it still requires significant effort (Rozengard-Pupko, 1948). As a result of such caregivers' efforts, infants come to respond more easily with smiles at caregivers' smiles, talk, and fondling. Finally, an important shift in the development of infant–caregiver emotional interactions takes place: Infants start smiling at caregivers on their own initiative rather than merely responding to loving actions. This shift indicates the beginning of the third stage in the development of infant–caregiver emotional interactions.

[3] These data are consistent with some of the observations made by Spitz (1945, 1946).

Earlier I noted problems associated with Bowlby's (1969/1982) interpretation of infant smiling as an innate behavior, which develops as a result of evolution and the role of which is to evoke parenting responses. The previous analysis of the dynamic of development of infant smiling supports the neo-Vygotskian position that, rather than being infants' "natural" reaction, their smiling is primarily the outcome of caregivers' initiatives aimed at involving infants in emotional interactions. An additional confirmation of this position can be found in studies of Russian and American researchers of blind (Fraiberg, 1974) and deaf and blind (Sokoliansky, 1962) infants. Unless caregivers managed to use specially designed techniques aimed at involving these infants in emotional interactions, the infants were at risk for not developing smiling at caregivers on their own initiative.

THE THIRD STAGE: 2.5 TO 6 MONTHS

As was mentioned, an important indication of infants' transition to the third stage of the development of emotional interactions with caregivers is their starting to smile at caregivers on their own initiative rather than just responding to caregivers' loving actions. American researchers refer to this kind of smiling as "social smiling" (Cole & Cole, 1993). The social smile, however, is just one of the components of a complex and intensive positive emotional reaction of infants to caregivers, which was called by Russian researchers "the state of excitement" (Figurin & Denisova, 1949). In addition to smiling, "the state of excitement" includes body gesturing and happy vocalizing. As soon as an infant notices a caregiver nearby, he or she starts smiling, vocalizing, and "expressing his joy with all the possible body gestures" (Rozengard-Pupko, 1948, p. 22). If caregivers respond to this infant reaction with smiling and talking, the infant expresses even more pleasure and joy. It is interesting that infants' interest in emotional interactions with caregivers may be even stronger than their physiological needs: The infant may interrupt sucking the nipple to smile at the mother

(Rozengard-Pupko, 1948). Often, the presence of a caregiver by itself is sufficient to make an infant stop crying and start demonstrating "the state of excitement."

This analysis of infant behavior during the discussed age period made it possible to conclude that "in the third month of life, the infant–adult relationships proceed on the infant's initiative" (Rozengard-Pupko, 1948, p. 25). This means that infants have developed a new motive, that is, the motive of emotional interactions with caregivers. As discussed in chapter 2, the development of a new motive is associated in activity theory with the development of a new activity. Therefore, the development in infants of the *motive* of emotional interactions with caregivers indicates that the *activity* of emotional interactions with caregivers has been developed in infants as their new activity.[4]

The further development of the activity of emotional interactions with caregivers during the discussed age periods proceeds in two main directions (Rozengard-Pupko, 1948). First, infants' reactions toward caregivers become less global. Rather than using all means (smile, vocalization, and body gestures) to express their joy and happiness at the sight of caregivers, infants may limit their reactions, for example, to happy vocalization. Second, infants are becoming more discriminating in their reactions to primary caregivers as opposed to strangers. At the beginning of the discussed age period, infants' positive reactions

---

[4] The development in infants of the activity directed toward the motive of emotional interactions with caregivers may serve as the ontogenetically first example of the phenomenon of conversion of goals into motives, and actions into activities, discussed in chapter 2. In the course of joint activity with infants aimed at the gratification of their physiological needs, caregivers mediate this activity, that is, enrich it with actions and goals of emotional interactions. As an outcome of such mediation, infants develop interest in emotional interactions with caregivers for their own sake, which means that the goals of emotional interactions have converted into their new motive. Accordingly, the actions of emotional interactions in the context of infant–caregiver activity aimed at gratification of infants' physiological needs have converted into infants' new activity of emotional interactions with caregivers.

toward caregivers are not much different from their reactions toward strangers. Later, however, whereas reacting joyfully toward primary caregivers, infants start to react more neutrally and sometimes even negatively (with crying) to strangers. This difference in infant reactions toward caregivers and strangers becomes obvious by the end of the sixth month, which indicates that attachment to primary caregivers has developed. The development of attachment manifests infants' transition to the next stage of development of their activity of emotional interactions with caregivers.

THE FOURTH STAGE: 6 TO 12 MONTHS

Russian neo-Vygotskians associate this age period with major transformations of infants' activity of emotional interactions with caregivers, which lead by the end of this period to the development of infants' new activity, namely, infant–caregiver joint object-centered activity (Elkonin, 1971/1972, 1989; Lisina, 1986; Zaporozhets & Lisina, 1974). What are these transformations?

It was during the previous stage of infant–caregiver emotional interactions that caregivers started to include objects and toys in the context of their interactions with infants. At that point, however, a toy was just "the means of [infants'] communication with adults" (Elkonin, 1989, p. 277), that is, infants' actions with objects were energized by their motive of emotional interactions with caregivers. Even 6-month-old infants could be easily switched from manipulation of toys to purely emotional interactions if caregivers started talking to them, fondling them, and smiling at them. The development of infants' attachment to caregivers, however, has made them especially susceptible to all the influences from caregivers, including the objects and toys that caregivers introduce to them in the context of emotional interactions. Therefore, "through manipulations of objects and drawing the child's attention to these manipulations, an adult can shift the child's interests and positive emotions from herself to these objects" (Zaporozhets & Lisina,

85

1974, p. 67). As a result of these caregivers' efforts, by the end of the first year, infants' interest in manipulations of objects becomes much stronger than their interest in purely emotional interactions with caregivers. They may even get irritated with an "idle caress" that has no relation to object-centered manipulations in which they are engaged (Lisina, 1986, p. 53). Thus, by the end of the first year, infants' motive of emotional interactions with caregivers is replaced by the motive of object-centered activity as their new leading motive.

The process of formation in infants of the new motive of object-centered activity is associated with a major change of the caregiver role in infant life. Rather than continuing to play the role of infants' partners in emotional interactions, caregivers, by the end of the first year, come to serve the role of mediators of infants' object-centered activity (Elkonin, 1971/1972, 1989; Lisina, 1985, 1986; Rozengard-Pupko, 1948; Zaporozhets & Lisina, 1974). The establishment of this new role of caregivers in infants' lives is prepared by both infants' attachment to caregivers and caregivers' efforts aimed at the change of meaning of their interactions with infants from emotional to object-centered. Thus, infant object-centered activity develops as infant–caregiver *joint* object-centered activity.

The shift from infants' activity of emotional interactions with caregivers to their joint object-centered activity requires new means of infant–caregiver communication. Whereas smiling, touching, and vocalization were sufficient means of infant–caregiver communication to serve their emotional interactions, these means of communication are obviously not sufficient to serve object-centered interactions. Therefore, infants master new means of communication to serve their object-centered joint activity with caregivers.

Thus, the neo-Vygotskians associate the second half of the first year with major transformations in infant life. First, infants develop the motive of object-centered activity, which gradually replaces the motive of emotional interactions with caregivers as their leading motive.

Second, caregivers come to serve the role of mediators of infants' object-centered activity. Third, infants master new means of communication to serve their object-centered joint activity with caregivers. What follows is a more detailed analysis of these transformations.

The Development of Infants' Motive of Object-Centered Activity

As was indicated, Russian neo-Vygotskians argue that the motive of object-centered activity develops in infants as an outcome of primary caregivers' efforts aimed at involving infants in joint object-centered actions in the context of their activity of emotional interactions. These caregiver efforts lead to a gradual transfer of infants' positive attitudes toward caregivers to the object-centered actions that caregivers introduce to infants. As a result, by the end of the first year, the goals of infants' object-centered actions convert into the motive of their new activity directed toward objects in the external environment (Elkonin, 1971/1972, 1989; Lisina, 1986; Rozengard-Pupko, 1948; Zaporozhets & Lisina, 1974).

As one can see, this interpretation of the origins of infants' motive of object-centered activity is a direct elaboration of Vygotsky's general theoretical position that "the relation of the child to the world depends on and is largely derived from his most direct and concrete relations with an adult" (Vygotsky, 1984/1998, p. 231). At the same time, this neo-Vygotskian position is in sharp opposition to the basic assumptions of Piaget's (1936/1952) developmental theory.

According to Piaget, infants' object-centered actions develop from innate reflexes. Although these reflexes serve survival purposes, it is already during the first month of life that they can be observed in situations in which they seem useless (for example, an infant may make sucking movements between meals). Between the ages of 1 and

4 months, these reflexes develop into body-centered actions (for example, an infant starts sucking the thumb). Between 4 and 8 months, infants' actions come to be directed toward objects in the external environment. The starting point in the development of an object-centered action is a situation in which an infant's action happens to cause a novel interesting result (for example, her arm movement has caused the rattle to sound). The infant notices the connection between her action and this interesting result and repeats this action again and again. The learned object-centered actions develop further during the age period of 8 to 12 months, and the combination of two or more actions into one behavioral pattern is the major direction of this development. For example, an infant removes a cushion to grasp a rattle and starts shaking the rattle.

Why, according to Piaget, do infants' innate reflexes develop into object-centered actions? Why do infants keep extending, first, their innate reflexes, and later, learned actions to deal with new objects? Piaget's (1936/1952) answer to this question is as follows. From the very first days of life, infants actively seek new stimulation, which is provided by new objects that do not fit exactly within infants' existing behavioral patterns. When coming across such objects, infants assimilate them into their existing behavioral patterns and accommodate these behavioral patterns to the new objects. As a result, these objects get fitted within infants' behavioral patterns, that is, they do not provide infants with new stimulation any more. This leads infants to resume their search for new objects that will provide them with new stimulation. Thus, according to Piaget (1936/1952), infants' innate curiosity, their search for new stimulation, is responsible for their engagement in object-centered behavior. In terms of activity theory, Piaget's position is that from the very beginning infants' object-centered behavior is their activity directed toward its motive.

Although both the Piagetian and neo-Vygotskian explanations of the development of infants' motive of object-centered activity can be supported with empirical data and observations, the neo-Vygotskian explanation seems preferable. To be sure, the neo-Vygotskians would not disregard numerous empirical data collected by Piaget (1936/1952) and other researchers (for example, by Muir & Field, 1979) that new-born infants are inherently responsive to new stimuli. Neither would they argue against the Piagetian contention that infants have an innate need for new stimulation, which results in the development of their innate reflexes into body-centered actions, such as sucking the thumb. What, however, the neo-Vygotskians would dispute is the Piagetian idea that infants' physiological innate need for new stimulation comes to play the role of the motive of their activity directed toward objects in the external environment (Galperin & Elkonin, 1967). The empirical data and observations that seem to support the neo-Vygotskian explanation of the development of infants' motive of object-centered activity can be summarized as follows.

First, as discussed, infants' interest in object-centered manipulations develops later than their positive attitudes toward caregivers. Of course, *post hoc* does not mean *propter hoc*. However, this sequence is totally consistent with the neo-Vygotskian view that the motive of infants' object-centered activity is the result of their transfer of positive attitude toward caregivers to object-centered actions, which leads to the conversion of the goals of these actions into infants' new motive of object-centered activity.

Second, there are many observations supporting Elkonin's (1989) statement that for young infants a toy is simply "the means of communication with adults" (p. 277). A good illustration of this point is the situation that is familiar to everybody who has observed young infants: An infant is shaking a rattle, smiling at the mother, and vocalizing happily. It is obvious that the center of the situation for the infant is the mother and that shaking the rattle is simply an action in the context of infant's activity of emotional interactions with the mother. Often, young infants engaged in object-centered actions cease their manipulations of objects once the caregiver leaves the room and resume them when the caregiver returns (Fayans's study quoted in Leontiev, 1959/1964).

The third series of data that seems to support the neo-Vygotskian explanation of the origins of infants' motive of object-centered activity was collected in orphanages. Infants in orphanages who did not develop attachment to caregivers were shown to demonstrate serious delays in, or even complete absence of, object-centered actions (Kistyakovskaya, 1970; Rozengard-Pupko, 1948; Spitz, 1945, 1946). Rozengard-Pupko (1948) summarized the observations of such children whose age was around 1.5 years:

> In the absence of child–adult emotional bonds, the child is joyless, blank-looking, motionless, often crying. All the child's actions are centered around his own body. These actions include touching and scrutinizing his own hands, touching his body, a shirt, or a blanket, and sucking his thumb and fist. (p. 21)

Thus, whereas the absence of infant–caregiver emotional bonds is not associated with the lack of infants' body-centered actions, it is highly associated with infants' lack of any interest in objects within their environment.

The fourth series of data that is relevant to the topic being discussed was obtained in Lisina's studies with 2.5-month-old infants raised in a group home whose parents came to visit them once a week (Lisina, 1986; Zaporozhets & Lisina, 1974). The researcher provided infants who belonged to the experimental group with 30 specially designed sessions of emotional interactions, spending 8 minutes every other day on smiling at, talking to, fondling, and stroking an infant. The sessions did not involve the use of any objects or toys. Two months later (that is, after the sessions of emotional interactions in the experimental group were over), two aspects of infants' behavior were evaluated. First, infants' "state of excitement" (that is, their positive emotional reaction to caregivers) was measured. Second, the researcher provided infants with several toys (a rattle, a toy car, etc.) and evaluated their object-centered actions. It turned out, first, that infants in the experimental group demonstrated a much more intensive, positive emotional reaction toward an adult than infants in the control group. Second, infants in the experimental group demonstrated higher interest in the manipulation of the toys and a better quality of such manipulation than infants in the control group. Thus, infants' increased positive attitude toward adults was shown to be associated with an increase in their interest in object-centered actions.

In conclusion, the data and observations described here are highly consistent with the neo-Vygotskian idea that the motive of object-centered activity develops as the result of transfer of infants' positive attitude toward caregivers to object-centered actions. Of course, these data leave room for alternative interpretations. For example, one may argue that infants' positive emotional attitude toward caregivers, rather than originating their interest in objects within the external environment, makes it possible for their "innate curiosity" to unfold successfully. Similarly, it may be argued that "maternal deprivation" suppresses infants "innate curiosity." It seems undisputable, however, that infants' emotional interactions with caregivers play the crucial role in the development of their motive of object-centered activity.

The Establishment of the Caregiver Role as Mediator of Infant Object-Centered Activity

The neo-Vygotskians associate the switch from the infant's motive of emotional interactions with caregivers to the motive of object-centered activity, which is completed by the end of the first year, with a major change in the role of caregivers in infant life (Elkonin, 1960, 1971/1972, 1989; Lisina, 1986; Rozengard-Pupko, 1948, Zaporozhets

& Lisina, 1974). Rather than continuing to play the role of the infant's partners in emotional interactions, caregivers establish their role as mediators of infant object-centered activity. Although not differentiated explicitly by the neo-Vygotskians, there are two factors that contribute most to the establishment of this new role of caregivers by the end of the first year of the infant's life.

The first such factor is the infant's attachment to caregivers that makes caregivers "the psychological center of every situation for the infant" (Vygotsky, 1984/1998, p. 231). Lisina (1985) wrote:

> It can be assumed that in the presence of a person to whom children are attached they will feel more unconstrained, will freely explore their environment.... The grounds for such an assumption can be found, in particular, in Mescheryakova's (1975) study that has demonstrated that, by the end of the first year, infants explore their environment more actively in caregivers' presence than if they are alone or in the presence of a stranger. (p. 22)

Attachment by itself, however, is not sufficient for infant "acceptance" of caregivers as mediators of object-centered activity. As Lisina (1985) indicated, a 1-year-old child "who has not enjoyed the experience of object-centered collaboration with adults ... is just seeking caresses from them ... but cannot get involved in joint [object-centered] activity" (p. 23). Thus, the second important factor that contributes to the establishment of the role of caregivers as mediators of infants' object-centered activity is the caregivers' efforts aimed at the change of meaning of their interactions with infants from emotional to object-centered.

As discussed, starting with the fourth month of infant life, caregivers enrich their emotional interactions with infants with object-centered actions. Elkonin (1989) wrote:

> Adults, when interacting with infants, often do not even realize that they are involving infants in joint exercise aimed at the development of grasping: Adults make infants concentrate on an object, bring the

object to a distance within which infants start reaching for the object, move away the object, making infants stretch for it,...and touch infants' hands with the object. (p. 125)

After infants have mastered voluntary grasping at a sufficient level, caregivers model for infants object-appropriate actions and encourage them to perform these actions on their own. For example, a mother, having involved her infant in emotional interactions, puts a rattle in the infant's hand, then takes the infant's hand and shakes it, encouraging the infant to repeat this action. When repeating such actions, infants manipulate objects in accordance with their physical characteristics, and caregivers' involvement, strictly speaking, is not a must for infants' successful performance of these manipulative actions: Infants can discover by themselves, for example, that a rattle will produce noise if they shake it. Caregivers' involvement in these actions, however, in addition to its motivational outcome (discussed in the previous section), leads to the establishment of their new role as mediators of infant object-centered actions.

This new role of caregivers becomes especially important by the age of 11 or 12 months, when infants start imitating caregivers' actions with objects and toys in accordance with their social meanings (for example, feeding a doll). As discussed in chapter 2, in contrast to physical characteristics of objects, their social meanings cannot be discovered by infants themselves. Therefore, caregivers' mediation of these object-centered actions becomes a must for their successful performance by infants. As Lisina observed,

Just modeling [an object-centered action] by itself increased infants' attention to adults and the objects that they had presented. If, in addition to modeling, adults encouraged infants to repeat the modeled actions and praised them for successful attempts, infants paid even more attention to adults' actions, tried even harder to repeat these actions...and expressed joy when praised by adults for their successful attempts. (Zaporozhets & Lisina, 1974, p. 145)

93

The outcomes of these caregivers' efforts are not limited to infants' successful mastery of new object-centered actions (Elkonin, 1960, 1989; Lisina, 1986; Zaporozhets & Lisina, 1974). A more important outcome of these efforts is that, by the end of the first year, when infants develop the motive of object-centered activity, they start taking initiative in involving caregivers in this activity. They try "to make the adult repeat an action, persistently moving a toy towards him, putting the toy in his hand" (Zaporozhets & Lisina, 1974, p. 145). In other words, caregivers' role as infants' partners in emotional interactions has been replaced by their new role as mediators of infant object-centered activity, which, therefore, develops as infant–caregiver joint activity.

The neo-Vygotskian view of the role of caregivers and infants' attachment to them in the development of infant object-centered activity differs from alternative theoretical positions that dominate contemporary Western psychology, but it is consistent with many empirical findings of American and Russian psychologists. What follows is a brief analysis of these theoretical positions and relevant empirical findings.

As noted earlier, Piaget (1936/1952) viewed the development of object-centered activity as the result of the infant's extension of innate reflexes to new objects in the course of independent exploration. In particular, he holds that voluntary grasping grows out of the infant's innate grasping reflex. Therefore, Piaget has limited the role of caregivers in the development of infant object-centered activity to providing the infant with opportunities for exploring the environment. This theoretical position does not leave room for acknowledgment of the importance of either caregivers or infant attachment to them for the development of infant object-centered activity. In fact, Piaget held that infants smiling at caregivers is their reaction to familiar images and is not any different from infants smiling at familiar toys and objects.

Some of the empirical data and observations that seem to be inconsistent with Piaget's view were discussed in the previous section. In particular, "maternal deprivation" was shown to be associated with serious delays in, or even complete absence of, infants' object-centered manipulations (Kistyakovskaya, 1970; Rozengard-Pupko, 1948; Spitz, 1945, 1946). In contrast, the enrichment of infant–caregiver emotional interactions resulted in a better quality of young infants' object-centered actions (Lisina, 1986; Zaporozhets & Lisina, 1974).

Piaget's (1936/1952) idea that voluntary grasping grows out of an innate grasping reflex has been challenged by Bruner (Bruner, 1973; Bruner & Koslowski, 1972) and Vygotskaya (quoted in Zaporozhets, 1986a). Their empirical findings have led to the conclusion that voluntary grasping develops as the result of infant early motor experience under the control of vision. This conclusion makes it possible to assume that adult mediation of infant early motor experience will facilitate the development of voluntary grasping. Indeed, Vygotskaya's study with 3- to 5-month-old infants demonstrated that organization and enrichment by adults of infants' motor experience under the control of their vision resulted in faster mastery by infants of independent voluntary grasping (quoted in Zaporozhets, 1986a).

Additional confirmation of the important role of infant–caregiver relationships in the development of infant object-centered explorations has been obtained in studies by American researchers (Frankel & Bates, 1990; Main, 1983; Matas, Arend, & Sroufe, 1978). These studies have demonstrated that the quality of attachment measured in 12- to 18-month-old children is associated with higher levels of their use of tools, exploratory behavior, and play with toys by the end of the second year. Although these studies were performed with children beyond the discussed first-year period, their results are highly relevant to the topic of this discussion. Proceeding from these results, Bowlby's (1969/1982) view on the role of infant attachment to caregivers in the development of object-centered exploration seems to overcome the limitations of Piaget's general theoretical position on this matter.

Similar to Piaget (1936/1952), Bowlby (1969/1982) viewed infant exploratory object-centered behavior as a natural phenomenon, which is of the same origin in animals and humans:

> Exploratory behaviour is elicited typically by stimuli that are novel and/or complex, characteristics that often go together. Any novel object left in the cage of an animal, be it monkey, rat or rhinoceros, sooner or later is inspected and investigated.... Humans, especially young ones, behave in the same way.... Such is the effect of novelty on a human child, indeed, that the phrase "like a child with a new toy" has come to express the epitome of concentrated absorption in some one item of the environment. (p. 238)

In contrast to Piaget, however, Bowlby (1969/1982) stressed that exploratory behavior "is greatly speeded up in the presence of a friend; and in a young creature especially it is notably accelerated by the presence of mother" (p. 239). This positive influence of caregivers' presence on infants' explorations takes place only if infants are attached to caregivers, however. Securely attached infants use caregivers as "a secure base" for exploration, whereas poorly attached infants "do not explore even when mother is present" (Bowlby, 1969/1982, p. 337). Thus, according to Bowlby, attachment to caregivers develops in infants the feeling of a safe, supportive environment, which is advantageous for their object-centered exploratory behavior.

Bowlby's (1969/1982) idea about infant use of caregivers as a secure base for exploration has found much empirical support in studies by American researchers. It has been shown that, starting at approximately 9 months, infants use caregivers' facial expressions, gestures, and actions to determine how to feel about a new strange event (this phenomenon has been called *social referencing*, Ainsworth, 1992;

Campos & Stenberg, 1981; Emde, 1992, Feinman & Lewis, 1983; Walden & Baxter, 1989). It has also been shown that infants' social referencing is directed toward infants' attached figures rather than toward strangers (Zarbatany & Lamb, 1985).[5]

Yet, can the role of caregivers in infants' object-centered exploratory behavior be reduced to providing infants with a secure base for exploration, as Bowlby suggested? Recently, American researchers have found that social referencing in infancy includes not only "emotional messages, which define 'how to feel' [but also] instrumental messages, which define 'what to do'" (Feinman, Roberts, Hsieh, Sawyer, & Swanson, 1992, p. 28). Infants' taking advantage of adult "how to feel" messages has been referred to as *emotional referencing*, whereas their utilization of "what to do" messages has been called *instrumental referencing* (Feinman et al., 1992).

Instrumental referencing, which develops by the end of the first year, refers to situations "in which the infant observes others to learn the actions to perform" (Parritz, Mangelsdorf, & Gunnar, 1992, p. 209). For example, having observed their mothers petting a rabbit and listened to mothers' explanations of this action, infants also petted the rabbit (Parritz et al., 1992). The situation of instrumental referencing often involves infants' attempts to have an adult model a desired object-centered action. For example, "an 11-month-old trying to get an unfamiliar adult to help him get bunny to pop out of the jack-in-the-box offered the toy as an invitation for the adult to act, and attempted to indicate what he wanted the adult to do" (Rogoff, Mistry, Radziszewska, & Germond, 1992, p. 325).

Whereas the phenomenon of instrumental referencing in infancy can hardly be explained within Bowlby's attachment theory

---

[5] For the analysis of data that seemingly contradict this statement, see Ainsworth, 1992, p. 362.

(Ainsworth, 1992, p. 365), it is highly consistent with the neo-Vygotskian analysis of the period of infancy. It is caregivers who introduce objects and toys to young infants, mediate infant object-centered actions, and change the focus of their interactions with infants from emotional interactions to object-centered interactions. Therefore, it is understandable that when infants develop the motive of object-centered activity by the end of the first year, they address caregivers when they need assistance in dealing with objects and toys.

At this point, however, caregivers lose their exclusive rights to mediate infant relationships with the external world. It has been shown that, in contrast to emotional referencing, which is typically "directed toward the mother but not to a familiarized stranger" (Ainsworth, 1992, p. 362), instrumental referencing can be directed toward a stranger as well (Rogoff et al., 1992). The neo-Vygotskians would interpret this phenomenon as an expectable outcome of the change of infant's motives from the motive of emotional interactions with caregivers to the motive of object-centered activity by the end of the first year. As Lisina 1986) indicated, "the main reason for infants' interactions with adults is now their joint object-centered activity" (p. 85). As van der Veer and van Ijzendoorn (1988) noted, however, "some mothers may provide a very good emotional climate while not being very adequate instructors" (p. 224). In this case, probably, infants can especially be expected to "accept" strangers as mediators of their object-centered activity.[6]

In conclusion, the neo-Vygotskian idea that, by the end of the first year, caregivers come to serve the role of mediators of infants' object-centered activity seems better substantiated than Piaget's and Bowlby's

---

[6] These observations, in addition to their theoretical value, lead also to terminological consequences. Starting with chapter 4, I use the term "adults" rather than "caregivers" when discussing children's relationships and joint activities with representatives of the older generation.

views of the period of infancy. The neo-Vygotskian explanation of the reasons for the establishment of this new role of caregivers as the outcome of both infants' attachment to them and caregivers' efforts aimed at the change of meaning of their interactions with infants from emotional to object-centered is consistent with recent experimental findings of American researchers discussed earlier.

Infants' Mastery of the Means of Communication With Caregivers to Serve Their Joint Object-Centered Activity

Any joint activity requires relevant means of communication between participants, and their transition from one joint activity to another requires that the means of communication be changed.

As discussed, the ontogenetically first infant–caregiver activity is aimed at the gratification by caregivers of infant physiological needs. Accordingly, infants' major "role" in this activity is to use their innate means of communication (crying, facial expressions, or body gestures) to express their physiological needs, which caregivers interpret and gratify. Rather than limiting their interactions with infants to gratification of their physiological needs, however, caregivers use the situation of feeding and changing to involve infants in emotional interactions. Infants' participation in these interactions requires that they use new means of communication with caregivers, such as smiling, vocalizing, and body gestures. Although these means of communication have, for sure, innate roots, the initial use of these means by infants is not spontaneous but, as discussed, is evoked through caregivers' substantial effort. "The state of excitement" described by the neo-Vygotskians manifests the mastery by infants of the means of emotional communication and their use of these means to participate in the new activity of emotional interactions with caregivers as well as

99

to initiate this activity. Then, again, for the second time during the discussed age period, caregivers provide infants with mediation that results in their transition to a new joint activity with caregivers. This time, caregivers use their emotional interactions with infants to involve them in joint object-centered actions, which leads to infants' transition to object-centered joint activity with caregivers by the end of the first year. Obviously, such means of communication as smiling, vocalizing, and body gestures, which could successfully serve infant–caregiver emotional interactions, are not sufficient to serve their joint object-centered activity. Therefore, infants should switch from the use of the means of emotional communication with caregivers to the use of the means of object-centered (or, as neo-Vygotskians have called it, "business-orientated"; Zaporozhets & Lisina, 1974, p. 147) communication. What follows is the neo-Vygotskian analysis of the development in infants of the means of object-centered communication.

The ontogenetically earliest type of object-centered communication is gestural communication. Vygotsky (1983/1997) described the major means of gestural communication that 9-month-old infants start to use to direct caregivers' attention to objects in their environment: the indicatory (or pointing) gesture. As was briefly discussed in chapter 1, Vygotsky found the origins of the indicatory gesture in the situation in which an infant tries to grasp an object and fails because the object is too far away. The mother interprets this grasping movement as the indicatory gesture and gives the object to the infant. Thus, the mother introduces *the indicatory meaning* into the infant's unsuccessful grasping movement. Only afterward, as the result of the mother's numerous responses to the infant's grasping movement as if it were the indicatory gesture, this movement transforms, reduces, and begins to be used by the infant as the truly indicatory gesture. Thus, according to Vygotsky, the means of gestural communication are learned by infants from caregivers in the context of their object-centered interactions, and then these means come to serve these interactions.

Following Vygotsky's (1983/1997) analysis of the indicatory gesture, the neo-Vygotskians hold that the major role of gestural communication is "to express the child's readiness for [object-centered] interactions with an adult and to indicate in what kind of interactions the adult is invited to become involved" (Lisina, 1986, p. 61). In addition to indicatory gesture, they have described some other means of gestural communication that infants use. For example, even holding out a toy or another object to an adult is a means of gestural object-centered communication because, when doing it, "the child, in a way, is describing a joint action that he wishes to perform, and he uses this object or toy as an invitation addressed to the adult to become involved in the performance of this action" (Lisina, 1986, p. 61).

The neo-Vygotskians strongly support Vygotsky's view that it is caregivers who provide infants with the means of gestural communication in the course of their object-centered interactions. They have described two major ways to provide infants with such means, although they have not differentiated explicitly between these two ways (Elkonin, 1960; Lisina, 1986; Zaporozhets & Lisina, 1974). The first way is to introduce a new meaning into an infant's "natural" movement, which is the case, for example, in the situation of infant mastery of indicatory gesture discussed earlier. The second way is to model a new object-centered action for an infant, which he or she then reproduces in an abbreviated or "sketchy" fashion to communicate to caregivers the desire to involve them in joint performance of this action (Lisina, 1986, p. 61). In both cases, the means of object-centered gestural communication that infants have mastered are "intentionally used by children *learned* [emphasis mine] movements" (Lisina, 1986, p. 63).

Thus, in contrast to the means of emotional communication, the means of gestural communication can successfully serve infants's object-centered interactions with caregivers. However, as infant–caregiver object-centered interactions develop and become more complicated, the means of gestural communication become insufficient to serve these interactions (Elkonin, 1960; Lisina, 1986). Therefore, by the end of the first year, infants start the mastery of a qualitatively new means of object-centered communication, that is, verbal means of communication. Verbal communication comes to serve children's object-centered interactions with caregivers during the second year, and children's mastery of its means is discussed in the next chapter.

The neo-Vygotskian ideas that, around the age of 9 months, infants become engaged in gestural communication with caregivers and that this communication plays an important role in the development of infant object-centered behavior are consistent with the ideas and findings of many non-Piagetian-oriented Western researchers (see, for example, Feinman, 1992; Gauvain, 2001; Newson, 1979; Rogoff, Malkin, & Gilbride, 1984; Snow, de Blauw, & van Roosmalen, 1979; Tomasello, 1999; Trevarthen, 1979, 1980, 1988.). Some of these researchers, similar to Vygotsky and his Russian followers, view the development of object-centered means of communication in infants as the direct outcome of caregiver mediation (Newson, 1979; Rogoff et al., 1984; Tomasello, 1999). In this respect, it is interesting to discuss Tomasello's (1999) analysis of the origins of infants' indicatory (or pointing) gesture as a means of gestural object-centered communication.

Tomasello (1999) offers two hypotheses to explain the origins of the indicatory gesture. The first is as follows:

> Many infants use arm and index finger extension to orient their own attention to things, and, if the adult reacts appropriately, this kind of pointing may become ritualized. In this scenario it would be possible for an infant to point for others while still not understanding their pointing gestures for her.... Infants who have learned to point via ritualization will understand it only as an effective procedure for getting others to do things. (Tomasello, 1999, pp. 87–88)

The alternative Tomasello's (1999) hypothesis is that

> the infant observes an adult point for her and comprehends that the
> adult is attempting to induce her to share attention to something;
> that is, she comprehends the communicative goal of the gesture. The
> child then imitatively learns the gesture by seeing that when she has
> the same goal she can use the same means. (p. 88)

As one can see, both Tomasello's hypotheses are different from
Vygotsky's (1983/1997) explanation of the indicatory gesture as rooted
in infants' unsuccessful grasping movement. These hypotheses, however, are highly consistent with the Vygotskian general theoretical
framework. In the first Tomasello scenario, caregivers introduce the
indicatory meaning into infants' "natural self-directed pointing," in
much the same way that "Vygotskian caregivers" introduce this meaning into infants' unsuccessful grasping movement. In the second
Tomasello scenario, caregivers introduce the indicatory gesture to infants as a new means of communication, which infants then master
and start to use to direct caregiver's attention. Thus, in both cases, it is
caregivers who provide infants with the means of gestural communication in the course of their object-centered interactions.

Not all the researchers, however, would agree with the idea of
the dominant role of caregivers in infants' development of new
means of object-centered communication. An example of the opposite position in this respect is the works of Trevarthen (1979, 1980,
1988), whose ideas are rather popular among contemporary Western
psychologists.

Similar to the neo-Vygotskians, Trevarthen (1979, 1980, 1988) discussed infants' transition from emotional communication with caregivers, which starts in the second month, to their object-centered communication by the age of 9 months. In contrast to the neo-Vygotskians,
however, he substantially underplays the role of caregivers in the

development of infant–caregiver communication. Trevarthen holds that "humans are born with a self-regulating strategy for getting knowledge by human negotiation and co-operative action" (1988, p. 39), that from the very beginning infants have "a clear commitment to intentional communication" (1979, p. 331), and that infants are engaged in communication with caregivers as "conscious and personal" participants (1980, p. 530). Although the development of infants' communication is "supported by responses older persons give to their communicative expressions" (Trevarthen, 1988, p. 39), this support, according to Trevarthen, is not a must. Because "there are intrinsic abilities in babies to be expressive in a human way" (Trevarthen, 1988, p. 44–45), their communications with caregivers "do not depend on maternal behaviours for their beginning and may develop autonomously through infancy as long as the human environment is 'good enough'" (Trevarthen, 1988, p. 45). Referring specifically to infants' object-centered gestural communication, Trevarthen (1988) indicated that "gestures have an expressive value that needs response from others for its maturation, but not for its initiation" (p. 80).

Trevarthen's ideas cited here seem highly arguable. As discussed, although the means of emotional communication (smiling, vocalizing, and body gestures) are, indeed, innately rooted, infants' use of these means, rather than being spontaneous, is evoked by caregivers through substantial effort. Therefore, it is hard to agree with Trevarthen's (1979) claim that "human beings are equipped at birth with a mechanism of personality which is sensitive to persons and expresses itself as a person does" (p. 321). Observations and empirical findings that he used to substantiate this claim are not convincing. For example, in one of his studies

> two-month-olds seemed to display an exquisite sensitivity to the contingencies of social interactions with others, which he interprets as

evidence that the infant understands the subjectivity of the other. However, a number of researchers who have recently attempted to replicate these results have had mixed success in doing so. (Tomasello, 1999, p. 66)

Even more arguable is Trevarthen's (1980, 1988) idea that the means of infant object-centered gestural communication, rather than being learned, are innately rooted and that these means' "expressive value ... needs response from others for its maturation, but not for its initiation" (Trevarthen, 1988, p. 80). Challenging this view, Tomasello (1999) indicated that 5-month-old infants already have all of the motor skills necessary to use the pointing gesture: They "both reach for objects and extend their index fingers quite often" (p. 66). They will not, however, use the pointing gesture until the age of approximately 9 months. Therefore, it is not motor limitations that prevent young infants from engagement in object-centered communication with caregivers.

Finally, an important limitation of Trevarthen's approach is that it fails to explain the reason for infant transition from emotional to object-centered communication. Trevarthen (1980) limited the analysis of this transition to the statement that "before the first year is out something happens to transform the infant's mind, and ... a uniquely human sharing of experience begins" (p. 561). The neo-Vygotskian explanation of this transition seems much more convincing than the view of Trevarthen on this matter.

In conclusion, the neo-Vygotskian analysis of the role of caregivers in the development of the means of object-centered communication in infants seems better substantiated than Trevarthen's nativist approach. Not only is their analysis consistent with empirical data and observations, it also explains infant transition from emotional to object-centered communication with caregivers, which Trevarthen's approach fails to do.

105

Why Is the Activity of Emotional Interactions With Caregivers Leading for Infants?

As discussed, by the end of the first year, caregivers' mediation and enrichment of their emotional interactions with infants result in the following outcomes. First, infants have developed the motive of object-centered activity. Second, they have "accepted" caregivers as mediators of their object-centered activity and mastered the gestural means of object-centered communication with caregivers. Infants' mastery of the means of gestural communication, in addition to its "communicational" value, also leads to major transformations of their mental processes, which should be discussed separately.

As mentioned in chapter 1, Vygotsky (1984/1998) emphasized the metacognitive value of the acquisition of the indicatory gesture by infants. He held that the mastery of the indicatory gesture makes it possible for infants to direct the attention of others, which is the starting point in the development of their ability to control and regulate their cognitive processes and their behavior in general. Similar ideas have been expressed by several American researchers, who associate infant mastery of gestural means of object-centered communication with the development of infant–caregiver *joint attention* (Bruner, 1995; Gauvain, 2001; Tomasello, 1999). Joint attention "is the tendency for social partners to focus on a common reference, which may be an object, person, or event, and *to monitor one another's attention* [emphasis mine] to this outside entity" (Gauvain, 2001, p. 86). Although Vygotsky's (1984/1998) speculation that infant–caregiver mutual attentional monitoring facilitates the development of infant self-regulation has not been empirically proven, the engagement of infants in joint attention experiences "has been shown to predict later development in several domains, especially language" (Gauvain, 2001, p. 86). The importance of infants' engagement in joint attentional behaviors for their further development has also been emphasized by Tomasello (1999), who has called the emergence of these behaviors "the nine-month revolution" (p. 61).

Important as it is, the development of infants' ability to be engaged in joint attention with caregivers is not *the most important* developmental outcome of their mastery of the means of object-centered communication. As discussed in previous chapters, Vygotsky and his Russian followers hold that the development of children's mental processes is the result of their acquisition of psychological tools, which creates the zone of proximal development of these mental processes. Until the child has mastered and internalized a new psychological tool that the adult provided, this tool does not belong to the child's consciousness but can be used by him or her only at the "interpsychological" (Vygotsky, 1981a, p. 163) level. As Bruner (1985) insightfully expressed this Vygotskian position:

> if the child is enabled to advance by being under the tutelage of an adult or a more competent peer, then the tutor or the aiding peer serves the learner as *a vicarious form of consciousness* until such a time as the learner is able to master his own action through his own consciousness and control. (p. 24, emphasis mine).

To gain access to this "vicarious form of consciousness," however, children have to acquire appropriate means of communication with adults. Thus, infants' acquisition of gestural means of object-centered communication is the first step in exceeding the bounds of their consciousness and creating the zone of proximal development of their mental processes.

The previous analysis has shown that mediation in the context of infant activity of emotional interactions with caregivers results, by the end of the first year, in the major transformations of infant motives, mental processes, and behavior in general. These transformations

107

create the basis for infant transition to object-centered joint activity with adults, which, as discussed in the next chapter, plays the leading role in child development during the next age period. Thus, infant activity of emotional interactions with caregivers meets all the requirements of the leading activity as formulated by the neo-Vygotskians.

4 Second and Third Years of Life: Object-Centered Joint Activity With Adults as the Leading Activity of Toddlers

According to Piaget (1936/1952), the development of children's manipulations of objects during the second year of life is simply a continuation of the development of their object manipulations as infants. He did not see a major qualitative difference between children's object-centered actions during the first and second years, which made it possible for him to designate the first 2 years of life as belonging to the same sensorimotor period of development. In contrast, following Vygotsky (1984/1998), Russian neo-Vygotskians emphasize a major difference between object-centered actions during the first and second years (Elkonin, 1978, 1989; Lekhtman-Abramovich & Fradkina, 1949; Zaporozhets & Lisina, 1974).

Until the end of the first year of life, infants manipulate objects in accordance with their physical characteristics: shaking a rattle, pushing a ball, and so on. Of course, Russian neo-Vygotskians would not deny that such independent manipulations of objects in accordance with their physical characteristics can often be observed during the second and even the third years of life. Neither would they undermine the importance of such manipulation for the child's learning different physical properties of objects and the environment in general.

The neo-Vygotskians, however, give major emphasis to another type of children's object-centered actions, which become typical of children during the second and third years of life. These are actions with objects in accordance with their social meanings, which include, but are not limited to, children's play actions with different toys. To understand this neo-Vygotskian position, it is important to return to the Vygotskian notion of mediation as the major determinant of children's development.

When manipulating objects in accordance with their physical characteristics, children, strictly speaking, do not need an adult nearby. Physical characteristics of objects are on the surface and visible and can therefore be revealed in the course of independent explorations. Therefore, children can discover by themselves, for example, that a ball rolls away if pushed or that a rattle makes a sound if shaken. When carrying out such independent actions, however, children are performing at the *actual* rather than *proximal* level of development of their mental processes, which is not particularly advantageous in terms of their mental development (see chapter 1 for a discussion of the notions of actual and proximal levels of development).

In contrast, as discussed in the previous chapters, when involved in actions with objects in accordance with their social meanings, children are in need of adult help: As opposed to physical characteristics of objects, their social meanings are not "written" (Elkonin, 1989, p. 48) on objects and therefore cannot be discovered by children independently. Such involvement of adults in children's actions with social objects provides the context for adult mediation of children's mental processes. Thus, child–adult joint object-centered actions are not only a must for children's mastery of the ways to use social objects, but they also lead to the creation of the zone of proximal development of the child's mental processes.

As discussed in chapter 3, by the end of the first year, infants have developed the motive of object-centered activity. They have also "accepted" adults as mediators of this activity and started to imitate adult actions with objects and toys in accordance with their social meanings. Finally, they have mastered the gestural means of object-centered communication with adults, which, in addition to its "communicational" value, has also led to the development of infant–adult joint attention and created a foundation for further development of children's mental processes.

Thus, according to the neo-Vygotskians, children's object-centered joint activity with adults is both advantageous for their development during the discussed age period and is already prepared for by their development during the previous age period. Proceeding from this understanding of child–adult joint object-centered activity, Russian neo-Vygotskians have suggested that this activity is leading for children during the second and third years of life. The major goals of their studies have been to analyze how this activity develops and in what developmental outcomes this activity results.

The Development of Children's Object-Centered Joint Activity With Adults

Summarizing the results of the neo-Vygotskians' major studies (Elkonin, 1978, 1989; Fradkina, 1946; Lekhtman-Abramovich & Fradkina, 1949; Mikhailenko, 1975; Zaporozhets & Lisina, 1974), one finds that the development of child–adult object-centered activity can be presented as proceeding through the following two stages.

THE FIRST STAGE: 1 YEAR TO 2 YEARS
At the beginning of this stage, children continue imitating adults' actions with objects and toys in accordance with their social meanings (for example, feeding a doll), which they started to do at the end of the period of infancy. Such imitations appear only if adults, having

111

demonstrated appropriate actions, then encourage children to imitate them. As a result of these adult efforts, the number of children's nonspecific manipulations of objects (shaking, banging) decreases, and they willingly imitate adult actions even without encouragement. These children's actions, however, are limited to exact imitations of actions with those toys and objects adults used in the course of their joint activity with children. For example, a 1-year-old girl

> always lulls and feeds only those toy-animals that her caregiver used to perform these actions. For the child of this age, it does not matter whether or not a toy resembles the object that it represents. What does matter is that this is the same toy with which an adult and the child jointly played. (Elkonin, 1978, p. 162)

In the course of mastery of a new action, children constantly refer to adults to get a confirmation of the correctness of their performance, and they actively seek an adult's help if they experience difficulties with imitation of a new action.

Later, children start to transfer the actions that they have mastered in the course of joint activity with adults to new objects and situations (for example, the action of feeding a doll with a spoon is transferred to using a spoon to feed a toy dog, a toy horse, etc.). The importance of children's transfer of their object-centered actions to new objects and situations is that these actions get generalized, which prepares the way for their separation from particular objects to which they initially were tied. The major step toward the separation of actions from objects, however, is associated with children's use of object substitutes, which increases dramatically by the end of the second year of life, indicating children's transition to the second stage of their object-centered joint activity with adults.

THE SECOND STAGE: 2 TO 3 YEARS

As Elkonin (1978) indicates, object substitutions appear in a situation in which a child is missing an object that is necessary for performance of a play action. For example, children may use a stick to substitute for a spoon when feeding a doll, or a stone to substitute for a piece of soap when washing a doll's hands. Observations and studies of Russian neo-Vygotskians have shown that initial use by children of object substitutes occurs only after an adult, having involved a child in joint play with objects, has suggested that the child use a certain object instead of a missing one (Bugrimenko & Smirnova, 1994; Elkonin, 1978; Fradkina, 1946; Lekhtman-Abramovich & Fradkina, 1949; Mikhailenko, 1975). Such experience of joint child–adult play with object substitutes leads later to children's independent imitation of object substitutions performed by adults and, still later, to children's creation of their own object substitutions. By the end of the third year, children demonstrate a high level of object substitutions, which reveals itself, in particular, in their ability to use the same object during the same play to substitute for different missing objects. For example, when performing a set of logically connected play actions (washing a doll's hands, feeding the doll, putting the doll to bed), they may use the same stone to substitute for a piece of soap when washing the doll's hands and for an apple when feeding the doll, with a renaming of the stone in accordance with what object (a piece of soap or an apple) it is representing. It is important, however, that children's first renaming of a substitute object after a missing object that it is representing occurs as the result of an adult's renaming this object.

Piaget (1945/1962) and many Western psychologists (see Fein, 1981, for an overview) associate object substitutions with children's transition to a new level of performance, which is defined by different researchers as symbolic (make-believe, imaginative, fantasy, dramatic, or pretend) play. Although Vygotsky (1966/1976; 1984/1998) and the neo-Vygotskians (Elkonin, 1978; Slavina, 1948; and others) agree that children's activity with the use of substitutes can be defined as play in the broadest sense of the word, they prefer to use the term play to define children's activity in which they take play roles and act in accordance with these roles. This activity emerges during the third year of life, when children start naming themselves as action performers. Initially, they name themselves with their real names (for example, a boy brings a cup to a toy horse's mouth and says "Bobby is feeding"; Elkonin, 1978). By the end of the third year, children begin to use the name of the adult (for example, a mother) whose actions they are imitating, which indicates their transition to role-play.[1] Initial assumption by children of play roles has been shown to be a result of adults' mediation aimed at the introduction of the world of social roles and relations to children (this mediation is discussed in the next section) (Elkonin, 1978; Mikhailenko, 1975; Slavina, 1948; Sokolova, 1973).

This analysis has shown that, according to the neo-Vygotskians, adult mediation is the major determinant of children's transition from object-centered manipulations in the beginning of the second year to role-play at the end of the third year. This theoretical view is the opposite of the position of Piaget, who emphasized as an important characteristic of play

> the child's refusal to allow the world of adults or of ordinary reality to interfere with play, so as to enjoy a private reality of his own. But this reality is believed in spontaneously, without effort, merely because it is the universe of the ego, and the function of play is to protect this universe against forced accommodation to ordinary reality. (Piaget, 1945/1962, p. 168)

As Fein (1981) indicated, in the early 1970s, "Piaget's work became the basis of systematic studies of pretend play" for Western researchers (p. 1097). According to Berk and Winsler (1995), "because the Piagetian perspective has been so widely accepted, not until recently have [Western] investigators seriously addressed the social context of

---

[1] Children's verbal naming of roles that they have taken is used as the criterion of role-play by some Western psychologists as well (Dunn & Dale, 1984; Huttenlocher & Higgins, 1978; Miller & Garvey, 1984).

children's play experiences" (p. 62). Not only did the Piagetian view of play as children's solitary activity strongly influence the studies of play by Western psychologists in the 1970s, but it even resulted in misinterpretation by some researchers of those studies that failed to confirm their disregard of the role of adults in children's play. For example, summarizing experimental data, Fein (1981) concluded:

> It is unlikely that parents play pretend games with their young children or model such games.... When pretend episodes occur in the home they are more likely to be initiated by the child than the mother, and although the mother may acknowledge the pretense or offer a verbal suggestion, she rarely joins or extends it. (p. 1106)

To support this conclusion, Fein (1981) referred, in particular, to the study of Dunn and Wooding (1977). Similar interpretation of this study can be found in Rubin, Fein, and Vandenberg (1983). As Smolucha (1992) correctly indicated, such an interpretation of the Dunn and Wooding study is simply wrong:

> In a review of play research, Rubin, Fein, and Vandenberg (1983) concluded that observational research has failed to show that children learn how to play through interactions with their mothers, but then erroneously cited the Dunn and Wooding (1977) study as supporting that conclusion (1983, pp. 728–729). Dunn and Wooding (1977) actually found that mothers of children aged 18 to 24 months initiated 39% of the pretend play episodes, and most of the child-initiated episodes were interactions with the mother. (p. 72)[2]

New challenges to the Piagetian understanding of play as children's solitary activity have been suggested by empirical findings and observations that Western researchers accumulated in the 1980s and thereafter. Summarizing the findings of the late 1970s and early 1980s,

---

[2] In the following section of the chapter, one can find more references to the results of the Dunn and Wooding (1977) study as supporting rather than contradicting the neo-Vygotskian view of play.

O'Connell and Bretherton (1984) wrote: "The significant differences in the children's performance in spontaneous and elicited play situations lend some support to Vygotsky's argument that activities conducted with the assistance of capable collaborators enable children to achieve more than they might on their own" (p. 343). They emphasized, at the same time, that to be efficient, adult mediation should be "in the zone of proximal development" of children (p. 365; this reservation explains the failure of some researchers to advance children's play through adult participation).

Observations and empirical findings of the late 1980s and early 1990s brought up still stronger support for the Vygotskian position in regard to the role of adults in children's play. Summarizing some of these findings, Wachs (1993) concluded that caregivers' mediation had been shown to be positively related to the advancement of children's play. Another such analysis by O'Reilly and Bornstein (1993) led them to the following conclusion:

> Maternal participation in child play lengthens play bouts, raises the level of sophistication of those bouts, and makes play more diverse, in comparison to solitary child play.... The highest level of child play occurs in direct response to maternal demonstrations and solicitations: When mothers prompt child play, child play is more sophisticated than either spontaneous child play with mother or play alone. (p. 58)

Discussing the results of their observations, Haight and Miller (1993) reached a similar conclusion:

> By observing young children in the family context we discovered that pretending was not only overwhelmingly social but that mothers served as the primary play partners from one to three years of age.... Mothers attended to and pursued the topics introduced by the child, while at the same time extending the play by elaborating upon and prompting the child. (pp. 6–7)

116

Thus, the data and observations of Western researchers have provided strong empirical support for the Vygotskian view that the advancement of children's actions with toys is determined by caregivers' mediation of these actions. It would not be an exaggeration to say that this Vygotskian view has come to influence not only more and more Western studies of child play but educational practices as well. For example, the major problem addressed in Welteroth's study (2002) is how the Early Head Start home visitors can encourage socially and economically disadvantaged parents to mediate their children's play so that the children's play competence is enhanced.

The development of play competence, however, is not the only outcome of adult mediation of children's play with toys; such mediation has also been shown to result in major changes in children's motivational and mental domains. These developmental outcomes of adult mediation are discussed in the following sections.

The Development of Children's Motive of Role-Play

One of the major developmental outcomes of adult mediation of children's object-centered activity is the development in children of the motive of role-play, which, by the end of the third year, replaces children's motive of object-centered activity (Elkonin, 1978, 1989; Fradkina, 1946; Lekhtman-Abramovich & Fradkina, 1949; Leontiev, 1959/1964; Slavina, 1948; Usova, 1976). This shift in children's motivation is not as obvious as, for example, their shift from the motive of emotional interactions with caregivers to the motive of object-centered activity, which was discussed in the previous chapter. Indeed, both 2- and 3-year-old girls may play the same mother daughter game with the use of the same doll and other toys. If analyzed, however, the characteristics of their play would be very different, which would make it possible to suggest that the motives that drive these girls' play are very different as well.[3]

As studies and observations of the neo-Vygotskians have demonstrated, the development in children of the motive of role-play proceeds through several steps (Elkonin, 1978, Fradkina, 1946; Lekhtman-Abramovich & Fradkina, 1949; Slavina, 1948; Usova, 1976). Initially, the major point of interest for children during the second year of life is the imitation of object-centered actions that have been modeled by adults. As discussed, after an adult has offered toys to children (for example, a doll and a spoon), modeled actions with these toys (feeding a doll with a spoon), and encouraged children to imitate these actions, children willingly engage in the performance of these actions.

The introduction by an adult of object substitutes to children and involving them in joint play with the use of these substitutes (for example, the use of a stick to substitute for a spoon when feeding a doll) help children separate actions from objects, which leads to a shift of children's interests. Elkonin (1978) described this shift as follows: "Before, a spoon or a comb was in the focus of children's action. Now, the focus of their action is the doll . . . whereas a spoon or a comb turns into the means of performing the action of feeding or combing the doll" (p. 186).

The final step in the development of the new role-play motive in children deals with their getting interested in the world of social roles and relations. The world of adults becomes very attractive to children, and they are looking forward to becoming a part of this world. Children, however, cannot fulfill this desire directly: They cannot be

---

[3] In Western psychology, qualitative characteristics of object-centered and exploratory play as measures of children's motivation were used by Jennings, Harmon, Morgan, Gaiter, and Yarrow (1979) and Belsky and Most (1981).

mothers, or doctors, or firefighters. Therefore, children's interest in the world of social roles and relations is gratified by their imitation of these roles and relations in the course of role-play. As Vygotsky (1966/1976) noted, role-play "must always be interpreted as the imaginary, illusory realization of unrealizable desires" (p. 539). Thus, the motive of role-play is "to act like an adult" (Elkonin, 1978, p. 150).

The Vygotskian explanation of the motive of role-play has found strong support in the ethnographic literature. In preliterate societies, children as young as age 3 may already participate in adult activities such as foraging (see, for example, Lancy, 2002). Therefore, proceeding from the Vygotskian perspective, they do not need to imitate these adult roles in role-play. Indeed, starting with Mead's (1930) observations of children in New Guinea, numerous data have been collected that children in preliterate societies either are not engaged in role-play at all (see Feitelson, 1977, for an overview), or their role-play involves imitation of those aspects of adult life that are not accessible for children in their actual lives, such as playing marriage among the children of Brazilian Indians (Gregor, 1977).

The development by children of the motive of role-play reveals itself in children assuming play roles and acting according to these roles. Whereas a younger girl would not accept an adult's invitation "to play at a mother" (although she would accept the invitation "to feed the baby"), a 3-year-old girl would willingly accept this role and act according to it. When asked What are you?, she would answer by naming the play role that she is performing ("I am the mother"). The major aspect of a mother–daughter game for her becomes the imitation of mother–daughter relationships (love, care, etc.), which are implied by the role of a mother that she has assumed. Of course, when playing, the girl may perform object-centered actions similar to those that she performed a year ago when playing the same game (i.e., feeding a doll or combing the doll's hair). The *meaning* of these actions for the child, however, is very different from what it used to be. Elkonin (1978) wrote:

> [Before], the child bathed the doll, fed it, put it in bed. Now, at first glance, she is performing the same actions with the same doll. What has changed? All these objects and actions are now incorporated into a new system of the child's relations to the world, into a new emotionally attractive activity. Therefore, these actions and objects have now a new meaning for the child. The child's turning into a mother and the doll's turning into a baby lead to turning the actions of bathing, feeding, and cooking into nursing the baby. These actions now reflect a mother's relations to a baby, her love and tenderness. (p. 276)[4]

Thus, the imitation of object-centered actions is not the major aspect of the child's play anymore:

> Actions that children perform in the course of play are subordinated to the plot of the game and the role assumed. The performance of these actions is not an end in itself; it always serves the realization of the role. These actions are generalized and abbreviated, and the older the children are, the more abbreviated their play actions. (Elkonin, 1978, p. 176)

This shift from the performance of object-centered actions as an end in itself to the performance of these actions in abbreviated form as serving the realization of a play role is an additional indicator that the motive of role-play has developed and replaced children's motive of object-centered activity.

Children's motive of role-play, however, does not develop automatically. To develop such a motive, the child, first, should "discover" the

---

[4] This observation by Elkonin is highly consistent with Smilansky and Shefatya's data (1990). Having observed that play of 3- to 6-year-old children from low-socioeconomic-status families often remains immature, they indicated: "The satisfaction for a child from a lower socioeconomic level comes from imitative activities, *from doing what adults do*. The closer his actions are to an adult's activities as the child perceives them, the more he enjoys them" (p. 58). In contrast, children of the same age from higher socioeconomic backgrounds, who demonstrate a mature role-play, "move from experiencing what adults do to *experiencing what adults are like and feel like*" (p. 58).

existence of the world of social roles and relations. As Elkonin (1978) insightfully noted, however, for a young toddler, "the world of adults with their activities, their responsibilities, and their relationships...is hidden under object-centered actions" (pp. 275–276). Thus, to facilitate the development in children of the motive of role-play, adults should help them "discover" the world of social roles and relations that is "hidden" under object-centered actions. The studies of Russian neo-Vygotskians made it possible to reveal two major components of adults' facilitation of this "discovery" (Elkonin, 1978; Mikhailenko, 1975; Slavina, 1948; Sokolova, 1973).

First, adults should involve children in joint performance of *different* actions that are relevant to a certain social role. For example, if the child is playing at "feeding a baby" (that is, is performing an action that is relevant to the role of a mother), an adult should involve the child in joint performance of other actions that are relevant to this role (washing the baby, putting the baby in bed, taking the baby for a walk, etc.). Second, while children are performing these actions, an adult should refer them to the role that they are performing without realizing it (for example, "You, *like a mother*, are washing your baby"). Such an enrichment of children's object-centered activity with actions and goals of the imitation of social roles and relations leads to a shift of children's interest from the imitation of object-centered actions to the imitation of social roles and relations as an end in itself. To describe this shift in the neo-Vygotskian terms, the goals of the imitation of social roles and relations convert into the motive of children's new activity directed toward the imitation of social roles and relations, that is, into the motive of role-play.

Thus, the development of the motive of role-play, rather than being spontaneous, is an outcome of adult mediation. As Elkonin (1978) noted, "the notion of spontaneous development of role play in children is the result of adults not noticing the guidance that they, in fact, provide children with" (p. 187).

121

In Western psychology, the problem of development of the motive of role-play in children is generally overlooked because play is often considered "a spontaneous and self-motivated activity" (Bondioli, 2001, p. 111). The empirical data of some of Western psychologists, however, are consistent with the neo-Vygotskian analysis of the role of adult mediation in the development of children's motive of role-play.

Observations by Haight and Miller (1993) of young children in a family context showed that 12-month-old children initiated only 1% of all episodes of mother–child pretend play, whereas 24-month-old and 36-month-old children initiated 41% and 58% of play episodes, respectively. If we interpret these data as characteristic of the dynamic of children's play motivation, as the researchers seem inclined to do, the conclusion can be drawn that pretend play is not from the very beginning a self-motivated activity. Rather than that, the motive of play gradually develops in children. The observations of the researchers that, at 24 and 36 months, the length of children's episodes of pretend play with their mothers was twice as sustained as their solo pretend play can be interpreted as an indication that mothers' participation in children's play increases children's interest in play.

As Dunn and Wooding (1977) observed, mothers' supportive presence even by itself resulted in an increase of the duration of 18- to 24-month-old children's pretend-play periods. The fact that a child's play "was substantially increased in length with adult attention certainly suggests that the child's interest and motivation were affected" (Dunn & Wooding, 1977, p. 50). Although this suggestion refers to the development of children's motive of object-centered play rather than their motive of role-play, the idea of the role of adults in the development of children's play motives is consistent with the general neo-Vygotskians perspective in this respect.

Miller and Garvey's (1984) longitudinal study of 2- to 3-year-old children involved in pretend motherese documented that, when playing with a 2.5-year-old child, caregivers "made explicit references to

child as mother, saying, for example, 'You're the mommy' (p. 119)."
When playing with a 23-month-old girl, her caregivers

> model and elicit from the child . . . what mothers are responsible for
> providing, what they must be concerned with, and how they should
> act. The instruction goes beyond the little scripts for practical action
> such as burping, diapering, or feeding to include the attribution of
> internal states and the demonstration of appropriately fond or affec-
> tionate attitudes. (Miller & Garvey, 1984, p. 128)

Miller and Garvey (1984) also detected "continuity from the earlier
mothering play of child and care giver and the subsequent social role-
play of peers" (p. 128). As Dunn and Dale (1984) concluded, these experimental findings have clearly indicated that "many months before
the children were able explicitly to adopt a pretend role identity, they
were involved in social exchanges and play activities that appeared to
be closely related to this ability" (p. 133).

Finally, as Smilansky and Shefatya (1990) observed, children's involvement in role-play is facilitated by parents' "reacting to a child
who is manipulating his toys as if they were a role player: 'How is your
baby today? Is she crying a lot? Did she eat her food? Did you do your
shopping today?'" (p. 130). Thus, observations and studies of Western
researchers have provided strong support for the neo-Vygotskian contention that children's assuming a play role is the result of adults referring them to the roles that they are performing without realizing it.

Object Substitutions and the Development
of Symbolic Thought

Both Vygotsky (1984/1998) and Piaget (1945/1962) viewed the ability to think symbolically as the major neo-formation that begins to
emerge by the end of the second year of life. Before this ability develops in children, they are "stuck" to reality and cannot imagine objects

or events that are not present. Moreover, these children cannot even repeat a statement that contradicts the reality they are perceiving. Vygotsky (1984/1998), who defined this limitation of children's thought as its being "subordinated to perception," (p. 263), observed:

> Two-year-olds repeat without any difficulty sentences such as: "The chicken is walking," "Koko is walking," or "The dog is running." But the child cannot say "Tanya is walking," when Tanya is sitting on a chair before him. This sentence gets the reaction, "Tanya is sitting."...Only by the end of [the third year of life] does the child develop a very elementary capacity to say something that is actually not so." (pp. 262–263)

Also, both Piaget and Vygotsky associated children's emerging ability to think symbolically with their use of object substitutes when performing pretend actions. They, however, gave contrasting explanations of the relationships between the development of symbolic thought in children and children's use of object substitutes.

According to Piaget (1936/1952, 1945/1962), symbolic thought is the result of maturation of children's sensorimotor schemas with the use of object substitutes being a consequence of, rather than the reason for, the development of symbolic thought. As he noted,

> the causality of symbolic play now becomes clear, since it derives essentially from the structure of the child's thought. Symbolic play represents in thought the pole of assimilation, and freely assimilates reality to the ego....Symbolic play is merely egocentric thought in its pure state. (Piaget, 1945/1962, p. 166)

In contrast, Vygotsky (1966/1976) held that the development of symbolic thought is far from being a spontaneous and "natural" process. Rather than that, it is heavily determined by children's use of object substitutes, which help children separate their thoughts from the perceived objects and events: "Separating words from things requires a pivot in the form of other things" (p. 547). To illustrate this idea, Vygotsky (1978) gave an example of a child who is "riding" using a stick as a horse:

> When the stick becomes the pivot for detaching the meaning of "horse" from a real horse, the child makes one object influence another semantically. He cannot detach meaning from an object, or a word from an object, except by finding a pivot in something else. Transfer of meanings is facilitated by the fact that the child accepts a word as the property of a thing; he sees not the word but the thing it designates. For a child, the word "horse" applied to the stick means "there is a horse," because mentally he sees the object standing behind the word. A vital transitional stage toward operating with meanings occurs when a child first acts with meanings as with objects (as when he acts with the stick as though it were a horse). (pp. 98–99)

Russian neo-Vygotskians have enthusiastically adopted Vygotsky's view of the role of object substitutes in the development of symbolic thought. Elkonin (1978) wrote:

> Considering play actions, one can easily notice that children already deal with meanings of objects but still use toys as object substitutes. Analysis of the development of play actions shows that children's actions with object substitutes become more and more abbreviated. Whereas initially children need an object substitute and a pretty extended action with this substitute ... later an object substitute through its name comes to play the role of an object's symbol, with actions transforming into abbreviated gestures accompanied by speech. Thus, play actions are of an intermediate nature. Gradually, they turn into mental actions with meanings of objects that are performed with the use of speech supported a bit by abbreviated gestures. Interestingly enough, children's speech in the course of play becomes abbreviated as well. For example, preparing himself for a "dinner," a child comes to the wall, performs one or two "hand-washing" movements, says "have washed," and then, having performed several "eating" movements with the use of a stick representing a spoon, says, "have had a dinner." This transition to the performance of actions with meaning detached from objects prepares, at the same time, the development of symbolic thought. (p. 284)

As already mentioned, the studies of the neo-Vygotskians have demonstrated that the development of children's ability to use object substitutes is crucially determined by adult mediation. In particular, initial use by children of object substitutes has been shown to occur only after an adult, in the course of joint play with a child, has suggested that the child use a certain object instead of a missing one and has named this object after the missing one (Bugrimenko & Smirnova, 1994; Elkonin, 1978; Fradkina, 1946; Lekhtman-Abramovich & Fradkina, 1949; Mikhailenko, 1975).

The results of several studies performed by Western psychologists in the 1970s seemed to support the Piagetian rather than the Vygotskian view of the role of adults' mediation in children's emerging ability to use object substitutes. The researchers observed children's independent use of object substitutes (Fein, 1975; McCune-Nicolich, 1977; Sinclair, 1970) and reported that an adult's modeling the use of object substitutes did not result in an advancement of children's object substitutions (Fein, 1975). A careful analysis of these studies by Smolucha and Smolucha (1998), however, has shown that "they do not provide the kind of incontrovertible evidence for the solitary origins of pretend play that they are often cited as presenting" (p. 38). In particular, Smolucha and Smolucha (1998) have concluded that none of the analyzed studies "take into consideration the possibility that their results may have been confounded by play interactions occurring outside of the parameters of the study" (p. 39). Smolucha and Smolucha (1998) have also correctly indicated that in Fein's (1975) study the experimenter just modeled object substitutions and suggested that the child imitate them, whereas the neo-Vygotskian contention of mediation

> would have involved not merely acting out a play behavior in front of the child, but rather engaging the child in a play *interaction* in which the adult *demonstrated an object substitution* and *then assisted the child in his/her reenactment* of the adult's behavior. (p. 41)

Therefore, Fein's (1975) study, rather than documenting that children's object substitutions are not determined by adult mediation, has confirmed the general neo-Vygotskian assertion that effective mediation cannot be provided without children's active engagement in joint activity with adults.

Empirical findings and observations collected by Western psychologists in the 1980s and thereafter are much more consistent with the Vygotskian rather than Piagetian views of the role of adult mediation of children's use of substitutes in the development of children's ability to operate with symbols. These findings and observations can be classified into three groups.

First, it has been documented that, when playing alone, children from 18 months to 30 months of age either are not involved in symbolic play, or their symbolic play is immature; in contrast, mothers' participation significantly raises the level of children's symbolic play (Beizer & Howes, 1992; Fiese, 1990; Haight & Miller, 1993; O'Reilly & Bornstein, 1993; Slade, 1987). In particular, O'Reilly and Bornstein (1993) indicated that "in two-year-olds' play in the home, nonsymbolic exploratory play characterizes child play alone and is rarely seen when mothers are playing with their children" (p. 59). Haight and Miller (1993) observed that, when playing alone, "children pretended predominantly with realistic objects...long past the point at which they became able to pretend with substitute objects" (p. 98).

Second, a strong correlation between the level of mother's engagement in symbolic play with their children and these children's level of symbolic play has been observed (O'Reilly & Bornstein, 1993; Tamis-LeMonda & Bornstein, 1991; Tamis-LeMonda, Bornstein, Cyphers, Toda, & Ogino, 1992; Unger & Howes, 1988). It is important to note that mothers' participation in joint play with their children has been shown to occur, using Vygotsky's terminology, at the level of proximal rather than actual development of the children's play. Haight and Miller (1993) wrote: "Of the eight children who were observed at twelve months, only four produced any pretending and their pretending occurred very infrequently. At this same age, however, all eight mothers produced some pretend play directed to and attended to by their children" (p. 40).

Finally, in several studies, the role of adults as initiators of children's object substitutions was specifically investigated (Bondioli, 2001; Bretherton, 1984; Fenson, 1984; Harris & Kavanaugh, 1993; Smolucha, 1992; Smolucha & Smolucha, 1998; Tomasello, Striano, & Rochat, 1999). These studies confirmed the Vygotskian idea that initial use of object substitutes by children is a direct outcome of adults' demonstrating object substitutions and further encouraging and scaffolding children's attempts to use object substitutes in the course of play. In particular, according to Smolucha's (1992) observation, "the majority of object substitutions during pretend play of children aged 14 to 25 months are initiated by the mother" (p. 73). Another longitudinal observation of 14- to 28-month-old children documented that "the children of the mothers who initiated the most object substitutions at the beginning of the study also initiated the most object substitutions by the end of the study" (Smolucha & Smolucha, 1998, p. 45).

Thus, empirical data and observations that have been collected by both Russian neo-Vygotskians and Western researchers have shown that adults' mediation of children's object substitutions in the context of joint object-centered play significantly determines the development of children's ability to perform at the symbolic level. Another major determinant of the development of this ability in children is their acquisition of language. The role of language acquisition in the development of children's symbolic thought is discussed in the next section.

Language Acquisition and the Development of Children's Mental Processes

One of the major features of the second and third years of life is, in Siegler's (1991) words, a "language explosion" (p. 146), that is, a remarkably fast acquisition of language by children. In contrast to Piaget (1945/1962), who viewed the development of language as a manifestation of children's emerging symbolic abilities, Vygotsky (1984/1998) explained this development as a result of children's need of new means of communication with adults that would serve their age-specific forms of collaboration. Vygotsky's Russian followers have elaborated on his explanation of the origins of children's speech.

DETERMINANTS OF LANGUAGE DEVELOPMENT

The neo-Vygotskians argue that nonverbal means of communication, which successfully served child–adult interactions during the first year of life, are not sufficient to serve their joint object-centered activity (Elagina, 1974, 1977; Elkonin, 1989; Lisina, 1986). Therefore, to take a part in this joint activity, in which children have developed a strong interest, they have to acquire language as a new means of communication. This happens, however, only if adults "don't understand" nonverbal means of communication that children try to use in the context of their object-centered joint activity and encourage children to use words. The following is a description of two classic studies that have supported the neo-Vygotskian view of children's language acquisition.

Fradkina (1955) compared the acquisition of new words by 1-year-old children in two situations. In the first situation, an adult repetitiously provided the child with the name of a new object. As a result, on the 10th or 11th day, the child acquired the new word. In the second situation, an adult involved the child in joint object-centered activity and, in the context of this activity, provided the child with the name

129

of the object. In this case, it took the child only 1 day to acquire the new word. Summarizing these empirical findings, as well as findings and observations of other neo-Vygotskians (Kaverina, 1950; Lyamina, 1960; Popova, 1968), Lisina (1986) came to the following conclusion: "The child's first words are addressed to the adult with whom the child is interacting. These words designate objects or actions and are used to express the child's wish which cannot be met without the adult's help" (p. 65).

A detailed analysis of how, in the course of joint object-centered activity, adults can facilitate children's language acquisition was done by Elagina (1977). In her study, 13- to 19-month-old children became involved in joint object-centered play with an adult, in the course of which the adult would name the play object. At a certain point, the adult interrupted the play and placed the object beyond the child's reach. The children's typical behavior in this situation was as follows. After several unsuccessful attempts to reach the object, the child started to use nonverbal means of communication (such as vocalizing and pointing gesture) in an attempt to have the adult give the object to him or her. The adult, however, rather than giving the object to the child, would pronounce the name of the object encouraging the child to repeat it. The child started to concentrate on the adult's articulation and tried to pronounce the word. After several attempts, the child correctly pronounced the name of the object, and the adult gave the object to the child. Importantly, when the children later came across a similar situation, they skipped all the attempts to reach an object by themselves or to influence the adult with nonverbal means of communication. Rather than that, they concentrated on the adult's articulation and tried to pronounce the name of the unreachable object. Elagina's (1977) finding, as well as similar data and observations of other researchers (Lisina, 1986; Rozengard-Pupko, 1963), made it possible for Lisina (1986) to conclude the following: "Nothing in the object reality would make children speak. Only adults' demands and the necessity created by them make children do the gigantic work of language acquisition" (p. 26).

This neo-Vygotskian explanation of the development of children's speech has been supported by empirical findings of Western researchers. These findings can be classified into three groups.

First, it has been demonstrated that the quality of children's pretend play is associated with, as well as predicts, their language development. In particular, the quality of 13-month-olds' pretend play was shown to be associated with their receptive language (Tamis-LeMonda & Bornstein, 1993) and to predict their language development at the end of the second year (Sigman & Sena, 1993; Tamis-LeMonda & Bornstein, 1993). Because, as already discussed, the quality of pretend play has been shown to be heavily determined by adults' mediation, these data, although indirectly, support the neo-Vygotskian contention of the major role of such mediation in children's language acquisition.

The second group of findings has provided even stronger support to the neo-Vygotskian contention discussed here. As documented in a variety of studies and observations, children's language acquisition is determined by adults' use of language in the context of their joint object-centered activity (Bruner, 1975a, 1975b; Haight & Miller, 1993; Olson, Bayles, & Bates, 1986; Tomasello & Farrar, 1986; Tomasello & Todd, 1983; Wells, 1985). In particular, as Haight and Miller (1993) summarized their observations, "substantial amount of children's talk accompanying pretend play replicated mothers' transformational talk at twelve and twenty-four months" (p. 67).

Finally, several studies have provided support for the neo-Vygotskian contention that, to facilitate the acquisition of language by children, adults should use joint activity with children to encourage them to use words rather than simply interpreting their gestures and vocalizations (the study by Moss & Dumas, 1988, described in Moss, 1992; Ninio & Bruner, 1978). Encouraging children to communicate at the level of *proximal* rather than *actual* development is especially important if children have disabilities. As Yoder's research (1992) indicated, when communicating with infants with disabilities, their mothers "are 'too' willing to interpret and respond [which] may actually result in taking away helpful incentives and information that helps babies with disabilities to learn to talk to communicate their needs" (p. 1). In contrast, providing children with mental retardation with verbal means of communication and then encouraging them to use these means to communicate their needs was shown to facilitate their language development (Warren, Yoder, Gazdag, Kim & Jones, 1993).

THE ROLE OF LANGUAGE ACQUISITION IN THE
DEVELOPMENT OF CHILDREN'S MENTAL PROCESSES

For Vygotsky, the importance of acquisition of language is not limited to children's mastery of the main means of social communication. As discussed in chapter 1, Vygotsky (1978, 1934/1986, 1984/1998) viewed verbal means of communication as major psychological tools that, having been mastered by children, come to mediate their mental processes. A similar position is held by Russian neo-Vygotskians (although, as discussed in chapter 2, they insist that verbal means of communication cannot serve as psychological tools unless children also have mastered the procedures of the use of these means of communication as tools; Elkonin, 1956; Galperin, 1957, 1966, 1969; Leontiev, 1959/1964; Zaporozhets, 1986b).

The importance of language acquisition for the development of children's mental processes has been confirmed in many empirical studies and observations. In chapter 1, I already discussed numerous findings of Russian and Western researchers that have provided strong support for the Vygotskian notion of the role of language in children's self-regulation. Having acquired verbal means, children start to use them for self-talk (so-called egocentric or private speech), which helps them regulate their performance. Later, children's private speech gets internalized and is used as an internal tool of self-regulation.

The second major developmental outcome of language acquisition is the development of children's symbolic thought. As discussed in the previous section, an important determinant of the development of symbolic thought is children's use of object substitutes, which serve the role of pivots helping children separate the names of objects from these objects. To accomplish such a separation, however, children have to know the names of these objects. Also, the use of language has been shown to enrich children's play actions enormously with the use of object substitutes. Following is an analysis of the role of language in enriching children's actions with the use of object substitutes.

As discussed earlier, children's initial object substitutions are simply exact imitations of adults' actions with the same toys and objects. Then, children come up with their own object substitutions, which, however,

> are not yet substitutions in the strict sense of the word, since they occur only in the child's actions and not in his mind. When an adult asks the child to name the objects the child is using in play, he gives their real and not play names. For instance, a boy is clearly cooking food: He stirs something in a pot, blows on it, tastes it. To a question from an adult, "What are you cooking in the pot?," he replies, "Sticks and rounds." (Bugrimenko & Smirnova, 1994, p. 292)

Thus, language has not yet come to mediate children's play actions. Later, however, children start to name object substitutes after missing objects, which

> radically changes the nature of the child's actions. The new meaning embodied in the word brings the object to life.... Let us consider a situation in which a little girl is feeding a doll with a little ball. When an adult asks, "What is the little doll eating? An egg?," the girl smiles and, as if recognizing a familiar object in the ball, begins to unfold a whole sequence of play actions with the ball. She blows on the "egg," saying, "It's hot; soon it'll be cool," she peels it, puts some salt on it, and only after this gives it to the doll to eat with the following words, "The egg is yummy, it isn't hot anymore..." and so on. When the

133

child renames an object during play for the first time – this usually happens when he accepts and repeats the renaming suggested by an adult – he discovers a new way of acting with objects, as it were. The child begins to introduce his own, sometimes very imaginative, re-placements [object substitutes] in his play. (Bugrimenko & Smirnova, 1994, pp. 292–293)

The statement of Bugrimenko and Smirnova that children's initial naming of object substitutes after missing objects is the result of re-naming suggested by adults has been supported by numerous obser-vations of Russian neo-Vygotskians (Elkonin, 1978; Fradkina, 1946; Lukov, 1937; Mikhailenko, 1975).

As Elkonin (1978) indicated, imposing new names on object substi-tutes becomes especially important by the end of the third year, when children start to perform a set of logically connected actions with the use of the same object to substitute for different missing objects. In this situation, naming the substitute object after the object for which it is being substituted within this particular play episode helps the child perform the relevant play action. Elkonin (1978) wrote:

As our studies and observations have demonstrated, objects used in play as substitutes for necessary but missing objects are very multi-functional and, at the same time, their resemblance to the missing objects is very relative. What, indeed, is the resemblance between a stick and a horse? A stick is not even a schematic image of a horse! The same stick can be used to substitute for a rifle, or a snake, or a tree.... This totally depends on what meaning the child is imposing upon the object substitute at this particular moment of play. The word that the child is using to name a multifunctional object substitute at a certain moment of play immediately limits the ways, in which this object can be used, and determines how this object can and should be used, that is, what actions should be performed with this object. If a brick has been named "an iron," that means that it should be used for ironing; if it is named "a cutlet," it should be eaten; and if it is named "a plate," it should be used for putting food on it and for carrying it as if it were a plate. *This is possible only because the word itself at this period of development contains the child's experience of acting with the object.* (p. 244–245; emphasis added)

Thus, when performing an action with an object substitute that has been renamed after a missing object, children proceed from the new meaning that has been imposed upon this object rather than being led by the object itself. Using Vygotsky's words (1978), the child's "thought as separated from objects and action arises from ideas rather than from things" (p. 97). As the quotation above from Elkonin (1978) highlights, however, to play such a mediational role in children's activity, the new name that the child is imposing on an object substitute has to be supported by the child' knowledge of the relevant procedure. For example, the word *iron* given to a brick will lead to the child's use of the brick as if it were an iron only if the child is familiar with the procedure of ironing. This reservation reflects the difference between Vygotsky and his Russian followers who, as previously discussed, insist that, in general, words cannot serve their mediational role unless children have also mastered the relevant procedures.

As several studies have documented, the role of verbal means of communication in the development of children's symbolic thought is not limited to their importance for children's object substitutions. Rozengard-Pupko (1948) studied perception of children around the age of 3 years with normal and delayed language development. Children were asked to find among different toy objects one that was similar to the given model (for example, the model – a big mouse; the objects – a little mouse and a big dog). The study revealed a major difference in the performance of children with normal language development compared with those having delayed language development. When solving the problems, children with normal language development, who knew the names of the objects, used the name of the model as the basis for their selection (for the example above, they selected a little mouse). In contrast, the selections of children with delayed language development were performed on the basis of such surface characteristics of an object as its size, color, and so on (for this example, they selected a big dog).[5]

The classical study of Luria and Yudovich (1956) was performed with twin boys who communicated mostly with each other (with the use of gestures and pseudo-words) but not with adults or other children. Because of a lack of communication, at age 5 years their language development was lower than that of 2-year-old children. The children's performance and problem solving also remained at a very low level. In particular, they could not solve at all those classification problems that children of the same age with normal language development could easily solve. The "intervention" that the researchers suggested was simple: The twins were separated and placed in different kindergarten settings. The need to communicate with peers resulted in both twins' rapid acquisition of communicative language, which reached the age-appropriate level after just 3 months of separation. Simultaneously, significant advancements in their behavior and problem solving were documented. After 7 additional months of separation, they became capable of doing object classification at the age-appropriate level. The researchers drew the reasonable conclusion that the major reason for these accomplishments was the acquisition by twins of communicative language, which became internalized and came to mediate their mental processes.

An additional confirmation of this conclusion was provided by comparative analysis of the advancements demonstrated by the twins.

---

[5] The knowledge of objects' names determines the perception of these objects not only by 3-year-old children but by adults as well. This fact was demonstrated in Luria's (1974/1976) famous study performed in the early 1930s with peasants in a remote village of Uzbekistan, one of the Asian republics of the former Soviet Union. When presented different geometric figures (circles, triangles, quadrangles, etc.) and asked which of them looked alike, illiterate peasants made their decisions on the basis of such features of the figures as their size, color, or mode of execution. In contrast, literate peasants made their decisions on the basis of the geometric classes to which these figures belonged.

The point is that one of them (initially the "weaker" one) had been provided with systematic training in the use of communicative language. After 10 months of training, this boy significantly exceded his brother not only in the use of communicative language but also in the level of problem solving, including object classification, as well.

As Tomasello (1999) indicated, many Western researchers "do not believe that acquiring a language has any great effect on the nature of cognitive representations because they view linguistic symbols as simply handy tags for already formulated concepts" (p. 124). Despite this general theoretical view, which has been heavily influenced by Piaget's (1936/1952, 1945/1962) view on this topic, the importance of language as a mediator of children's mental processes has been documented in several studies of Western researchers as well. As Kuczaj, Borys, and Jones (1989) demonstrated, teaching children names of objects facilitates their ability to classify these objects. In contrast, children's specific language impairment has been shown to be associated with different kinds of cognitive problems and delays (Leonard, 1998). Summarizing his own empirical data, as well as data of some other Western researchers, Tomasello (1999) concluded:

> Acquiring language thus leads children to conceptualize, categorize, and schematize events in more complex ways than they would if they were not engaged in learning a conventional language, and these kinds of event representations and schematizations add great complexity and flexibility to human cognition. (p. 159)

Why Is Object-Centered Joint Activity With Adults Leading for Toddlers?

As discussed, adults' mediation of children's object-centered activity results, by the end of the third year, in major transformations of children's motivational and mental spheres. First, children have developed a strong interest in the world of social roles and relations. As a result, the motive of imitation of social roles and relations in the course of role-play has arisen and become much stronger than children's motive of object-centered activity. Second, children have mastered language as the major tool for social communication. Third, they have become capable of self-regulation through the use of private speech. Fourth, they have developed the capacity for symbolic thought, which makes it possible for the child "to act independently of what he sees" (Vygotsky, 1978, p. 97). All these outcomes lead to children's transition to sociodramatic play (that is, role-play with peers), which, as discussed in the next chapter, will become their leading activity during the period of early childhood. Thus, toddlers' object-centered joint activity with adults meets all the requirements of the leading activity as formulated by the neo-Vygotskians.

5 Three- to Six-Year-Olds: Sociodramatic Play as the Leading Activity During the Period of Early Childhood

Sociodramatic play is a joint activity of children in which they choose a plot that reflects a certain aspect of social relations (i.e., buying something in a store), distribute roles (i.e., a seller and buyers), and play together imitating the chosen aspect of social relations. Although the most influential approaches to sociodramatic play give different explanations of the appearance of such play and its role in children's development (Erikson, 1963; A. Freud, 1927; S. Freud, 1920/1955; Piaget, 1945/1962), all of them share one major idea. Sociodramatic play is considered to be children's free and spontaneous activity in which they do whatever they want, liberating themselves from any rules and social pressure; therefore, adults are not supposed to interfere with children's play.

Vygotsky (1966/1976) and Russian neo-Vygotskians (Elkonin, 1948, 1971/1972, 1978, 1989; Leontiev, 1959/1964; Usova, 1976; Zaporozhets, 1978/1997) developed a quite different approach to sociodramatic play. From their point of view, children play not because they want to liberate themselves from social pressure. The opposite is true, for by the age 3 years, as discussed in the previous chapter, children develop a strong interest in the world of social relations. The world of adults becomes very attractive for children, and they are looking forward to becoming a part of this world. In industrialized societies, however, children cannot fulfill this desire directly: They cannot be doctors or a firefighters. That is why they "penetrate" the world of adults by imitating and exploring social roles and relations in the course of sociodramatic play. Thus, the motive of sociodramatic play is "to act like an adult" (Elkonin, 1978, p. 150).

An explanation very similar to the neo-Vygotskian explanation of the motive of sociodramatic play has been suggested by the Israeli researchers Smilansky and Shefatya (1990). Having observed that children's "most popular roles are those of *adults*, the grown-ups, the people who are actively doing 'real' things" (p. 20), the researchers concluded, "Sociodramatic play is a micro-world of active experiencing of social roles and relationships" (p. 224). Furthermore,

> through imitation behavior the child is attempting to interweave himself into the interactions of the adult world. . . . He does not try to distort the play reality to suit his ego or other psychological needs. On the contrary, *in sociodramatic play the child aims at reproducing, as exactly as possible, the world as he observes it, as he understands it, and insofar as he remembers it.* (p. 111)

Children's need to imitate social roles and relations, as well as their ability to enact such imitation in the course of sociodramatic play, does not develop spontaneously, however. Indeed, as discussed in the previous chapter, the motive of role-play develops in 3-year-old children as the result of adult enrichment of children's object-centered activity with actions and goals of the imitation of social roles and relations. Children's symbolic thought (which makes it possible for them to create an imaginary situation as the basis of sociodramatic play) has also been shown to develop as a result of adult mediation. Finally, adult mediation has been shown to determine the development of language and rudiments of self-regulation in children, which are also necessary prerequisites for their involvement in joint play. Thus, rather than being a spontaneous and natural phenomenon, children's transition to sociodramatic play is an outcome of adult mediation during the previous period of development. As will be further discussed, the development and advancement of sociodramatic play during the period of early childhood, according to the neo-Vygotskians, is also crucially determined by adult mediation (Elkonin, 1948, 1971/ 1972, 1978, 1989; Leontiev, 1959/1964; Usova, 1976; Zaporozhets, 1978/1997).

The neo-Vygotskian view of the leading role of adult mediation in the origins and development of sociodramatic play has found strong support in studies and observations of Western researchers. As they have documented, many preschoolers do not participate in sociodramatic play at all. Summarizing observations on British children, Tizard (1977) wrote:

> Much of the play in the nursery school tends to be repetitive and of a rather low level. We found that 84 percent of the play in nursery schools involved the child in only one action, e.g., swinging, or digging in the sand or perhaps running round saying, "I' m a Dalek." The kind of elaborate socio-dramatic or constructional play which involves a sequence of relatively integrated activities linked by an idea was really relatively infrequent. (p. 206)

Observations performed in Israeli kindergarten classes and nursery schools "indicated that play was becoming extinct.... Most of the play scripts of those who were playing were dull and repetitive, showing the same roles and actions day after day and using play objects mainly at the level of object transformations" (Glaubman, Kashi, & Koresh, 2001, p. 137). American preschoolers have also been shown to demonstrate a very low level of involvement in sociodramatic play (Elkind, 1987; Sylva, Roy, & Painter, 1980). These observations, as well as similar observations collected in various Western societies (Elkind,

1990), hardly support the view of sociodramatic play as a "spontaneous" and "natural" activity as it is claimed to be in the most influential theories of play. Having reviewed these theories, Smilansky and Shefatya (1990) indicated: "None of the play theories provide an explanation for the fact that certain groups of children do not engage in sociodramatic play activities" (p. 103).

Many researchers have put blame for the extinction of sociodramatic play on children's spending their free time on watching TV and playing computer or video games (Guddemi & Jambor, 1993). In particular, Johnson, Christie, and Yawkey (1987) wrote: "The bulk of research conducted on television viewing and the play of young children suggests that television is a negative influence, preempting play time and possibly impending creativity" (p. 213). A similar point of view is expressed by Provenzo (1998): "Contemporary culture is a turning point in the history of play. Electronically mediated playscapes shaped by television, video games, and new technologies such as virtual reality are drawing children away from more traditional and tactually oriented models of play" (p. 517).

Another (and, proceeding from the neo-Vygotskian approach, the main) reason for the extinction of sociodramatic play is that more and more parents in Western societies, rather than mediating sociodramatic play of their children, discourage them from engaging in play, considering it a waste of time (Elkind, 1987). Teachers have been shown to demonstrate a similar attitude toward sociodramatic play. A survey of attitudes of teachers in the United States and Israel toward sociodramatic play showed that "90% of the teachers did not regard sociodramatic play to contribute to the children's future learning and school readiness; the remaining 10% perceived the value of sociodramatic play in terms of socio-emotional adjustment" (Smilansky & Shefatya, 1990, p. 232). Even if teachers do not discourage children from engaging in sociodramatic play, in their educational practices, "there is an absolute value placed on the *nonintervention of the adult* when using play for furthering intellectual and socio-emotional development" (Smilansky & Shefatya, 1990, p. 141).

Additional data on the importance of adult mediation for children's engagement in sociodramatic play have been provided by the comparative analysis of the play of low-socioeconomic-status (SES) children and the play of children from higher socioeconomic backgrounds. For example, whereas the majority of high-SES Israeli children were observed to be actively engaged in sociodramatic play, the majority of their low-SES compatriot peers

> did not take advantage of the equipment provided for pretend play (the doll or hospital corners, etc.), despite the fact that they had been coming to preschool classes daily from the age of three or four. Those few who did go into the play corners engaged mainly in solitary manipulation of the toys for short periods of time. (Smilansky & Shefatya, 1990, p. xi)

Similar observations in regard to American children from low-SES and high-SES families have been reported by Griffing (1980). The importance of these observations becomes obvious if they are interpreted in light of the data that high-SES parents are much more likely to encourage, mediate, and join their children's play than low-SES parents (Smilansky & Shefatya, 1990).

Thus, the data and observations discussed have provided strong support to the neo-Vygotskian view of sociodramatic play as anything but a "natural" phenomenon in children's life. The association between adult mediation of sociodramatic play and children's engagement in such play is consistent with the neo-Vygotskian contention of mediation as the major determinant of sociodramatic play. An additional strong support to this contention has been provided by interventional studies, which are discussed in the next section.

Adult Mediation as the Major Determinant of Sociodramatic Play

Because sociodramatic play deals with children's imitation of social roles and relations, children need to know these roles and relations to be able to imitate them. Social roles and relations, however, cannot be discovered by children through mere observation of adult behavior. Indeed, what children can observe are adult actions. But *why* adults enact these actions and how these actions are related within the given episode of social life remains hidden from children. Therefore, the neo-Vygotskians hold that the explanation to children of different social roles and relations is the major content of adult mediation of sociodramatic play (Elkonin, 1978). This neo-Vygotskian contention has been confirmed in several studies and observations. What follows is a description of one of these studies (Koroleva, 1957, reviewed in Elkonin, 1978).

A group of 5- to 6-year-old kindergarten children went to a summer camp by train. They were then given different toys (a model of the train, a model of a railway station, etc.), and the teacher suggested that they play at a railway station. The children manipulated these toys but did not engage in sociodramatic play even after the teacher helped them distribute the roles (the station master, a conductor, passengers, etc.). After that, the children were taken to the railway station again, and the teacher explained to them the social roles of different people at the station (this is the station master – he is receiving a train; these are passengers – they are buying tickets; this is an engineer – he is preparing a locomotive engine for a trip; this is a conductor – he is checking the passengers' tickets; etc.). The teacher also explained to children the relationships between different episodes that they were observing (i.e., first, the passenger should buy a ticket, and then he should show it to the conductor to be let into the train). After returning to the kindergarten, the children assumed the roles and started to play at a railway station enthusiastically and on their own initiative.

The neo-Vygotskian contention of the importance of introducing and explaining social roles and relations to children for their engaging in sociodramatic play has been confirmed in several studies and observations of Western researchers. *First*, it has been demonstrated that lack of knowledge of social roles and relations ruins sociodramatic play. Johnson et al. (1987) summarized:

> Role playing requires that children draw on their prior knowledge and act out roles as they understand them. If children have had little experience with the roles they are attempting to portray, sociodramatic play can become difficult or impossible to sustain. Most children have had adequate experience with the roles of family members, but they may be unfamiliar with many work-related roles. Woodard (1984), for example, relates how preschoolers became confused when attempting to act out roles of chef and dishwasher in a restaurant theme area. (p. 29)

Second, Western studies and observations have confirmed the neo-Vygotskian contention that children cannot discover through observation social roles and relations that are "hidden" under adult's actions. In particular, Levin (1998) described the play of two boys that was inspired by a TV show. The play involved a repetitive imitation of the same violent actions over and over again without any attempt "to explore that violence, its effect on others, or alternatives to it" (p. 351). Summarizing their observations, Smilansky and Shefatya (1990) indicated that to play the role, for example, of a father, the child

> must understand, to a certain extent, the activity or behavior trait that he wishes to imitate. Without such understanding he will only be able to imitate external, physical gestures – he will walk as he sees his father walk, move his hands or face in the fashion characteristic of his father, etc.... It is impossible to derive the amount of understanding

> of parental behavior required in order to imitate this image from observation alone, but the child needs explanation, direct guidance and joint parent–child cooperation in certain activities. (p. 127)

This explains why no one child observed by Smilansky and Shefatya (1990) "based his sociodramatic play solely on the theme of a movie or story which may have been read to him" (p. 52).

Third, several studies and observations of Western researchers have demonstrated that, indeed, introducing and explaining social roles and relations results in children's enacting these roles and relations in play. Having observed 2.5- to 6.5-year-old children, Marshall (1961) found that "if parents and other important adults talk with the child about more topics the child can use in play with other children, the child will talk about and play these topics more frequently with peers" (p. 72). In contrast to children's independent TV viewing, which, as discussed, does not lead to the enrichment of children's sociodramatic play, their TV viewing that involved an adult's explanation of the meaning of certain episodes was shown to contribute positively to children's play (Singer & Singer, 1976, reviewed in Johnson et al., 1987). Finally, over a school year, Saltz, Dixon, and Johnson (1977) enriched 3- to 4-year-old children's knowledge of social roles and relations in the context of visiting a doctor's office, a grocery store, a fire station, and so on. Then the researchers encouraged the children to discuss their new experiences. As a result, almost all the children engaged spontaneously in sociodramatic play that reflected the observed social situations. Summarizing their review of studies of the adult role in the development of children's play, Johnson et al. (1987) wrote: "Teachers can help clarify children's understanding of themes and roles by providing relevant experiences such as field trips, classroom visitations by people in different occupations, and stories about different jobs. Parents, of course, can provide similar experiences for their children" (p. 29).

Although, as discussed, the neo-Vygotskian contention of the importance of introducing and explaining social roles and relations to

146

children for their engaging in sociodramatic play has been confirmed in Western studies, many Western researchers stress the importance of another form of adult mediation of sociodramatic play, that is, teaching children how to play. They have performed various interventional studies aimed at facilitating major aspects of sociodramatic play (for overviews and descriptions of selected studies, see Glaubman et al., 2001; Johnson et al., 1987; Smilansky & Shefatya, 1990). In these studies, adults mediated children's play by suggesting and elaborating the plot of the play; helping children distribute, adopt, and enact the play roles; facilitating children's use of object substitutes; modeling advanced types of play behavior; and engaging children in play-related conversation. Such mediation has been shown to increase substantially the duration and quality of children's sociodramatic play.

A comparative analysis of the two forms of mediation of sociodramatic play just discussed was performed in the impressive study of the Israeli researchers Smilansky and Shefatya (1990). The study was performed with 3- to 6.6-year-old children from low-SES backgrounds. Only about 30% of them were engaged in any sort of dramatic play, and only 10% engaged in sociodramatic play. The children were divided into three experimental groups and provided with a 6-week-long intervention (45 hours in total) aimed at the promotion of their sociodramatic play at "a clinic" and "a grocery store." Different intervention strategies were used in each of the three experimental groups.

In the *first group*, children visited a clinic and a grocery store and were provided with all kinds of explanations, including explanation of relevant social role and relations. For example, during the visit to a clinic, the teacher gave an explanation of

> the clinic equipment, the various waiting and treatment rooms, the different staff members and what they did, the teamwork, the interrelationships of the various staff members . . . the reasons that people came to the clinic, what people are supposed to do in order to get help,

what they might expect to happen when they come to the clinic, etc. (Smilansky & Shefatya, 1990, p. 148)

In the *second group*, children did not visit a clinic and a grocery store. Rather than that, the teacher helped them engage in and sustain sociodramatic play at a clinic or a grocery store with the teacher intervening from both "outside" and "inside" the play situation. For example, in the case of play at "a clinic," the intervention from "outside" included

> questions ("How is your baby today?"), suggestions ("Let's take your baby to the clinic."), clarification of behavior ("I did the same when my baby was ill."), establishing contact between players ("Can you please help her, nurse?"), and straightforward directions ("Show the nurse where it hurts your baby. Tell her all about it.") (Smilansky & Shefatya, 1990, p. 151)

In the case of intervention from "inside" the play situation the teacher joined the children's play by assuming and enacting a role relevant to the theme of the play. The teacher can

> activate a whole group of children, emphasizing the missing play components for each child in her contact with the child. Thus, if she knows that Miriam, who is playing a mother, does not use make-believe with regard to objects, the teacher can say to her, from within her role as a nurse, "Here is the medicine, Mrs. Ohajon" and pretend to give her something. She can elaborate further: "Give two spoonfuls to your baby twice a day. Now call a taxi to take you home since your baby is very ill and should not go out in this cold. Here is the telephone." (Smilansky & Shefatya, 1990, pp. 151–152)

Finally, in the *third group*, the teacher's intervention was a combination of the interventions used in the first and second groups.

The outcomes of the interventions were as follows. The intervention in the *first group* had not resulted in a significant improvement of the children's sociodramatic play (only 12% of the children became engaged in sociodramatic play). The intervention in the *second group* had resulted in a significant improvement of the children's play: 34% became engaged in sociodramatic play. Even more impressive improvement was documented in the *third group*: 48% of the children became engaged in sociodramatic play as a result of the intervention with which they had been provided.

How can these results be interpreted? The comparison of the intervention outcomes in the first and second groups seems to lead to the conclusion that, to become engaged in sociodramatic play, children should be taught play skills on how to assume and enact play roles rather than being introduced to social roles and relations to be imitated in play. Such an interpretation, however, does not explain why the outcome of intervention in the third group was much more impressive than that in the second group. Neither does this interpretation explain experimental findings by both Russian neo-Vygotskians and Western researchers discussed earlier that introducing and explaining social roles and relations to children leads by itself to their engaging in sociodramatic play.

Smilansky and Shefatya (1990) themselves seem to have found their results a bit contradictory. In one place in the book, they were inclined to interpret their results as an indication that both kinds of intervention are necessary to promote children's sociodramatic play (p. 179). In another place in the book, however, they wrote: "It is important that intervention should be skill-centered and not content-centered. The teacher has to help the child to develop skills that will enable him to express the content that interests him in his play and not to impose on him roles and themes from outside sources" (pp. 229–230). From my point of view, the data of Smilansky and Shefatya (1990) are anything but contradictory, and they are quite consistent with the data of other researchers discussed earlier.

Indeed, low-SES children in Smilansky and Shefatya's (1990) study were clearly lacking the necessary play skills. As the authors indicated, however, in their everyday life, the children had accumulated substantial experience in both attending a clinic and shopping in a grocery store, which, for sure, had been accompanied by at least some adult explanations of social roles and relations in those contexts. Therefore, teaching play skills to the children in the second group was sufficient to make it possible for many of them to become engaged in sociodramatic play at "a clinic" or "a grocery store," whereas the enrichment of the first-group children's experiences in attending a clinic and shopping was, by itself, useless. The importance of such enrichment of children's social experience became obvious, however, as soon as children had mastered play skills (see the results of the third group).

In contrast, the success of the studies in which the major form of intervention was the enrichment of children's knowledge of social roles and relations (i.e., Koroleva, 1957, reviewed in Elkonin, 1978; Saltz et al., 1977; and others) makes it possible to assume that children in those studies possessed play skills but were not familiar with social roles and relations to be imitated in sociodramatic play. Therefore, the explanation of these social roles and relations was by itself sufficient for those children's engagement in play.

In conclusion, this analysis supports the view that adult mediation is the major determinant of children's sociodramatic play. What kind of mediation should be used in every particular case, however, will depend on what exactly are the limitations of children's knowledge that prevent them from engaging in sociodramatic play. In some cases, children may need to be trained in play skills; in others, children may need to be acquainted with social roles and relations to be imitated; in still other cases, children may need both forms of intervention. Properly organized adult mediation of sociodramatic play is especially important in light of the fact that, as discussed subsequently, it results in major developmental accomplishments by the end of the period of early childhood.

The Role of Sociodramatic Play
in Children's Development

In contrast to Piaget, who "showed little interest" in sociodramatic play (Fein, 1981, p. 1100), Vygotsky (1966/1976) emphasized that "a child's greatest achievements are possible in play – achievements which tomorrow will become his average level of real action" (Vygotsky, 1966/1976, p. 549). Therefore,

> play ... creates the zone of proximal development of the child. In play a child is always above his average age, above his daily behaviour; in play it is as though he were a head taller than himself. As in the focus of a magnifying glass, play contains developmental tendencies in a condensed form; in play it is as though the child were trying to jump above the level of his normal behaviour. (Vygotsky, 1966/1976, p. 552)

One of the earliest neo-Vygotskian studies aimed at testing Vygotsky's (1966/1976) view of sociodramatic play as "the leading source of development in pre-school years" (p. 537) was performed by Istomona (1948). She compared how many words 3- to 7-year-old children could memorize in two situations. In the first situation, the experimenter read a list of words that the child had to remember and recall. In the second situation, the experimenter was playing "at kindergarten" with a group of children. In the context of play, she asked one of the children to go to a "grocery store" to do shopping for "the kindergarten," and she read the list of items to be bought. When the child came to the "grocery store," "the seller" (the experimenter's assistant) asked the child what items he or she would like to "buy." The study showed, that, with age, the number of words that the children were able to recall in both situations increased. In the play situation, however, the children of all the age groups were able to recall substantially more words than in the situation of the laboratory experiment.

The difference in recall between these two situations was the most significant (100% increase in the number of words) for 4- to 5-year-old children, with a 60% increase for older children. Thus, Istomina's study confirmed both components of Vygotsky's contention: First, in play, children do perform at the proximal rather than actual level of their development; second, the level of performance that children initially demonstrate in play turns gradually into the level of their performance in nonplay situations.

Similar data were obtained in other neo-Vygotskian studies on sociodramatic play. In particular, it has been shown that in sociodramatic play children develop friendly relationships and learn to negotiate and concede to each other not only in the context of play but in a real-life context as well (Zalogina, 1945, reviewed in Elkonin, 1960). Another study showed that children in play demonstrate a much higher level of cooperation, coordination of their actions, and mutual help than they do in real-life situations (Koroleva, 1957, reviewed in Elkonin, 1960). As Karpova and Lysyuk (1986) demonstrated, mediation of sociodramatic play substantially influences the acquisition and mastery by children of moral norms. As is discussed in detail later, the neo-Vygotskian studies have also revealed the importance of sociodramatic play for the development of children's self-regulation, perspective taking, and symbolic thought.

Similar findings about the importance of sociodramatic play for children's development have been collected by Western researchers. Sociodramatic play has been shown to contribute substantially to children's intellectual, cognitive, emotional, and language development; to their social competence, perspective-taking skills, school achievement; and to other developmental accomplishments during this period (for overviews, see Berk & Winsler, 1995; Cheah, Nelson, & Rubin, 2001; Fisher, 1992; Smilansky & Shefatya, 1990). In contrast, children who do not engage in sociodramatic play "appear to be at risk for contemporaneous difficulties and long-term maladaptive outcomes"

(Cheah et al., 2001, p. 61). Numerous research findings have also indicated not only that mediation of sociodramatic play leads to higher quality children's play, but that it also results in children's development in the various domains just described (for an overview, see Smilansky & Shefatya, 1990).

Discussing developmental outcomes of children's engagement in sociodramatic play, the neo-Vygotskians especially stress the significance of those developmental outcomes that, in their view, are most important for children's transition to the next period of development. An analysis of these developmental outcomes is presented in the following sections.

The Development of the Motive to Study at School

One of the major outcomes of sociodramatic play is that, by the end of the period of early childhood, children become dissatisfied with such a pseudo-penetration into the world of adults. As Elkonin (1978) wrote,

> [the child] looks at himself through the role he has taken, that is, through the role of an adult, emotionally compares himself with an adult, and discovers that he is not an adult yet. The realization of the fact that he is still a child comes as a result of play and leads to the development of the child's new motive to become an adult and to fulfill adult responsibilities in reality. (p. 277)

The only "real" and "serious" role that is available for the child in an industrialized society and that will bring him or her nearer to an adult position in society is the role of a student in school. Therefore, the motive to fulfill adults' responsibilities is concretized in children's strong desire to study at school (Bozhovich, 1948, 1968, 1995; Elkonin, 1978, 1989). Thus, according to the neo-Vygotskians, sociodramatic play leads to the development in children of the motive to study at school (Bozhovich, 1995; Elkonin, 1989).

To test the neo-Vygotskian explanation of the role of sociodramatic play in the development of children's motive to study at school, the following two questions have to be answered. First, do children indeed develop the motive to study at school by the end of the period of early childhood? Second, is the development of this motive determined by children's engagement in sociodramatic play?

DO CHILDREN DEVELOP THE MOTIVE TO STUDY AT SCHOOL BY THE END OF THE PERIOD OF EARLY CHILDHOOD?

Neo-Vygotskian studies and observations make it possible to give a positive answer to this question. Numerous observations have been collected demonstrating that, by the end of the period of early childhood, children start expressing dissatisfaction with their preschool occupations and a strong desire to study at school (Bozhovich, 1948, 1968). Often this desire is expressed directly by children's statements to the effect that they want "to go to school and start to study as soon as possible" (Bozhovich, 1968, p. 218).

Another indicator of the development of this new motive in children is that, in contrast to 4- to 5-year-old children, 6-year-olds are very interested in playing at school. Bozhovich (1968) observed that, when playing at school, "as a rule, all the participants want to play the role of pupils; nobody wants to assume the role of the teacher, and, usually, this role is assigned to the youngest or meekest child" (p. 221). This observation is especially interesting because in all the other sociodramatic games the situation is just the opposite: The most prestigious roles are those of adults, and children "do their best to refuse playing roles of children; these roles are not attractive for them" (Elkonin, 1978 p. 200).[1]

---

[1] When Bozhovich made this observation, schooling in Russia started at age 7 years, and children were not introduced to formal schooling at preschool settings. Such observations can hardly be made these days because schooling starts at age 6, and it

An interesting study aimed at the evaluation of Russian 6-year-old preschoolers' motive to study at school was performed by Ginzburg (for a review, see Elkonin & Venger, 1988). The researcher selected 11 pairs of adjectives (clean–dirty, good–bad, fast–slow etc.), and each of the adjectives was written on a separate card. In front of the child were two boxes with attached pictures: On one picture were school students with briefcases; on the other, playing children. The researcher said to the child, "These are school students, who study at school; and these are preschoolers, who are playing. I will be reading different words. You should think whether each word suits better a school student or a preschooler and put the card with this word into the proper box." After that, the experimenter read aloud the adjectives in random order. After reading an adjective, the experimenter gave the card to the child, who put it into one of the boxes.

The results of this study demonstrated that almost all the preschoolers attributed the "positive" adjectives (clean, good, fast, etc.) to school students and the "negative" adjectives (dirty, bad, slow, etc.) to preschoolers. Thus, these results have provided an additional confirmation to the neo-Vygotskian contention that, by the end of the period of early childhood, children get dissatisfied with their status as preschoolers and develop the motive to study at school.

DOES SOCIODRAMATIC PLAY DETERMINE
THE DEVELOPMENT OF CHILDREN'S MOTIVE
TO STUDY AT SCHOOL?

This question still remains open. Surprisingly enough, the neo-Vygotskians have never performed empirical studies aimed at testing their theoretical speculation of the importance of sociodramatic play for the emergence of children's motive to study at school.

is already at kindergartens that children are introduced to some elements of formal schooling. Obviously, kindergarten children are not interested in assuming the play roles of pupils because they are already enjoying these roles in their actual lives.

Certainly, this weakens their analysis of the role of sociodramatic play in children's development during the period of early childhood and their transition to the next period of development. Recent studies of American researchers, however, have provided some empirical support for this theoretical speculation of the neo-Vygotskians. In particular, Fantuzzo and McWayne (2002) have revealed a significant association between preschoolers' peer play and their learning motivation.

The Development of Self-Regulation

In contrast to Erikson's (1963), A. Freud's (1927), S. Freud's (1920/1955), and Piaget's (1945/1962) views of sociodramatic play as children's free activity, Vygotsky (1966/1976) and his Russian followers (Elkonin, 1960, 1978; Leontiev, 1959/1964) stressed that children are not free in play. In play, every child is supposed to act in accordance with his or her role. Every role contains some implicit rules, however:

> If the child is playing the role of a mother, then she has rules of maternal behaviour. The role the child fulfils . . . will always stem from the rules, i.e. the imaginary situation will always contain rules. In play the child is free. But this is an illusory freedom. (Vygotsky, 1966/1976, p. 542)

Thus, when acting out a play role, a child follows the rule, which is "hidden . . . under the role" (Elkonin, 1978, p. 248).[2]

Not all the play rules, however, are pleasant for the child. Often, playing children have to suppress their immediate desires and bend their behavior to an "unpleasant" rule for play to be sustained. Elkonin (1960) gives an example of mother–daughter play in which "mothers" brought their "children" (dolls) to "the kindergarten" and had to hand

---

[2] Of course, this does not exclude the freedom for children's creative improvisations within the framework of the roles they have assumed.

them over to "the teacher." The girls, especially the younger ones, were very reluctant to hand over their favorite dolls to "the teacher," but they managed to overcome their desire to keep the dolls and bent their behavior to the rules of the play. This and similar observations have supported Vygotsky's (1978) evaluation of sociodramatic play, which he formulated back in the 1930s:

> Play continually creates demands on the child to act against imme-
> diate impulse. At every step the child is faced with a conflict between
> the rules of the game and what he would do if he could suddenly
> act spontaneously. In the game he acts counter to the way he wants
> to act. A child's greatest self-control occurs in play. He achieves the
> maximum display of willpower when he renounces an immediate at-
> traction in the game (such as candy, which by the rules of the game he
> is forbidden to eat because it represents something inedible). (p. 99)

What makes it possible for children to bend their behavior to the rules of the play? Certainly, because children have strong play motives, they are doing their best to sustain the play with the use of those self-regulatory tools that, as discussed in the previous chapter, they have already mastered. There is, however, another factor, which crucially determines children's ability to suppress their immediate impulses and follow the rules of play. All the children who participate in a play are strictly regulating each other's behavior in regard to following the play roles. The following observation by Elkonin (1978) illustrates this point.

Six-year-old boys were playing at firefighters. They distributed the roles: One of them was "the chief firefighter," another was "the driver of the fire engine," and the others were "firefighters." The play started. The chief shouted, "Fire!" Everybody grasped a tool and took a seat in the fire engine. The driver drove the fire engine. When they got to the point of destination, the chief gave the order, and all the firefighters started to run to extinguish the fire. The first impulse of the driver was to follow everybody: After all, the most interesting part of the play was about to get started! But the other children reminded him that, according to his role, he had to stay in the engine. The child had to suppress his desire to follow everybody, and, instead, he returned to the fire engine.

The importance of children's involvement in mutual regulation in play is not limited to the development of their ability to suppress immediate impulses and follow the rules of the play. As discussed in chapter 1, according to Vygotsky (1981a), a major determinant of children's transition to self-regulation is their use of verbal tools for regulating the behavior of others. Proceeding from this contention of Vygotsky, it can be assumed that children's mutual regulation in play results in further development of their ability for self-regulation in nonplay situations, that is, in terms of Vygotsky (1966/1976), that play creates the zone of proximal development of children's ability for self-regulation.

To test this assumption, Manuilenko (1948) studied how long 3- to 7-year-old children were able to stand motionless in six different situations. Three of these situations turned out to be the most interesting for comparison. In the first situation, the child was instructed by the experimenter to stand motionless for as long as he could. In the second situation, the child, in the context of sociodramatic play, was performing the role of a sentry (which required that he stand motionless) in an empty room. The third situation replicated the second one with one difference: The child was "standing sentry" in the same room in which his playmates were playing.

The study documented that, in all three situations, the time that children were able to stand motionless increased with age. In all the age groups except for 6- to 7-year-olds, however, children demonstrated the greatest ability to stand motionless in the third situation. The explanation of these results became clear in light of the researcher's observation that, when playing in the same room, the playmates were monitoring the "sentry's" performance. As for a 6- to 7-year-old "sentry," who demonstrated approximately the same results in all three situations (12 minutes in both play situations and 11 minutes when asked to stand motionless), such monitoring by playmates was not necessary: Apparently, he had already developed a level of self-regulation sufficient for nonplay situations.

The results of Manuilenko's study (1948) have supported Vygotsky's contention that, in sociodramatic play, 3- to 6-year-old children perform at the proximal rather than actual level of the development of their self-regulation, which gradually turns into the actual level of the development of their self-regulation by the end of early childhood. Also, this study has supported the notion that children's ability to do self-regulation in play is crucially determined by playmates monitoring their behavior. Neither Manuilenko's study nor other neo-Vygotskian studies, however, have directly confirmed the Vygotskian contention that sociodramatic play *leads* to the development of children's self-regulation in nonplay situations, that is, *creates* the zone of proximal development of children's self-regulation.

Conformations of Vygotsky's contention that sociodramatic play leads to the development of children's self-regulation can be found, however, in studies of American researchers. The study by Elias and Berk (2002) has documented that children's engagement in sociodramatic play predicts further development of their self-regulation. Even a stronger confirmation of this Vygotskian contention can be found in the study of Saltz et al. (1977). As discussed, the researchers enriched 3- to 4-year-old children's knowledge of social roles and relations and further encouraged them to discuss their new experiences and enact the roles and relations observed, which resulted in the children's engagement in sociodramatic play. Then, the children were posttested on several tasks. The most important for this discussion are the posttest data on the children's impulse control: These data turned out to be much better than the impulse-control data of the children from the control group.

To discuss additional confirmation of the Vygotskian contention of the major role of sociodramatic play in the development of children's self-regulation, I want to return to numerous studies and observations by Western researchers, which have suggested that sociodramatic play is becoming extinct. Proceeding from this Vygotskian contention, one can predict that children's nonengagement in sociodramatic play during the period of early childhood will result in deficiencies of their self-regulation by the end of this period. Indeed, a survey of kindergarten teachers conducted by the National Center for Early Development and Learning "suggests that many children are arriving at school without effective self-regulation skills" (Blair, 2002, p. 112). It has also turned out that one of the major complaints of American elementary school teachers is that "they have to 'sing, dance, or act like Big Bird' in order to teach" (Bodrova & Leong, 1996, p. 4). To "translate" this complaint into psychological language, children come to school with a very poor level of self-regulation, and, therefore, they cannot attend to the teacher's explanations unless the teacher uses some "tricks" to attract and maintain their attention. As discussed in chapter 1, Vygotsky referred to this type of attention as a lower mental process, which has to be replaced by children's self-regulation by the end of the period of early childhood. Thus, not only does sociodramatic play lead to the development of children's self-regulation, but the lack of sociodramatic play is associated with deficiencies of their self-regulation as well.

Further Development of Symbolic Thought

As discussed in chapter 4, by the end of the second year, children start to use object substitutes, that is, objects that stand for other objects. Also, as studies cited in chapter 4 have demonstrated, children's engagement in object substitutions as mediated by adults is instrumental in the development of children's symbolic thought during the third year of life.

The use of object substitutes continues, although in a different context, during the period of early childhood (Elkonin, 1978; Smilansky & Shefatya, 1990). Now children use object substitutes in the course of sociodramatic play; for example, when playing at war, children may use sticks to substitute for guns. Although in many cases children are capable of coming up with their own object substitutions, in some cases the use of object substitutes still requires adult mediation (Elkonin, 1978; Smilansky & Shefatya, 1990).

Developmental outcomes of object substitutions in sociodramatic play have not been specifically investigated by the neo-Vygotskians. Proceeding from the experimental data and observations discussed in chapter 4, however, it is reasonable to assume that such objects substitutions continue to contribute to further development of children's symbolic thought.

A possible objection to this assumption is that, although object substitutions have been proved to be instrumental in the development of symbolic thought during the third year of life, they no longer play this role during the period of early childhood. In an attempt to address this possible objection, what follows is a brief description of Dyachenko's study (1980, 1986).[3] Although the goal of the study was to teach children to retell the plot of a tale rather than to mediate their play, its findings are relevant to the topic under discussion here.

Analysis of the assignment to retell the plot of a tale shows that such an assignment imposes a demanding cognitive task on the child. While listening to a tale, the child has to construct a symbolic model of it, which involves the representations of the sequence of episodes with characters and actions engaged in each episode. No wonder not only first-graders but even much older children find this task too

---

[3] For a detailed description of this study in English, see Karpov, 1995.

difficult to perform. Proceeding from the Vygotskian idea of the role of object substitutes as pivots for the construction of symbolic representations, the researcher taught 5- to 6-year-old children to use substitutes (sticks, paper cutouts, etc.) to reproduce the main episodes of a tale on a table and then to retell the tale using these substitutes as pivots for the retell. Then, rather than giving ready-made substitutes, the researcher facilitated the children's invention of their own drawn substitutes, which they used to retell the plot of a tale. As a result of this mediation, the children's ability to retell the plot of a new tale even without substitutes was considerably improved, which indicated that they developed the ability to construct the model of a tale at the symbolic level.

Thus, Dyachenko's (1980, 1986) study has demonstrated that the use of object substitutes in an instructional context facilitates the development of symbolic thought during the period of early childhood. There is, then, reason to believe that children's use of object substitutes in the course of sociodramatic play leads to the same developmental outcome.

Overcoming of Egocentrism

As introduced by Piaget (1923/1959), the concept of egocentrism describes the major shortcoming of preschooler thinking: the inability to take into account the position of another person, or to look at a certain event or object from perspectives different from one's own.[4]

---

[4] Some researchers do not agree with Piaget's contention that egocentrism is the dominant feature of preschoolers' thinking, arguing that, depending on the nature of the task, both preschoolers and adults may demonstrate egocentrism (see, for example, Donaldson, 1978). These researchers, however, do agree that preschoolers demonstrate egocentrism more often than adults.

At the end of the period of early childhood, children overcome their egocentrism, which indicates their transition to the next period of development.

Piaget did not see any connection between children's engagement in sociodramatic play and overcoming their egocentrism. He believed that sociodramatic play is just a continuation of children's solitary symbolic play, which "is merely egocentric thought in its pure state" (Piaget, 1945/1962, p. 166). Therefore, "collective play either has no effect on the egocentric symbolism or, when there is imitation, it enhances it" (Piaget, 1945/1962, p. 168).

In contrast to this position of Piaget, Russian neo-Vygotskians stress the importance of sociodramatic play for children's overcoming of their egocentrism (Elkonin, 1960, 1978; Nedospasova, 1972). Indeed, when playing, children have to treat their playmates not according to their real-life names and relations but according to their play roles. In real life, Tom and John may have very bad relations; in play, however, they will treat each other in a collaborative and friendly manner if their roles require it. Also, playing children have to coordinate their play actions with the play actions of playmates. For example, if Phil has "shot" Steve when playing at war, Steve has to fall down and remain "dead." Finally, children have to accept the meanings their playmates have assigned to object substitutes that they are using. For example, in a "doctor–patient" play, the "doctor" may decide to use a stick to stand for a syringe. For the "patient," however, the stick "may become a syringe only if he takes into account the doctor's position" (Elkonin, 1978, pp. 281–282). Thus, in sociodramatic play "the child's position toward the external world fundamentally changes . . . and the ability to coordinate his point of view with other possible points of view develops" (Elkonin, 1978, p. 282).

This contention of the importance of sociodramatic play for children's overcoming of their egocentrism has been supported to some extent by neo-Vygotskian studies (Filippova, 1976; Nedospasova, 1972). The major empirical support for this contention, however, has been obtained in studies and observations by Western researchers.

As has been documented, sociodramatic play is associated with a reduction of children's egocentricity and an increase in their perspective-taking abilities (Connolly & Doyle, 1984; Van den Daele, 1970, quoted in Fein, 1981). The more time children spend on sociodramatic play, the more substantial is the increase in their perspective-taking abilities (Rubin et al., 1983).

Predictive relationships between sociodramatic play and children's egocentrism were studied by Youngblade and Dunn (1995). The researchers observed 3-year-old children's play with mothers and siblings and recorded all the instances of their assuming play roles in the context of play. Then, 6 months later, the children's ability to take into account another person's point of view was evaluated. It turned out that this ability was correlated with the frequency of children's assuming play roles that had been measured earlier.

In two interventional studies (Burns & Brainerd, 1979; Rosen, 1974), adults mediated 5-year-old children's sociodramatic play (helped children elaborate the topic of play, assume and enact play roles, use substitutes, etc.). Even a short-term mediation was proved to be sufficient to increase substantially the children's perspective-taking abilities.

The explanations by Western researchers of the reasons for children's overcoming their egocentrism in the course of sociodramatic play are very close to the explanations of these reasons by Russian neo-Vygotskians discussed earlier. Smilansky and Shefatya (1990) indicated that, in play, "the child is willing to suppress egocentric fancies, accept the suggestions of his co-players, and be attentive to their interpretations in order to have the pleasure of participating" (p. 122). Göncü (1993) argued that sociodramatic play requires shared understanding and adjusting to the perspectives of play peers. A similar view was expressed by Glaubman et al. (2001): "In socio-dramatic play, children construct cognitive and emotive meanings through continual communicative and metacommunicative negotiations. . . . Children construct meanings in the form of common play narratives, and they do so by mutual negotiations" (p. 135). Finally, it is argued that sociodramatic play requires that playmates agree to the meanings assigned to object substitutes that they use in play (Glaubman et al., 2001; Winnicott, 1982).

Thus, engagement in sociodramatic play literally forces children to overcome their egocentrism. Therefore, this play results in "developing the child from being predominantly egocentric into being capable of cooperation and social interaction" (Smilansky & Shefatya, 1990, p. 32).

Why Is Sociodramatic Play the Leading Activity During the Early Childhood Period?

By definition, children's activity is leading during a given age period if it prepares children for the transition to the activity that becomes leading during the next period of development. As discussed in the next chapter, the neo-Vygotskians argue that children's leading activity during the period of middle childhood is learning at school. Therefore, to define sociodramatic play as the leading activity during the period of early childhood, it is necessary to demonstrate that children's engagement in sociodramatic play prepares them for successful transition to learning at school, that is, that sociodramatic play strongly contributes to the development of *school readiness*.

Discussing the term school readiness, both Russian neo-Vygotskians and Western scholars have concluded that there is no consensus on how it should be defined (Carlton & Winsler, 1999; Kravtsov & Kravtsova, 1987; La Paro & Pianta, 2000; Pyle, 2002; Talyzina, 2001). Often, school readiness is associated with children's mastery of such academic skills as counting, elements of reading and writing, and so on (for reviews, see Kravtsov & Kravtsova, 1987; La Paro & Pianta, 2000; Talyzina, 2001). This understanding of school readiness is especially popular among parents who often train their children in academic skills (sometimes, as discussed earlier, at the expense of socio-dramatic play) with the hope that this training will result in children's more successful learning at school. Initially, indeed, these children demonstrate better success at school than their "nontrained" peers. Often, however, in several months, these children begin to demonstrate less and less interest in learning, and their learning becomes less and less successful (Kravtsov & Kravtsova, 1987). Proceeding from these observations, the neo-Vygotskians have come to the conclusion that the mastery of basic academic skills by itself does not make preschoolers ready for learning at school (Elkonin, 1989; Kravtsov & Kravtsova, 1987; Talyzina, 2001). Some American researchers have reached a similar conclusion. Having analyzed the outcomes of typical school-based preventive intervention programs, La Paro and Pianta (2000) indicated that they focus primarily on "teaching the child to spell his or her name, how to count, or the letters of the alphabet (Kagan, 1990). Again, our data suggest that this is only part of the story of these children's success in later grades, even in the same performance domain" (p. 476).

Having analyzed the process of learning at school, Russian neo-Vygotskians have defined the major characteristics of children's motivational and mental domains that are necessary for children's successful learning and, therefore, are the components of school readiness (Bozhovich, 1968; Elkonin, 1978; Kravtsov & Kravtsova, 1987; Talyzina, 2001; Venger & Kholmovskaya, 1978). Although there are differences in the lists of the components of school readiness as suggested by different neo-Vygotskians, they are consistent in stressing the importance of the following characteristics of children's motivational and mental domains for school readiness.

THE MOTIVE TO STUDY AT SCHOOL

The importance of children's motive to study as a component of their school readiness was emphasized by Vygotsky (1984): "The problem of interest in instruction is not whether or not children learn with interest; they never learn without interest" (p. 35). Numerous empirical data and observations of Russian neo-Vygotskians have confirmed the notion of the crucial role of children's motive to study in their successful learning (Bozhovich, 1948, 1968, 1995; Elkonin, 1989; Elkonin & Venger, 1988; Kravtsov & Kravtsova, 1987; Leontiev, 1959/1964; Talyzina, 2001). A similar position, although in different words, was expressed by 76% of surveyed American kindergarten teachers, who "endorsed the idea that children need to be enthusiastic and curious" to learn successfully (Blair, 2002, p. 112).

SELF-REGULATION

Research and observations of both Russian neo-Vygotskians and Western scholars have demonstrated that children's ability to self-regulate (to bend their behavior to school rules and regulations, to follow directions, and to attend to the teacher's explanation) is extremely important for their learning at school (Blair, 2002; Bozhovich, 1968; Elkonin, 1978; Normandeau & Guay, 1998; Talyzina, 2001; Venger & Kholmovskaya, 1978). The same conclusion has been reached by educational practitioners. Earlier, I mentioned that one of the major complaints of American elementary school teachers is that many children come to school with a very poor level of self-regulation, which makes the process of teaching extremely difficult (Bodrova & Leong, 1996). The results of two surveys of American teachers "clearly indicate that kindergarten teachers are concerned with children's regulatory readiness for school activities rather than with more strictly cognitive and academic aspects of readiness" (Blair, 2002, p. 112).

SYMBOLIC THOUGHT

As discussed in detail in the next chapter, Vygotsky (1978, 1934/1986, 1982/1987) and his Russian followers (Davydov, 1972/1990, 1986; Elkonin, 1989; Galperin, 1985; Leontiev, 1983; Talyzina, 1975/1981) have stressed the difference between the learning of preschoolers and school students. Preschoolers' learning is mostly a collateral product of their engagement in other activities (such as play), and they learn through practical exploration of separate objects and events. As discussed earlier, even at this level of children's functioning, symbolic thought is important for their successful performance (for example, it is essential for children's creation of an imaginary situation as the basis of sociodramatic play). In contrast to preschoolers' learning, learning at school deals with the acquisition by students of scientific, theoretical knowledge, which is presented to students in the form of concepts, rules, and laws. Therefore, symbolic thought is not just important but literally a must for children's successful learning at school (Elkonin, 1978; Kravtsov & Kravtsova, 1987; Talyzina, 2001; Venger & Kholmovskaya, 1978).

NONEGOCENTRIC POSITION

School students' nonegocentrism is important for their successful learning in two respects. First, the acquisition of scientific knowledge requires that children be ready to perceive, understand, and explain the world not from their own perspective but from the perspective of scientific rules and laws they have been taught by the teacher (Elkonin, 1989). Unfortunately, students' reluctance to accept scientific knowledge that comes to contradict their personal beliefs can be observed even at the college level. For example,

> students in teacher education programs may disregard a professor's definition of a concept, instead using their own (perhaps, erroneous) understanding of what that concept means. And they are likely to ignore any recommendations for teaching practice that are inconsistent with their own beliefs about what "good teaching" is ... And, despite the evidence I present on the effectiveness of meaningful learning, some of them stubbornly continue to believe that rote learning is a better approach. (Ormrod, 1995, p. 267)

Second, classroom learning requires that children be able to work as a group, which implies that they are capable of coordinating their actions with the actions of their classmates (Kravtsov & Kravtsova, 1987). It is worthy of note that, according to a national survey of American kindergarten teachers, 20% to 30% of them "report that about half of their students or more have difficulty working as part of a group" (La Paro & Pianta, 2000, p. 475).

Although these characteristics of children's motivational and mental domains do not, probably, constitute the full list of components of school readiness, as shown, they substantially determine children's transition to learning at school as their leading activity during the period of middle childhood. Furthermore, as discussed in this chapter, these characteristics are direct developmental outcomes of children's engagement in sociodramatic play. Thus, sociodramatic play meets the requirements of the leading activity as formulated by the neo-Vygotskians.

Some Western researchers share the neo-Vygotskian contention of the leading role of sociodramatic play in preparing children for the transition to learning at school. Summarizing empirical data of Smilansky and Feldman, Smilansky and Shefatya (1990) have reported an "astonishingly high" (p. 44) correlation between the quality of sociodramatic play of kindergarteners and their further achievement in reading comprehension and arithmetic in the second grade. These and similar findings have made it possible for Smilansky and Shefatya (1990) to conclude that "in many ways sociodramatic play means direct preparation of school behavior" (p. 20). Recent data of American researchers also lead to this conclusion. For example, the study of Fantuzzo and McWayne (2002) has revealed a significant association between preschoolers' peer play and their motivation to learn, their self-regulation, and their engagement in prosocial behavior in the classroom.

6 The Period of Middle Childhood: Learning at School as Children's Leading Activity

As briefly discussed in chapter 1, Vygotsky (1978, 1934/1986) viewed school instruction as the major avenue for mediated learning and, therefore, as the major contributor to children's cognitive development during the period of middle childhood. According to Vygotsky (1978, 1934/1986), the major reason for the development-generating effect of school instruction relates to students' acquisition of so-called scientific concepts, which can be contrasted with the spontaneous concepts of preschoolers.

Spontaneous concepts are the result of generalization and internalization of everyday personal experience in the absence of systematic instruction. Therefore, such concepts are unsystematic, empirical, not conscious, and often wrong. For example, a 3-year-old child, having observed a needle, a pin, and a coin sinking in water, comes to the wrong conclusion – that "all small objects sink" – and begins to use this concept for predicting the behavior of different objects in water (Zaporozhets, 1986c, p. 207). Despite their "unscientific" nature, spontaneous concepts play an important role in children's learning as a foundation for the acquisition of *scientific concepts*. For example, "historical concepts can begin to develop only when the child's everyday [spontaneous] concept of the past is sufficiently differenti-ated" (Vygotsky, 1934/1986, p. 194).

In contrast to spontaneous concepts, *scientific concepts* represent the generalization of the experience of humankind that is fixed in science (understood in the broadest sense of the term to include both natural and social sciences as well as the humanities), and they are acquired by students consciously and according to a certain system. In the example given here, the scientific concept that would make it possible to predict the behavior of objects in water is Archimedes' law.

Once scientific concepts have been acquired, they transform stu-dents' everyday life knowledge: The students' spontaneous concepts become structured and conscious. Thus, the acquisition of scientific concepts creates the zone of proximal development of spontaneous concepts (see chapter 1 for the analysis of Vygotsky's concept of the zone of proximal development). The importance of the acquisition of scientific concepts, however, is not limited to the fact that they "restructure and raise spontaneous concepts to a higher level" (Vygot-sky, 1982/1987, p. 220). Once acquired by students, scientific concepts come to mediate their thinking and problem solving. That is why "in-struction in scientific concepts plays a decisive role in the child's men-tal development" (Vygotsky, 1982/1987, p. 220). Specifically, "reflec-tive consciousness comes to the child through the portals of scientific concepts" (Vygotsky, 1934/1986, p. 171). As a result, students' thinking becomes much more independent of their personal experience. They become "theorists" rather then "practitioners" and, by the end of the period of middle childhood, develop the ability to operate at the level of formal–logical thought.

Thus, in contrast to Piaget's general disregard of the role of school instruction in children's cognitive development (Piaget, 1923/1959; Piaget et al., 1988), Vygotsky (1934/1986, 1982/1987) viewed school instruction as the major determinant of the development of children's ability to operate at the level of formal–logical thought. As discussed in the next section, cross-cultural studies of formal–logical thought have provided strong empirical support to this Vygotskian view.

Cross-Cultural Studies of Formal–Logical Thought

Rapid social changes, which were taking place in the early 1930s in Uzbekistan and Kirghizia, Asian Republics of the former Soviet Union, made it possible for Luria, Vygotsky's closest friend and colleague, to perform a classical study of the role of schooling in the development of the ability to engage in formal–logical thought (Luria, 1974/1976, 1979). The study was performed with adults in remote villages of those Asian Republics; some of the subjects were illiterate, and some had already taken advantage of the system of school instruction that had just been established there and had enjoyed 1 or 2 years of schooling. Rather than using standardized tests, the members of Luria's research team established friendly relations with the subjects and then involved them in informal conversations in their native language. In the context of such conversations, the researchers presented different syllogisms to the subjects and asked them to provide an answer to the question completing the syllogism and to explain this answer. The content of some of the syllogisms was familiar to the subjects, whereas the content of other syllogisms was unfamiliar to them.

The study revealed a qualitative difference between educated and illiterate subjects in answering the syllogism questions. The educated subjects correctly solved all the syllogisms with both familiar and un-familiar contents. In contrast, the typical responses of their illiterate neighbors even to syllogisms with familiar contents (such as cotton raising) were as follows:

> "Cotton can grow only where it is hot and dry. In England it is cold and damp. Can cotton grow there?"

"I don't know."

"Think about it."

"I've only been in the Kashgar country. I don't know beyond that."

"But on the basis of what I said to you, can cotton grow there?"

"If the land is good, cotton will grow there, but if it is damp and poor, it won't grow. If it's like Kashgar country, it will grow there too. If the soil is loose, it can grow there too, of course."

The syllogism was then repeated. "What can you conclude from my words?"

"If it's cold there, it won't grow. If the soil is loose and good, it will."

"But what do my words suggest?"

"Well, we Moslems, we Kashgars, we're ignorant people; we've never been anywhere, so we don't know if it's hot or cold there." (Luria, 1979, p. 78)

When presented syllogisms with unfamiliar contents ("In the Far North, where there is snow, all bears are white. Novaya Zemlya is in the Far North. What color are bears there?"), the illiterate subjects "refused even more decisively to draw inferences.... As a rule, many refused to accept the major premise, declaring that they 'had never been in the North and had never seen bears; to answer the question you would have to ask people who had been there and seen them'" (Luria, 1974/ 1976, p. 107). Summarizing the most typical responses of illiterate subjects, Luria (1974/1976) concluded that they

> were a complete denial of the possibility of drawing conclusions from propositions about things they had no personal experience of, and suspicion about any logical operation of a purely theoretical nature, although there was the recognition of the possibility of drawing conclusions from one's own practical experience. (p. 108)

Thus, the results of Luria's (1974/1976) study have provided strong empirical support to the idea of the dominant role of schooling in development of formal–logical thought.

Luria's (1974/1976) study was followed by many cross-cultural studies of solving syllogistic problems by educated and illiterate people in different traditional societies (for descriptions and overviews, see Cole, 1996; Cole, Gay, Glick, & Sharp, 1971; Cole & Scribner, 1974; Scribner, 1975, 1977; Scribner & Cole, 1981; Segall, Dasen, Berry, & Poortinga, 1990/1999; Sharp, Cole, & Lave, 1979; Tulviste, 1991). The results of these studies were highly consistent with the results of Luria's research discussed earlier: In contrast to educated subjects, illiterate people solved simple syllogistic problems "at a chance level" (Tulviste, 1991, p. 124) even if a syllogism was built around a content familiar to them. A more detailed analysis of differences between educated and illiterate subjects in solving syllogisms confirmed another of Luria's (1974/1976) findings: When asked to explain their responses, educated subjects proceeded from the premises of the given syllogism, whereas illiterate people, even if their answer was correct, substantiated their responses by referring to their personal experience.

Despite the consistency of these findings with the data of Luria's (1974/1976) study, not all researchers have subscribed to his conclusion of the dominant role of schooling in the development of formal–logical thought. The most prominent advocate of an alternative explanation of these findings is Cole (Cole, 1976, 1990, 1996; Cole & Scribner, 1974; Cole et al., 1971; Scribner & Cole, 1973). Cole believes that people in all cultures have the same basic cognitive processes or abilities (including the ability to operate at the formal–logical level), but their manifestation of these abilities is determined by their cultural experiences. Therefore, "cultural differences in cognition reside more in the situations to which particular cognitive processes are applied than in the existence of a process in one cultural group and its absence in another" (Cole et al., 1971, p. 233). Schooling, from this point of view, does not lead to the development of new formal–logical abilities but rather leads to the extension of already existing formal–logical abilities to solving school-content problems.

An insightful analysis of the preceding theoretical position has been provided by Tulviste (1991). Discussing its methodological weaknesses,

175

Tulviste (1991) wrote:

> Let us suppose that having carefully studied the activity of people in a certain traditional group, we did not find that they use, let us say, Piaget's formal operations . . . According to Cole, even in this case we still do not have the right to assert that there are no formal operations in the thinking of people in this culture or group. He believes that on the basis of experimental data judgments can be made only about what subjects can do, but not about what they cannot do. . . . [S]uch an approach will lead an investigator into an endless search. With negative results, we can always say that we were simply not successful in setting experimental conditions in which the subjects would apply the abilities or processes they have, but which they were not able to exhibit. And substantial differences in thinking, if they do exist, remain undiscovered. (p. 59)

Evaluating Cole's assumption that schooling, rather than creating new formal–logical abilities in children, just extends the sphere of application of these already existing abilities to solving new kind of problems, Tulviste (1991) described his own study performed in the 1970s. The study was performed with 8- to 15-year-old schoolchildren who belonged to a traditional Eurasian nation. The children were presented with syllogistic problems of everyday content (e.g., "Saiba and Nakupte always drink tea together; Saiba drinks tea at 3 P.M.; does Nakupte drink tea at 3 P.M. or not?") as well as of school content (e.g., "All precious metals do not rust; Molybdenum is a precious metal; does molybdenum rust or not?"). Having answered the questions, the children were asked to explain their answers. The study demonstrated that the children, on average, successfully solved 74% of syllogisms with everyday content and 82% of syllogisms with school content. Much more interesting, however, was the analysis of the children's explanation of their answers. It turned out that 65% of the children's explanations of their correct answers to school-content syllogisms were based on the premises of the syllogism, whereas only 32% of their explanations of the correct answers to everyday-content syllogisms were based on the premises of the syllogism. Certainly, these results are not consistent with Cole's theoretical position that schooling just extends the area of applying children's existing formal–logical abilities from solving everyday problems to solving school-content problems. Rather than that, these results "lead to the conclusion that practically error-free solution of simple syllogistic problems based on relating deduction to premises initially emerges in the sphere of school (scientific) information and is transferred only later to the everyday sphere" (Tulviste, 1991, p. 127).[1]

In light of this discussion, the contention of Vygotsky and his followers of the dominant role of school instruction in the development of formal–logical thought seems much better grounded than Cole's alternative idea of formal–logical thought as a "basic" and universal cross-cultural ability. As Tulviste (1991) wrote, "the impression is formed that Cole's conviction of the universality of 'basic' processes... flows not so much from some theoretical notions or even from experimental data... as from nobleness, from a desire... to consider all cultures and all mental types as 'different but equal'" (1991, p. 61). In other words, the basis for such a theoretical position is ideological rather than scientific; its advocates "perceive the manifestation of Eurocentrism in the identification of qualitative differences in thinking" (Tulviste, 1991, p. 124).[2] Leaving aside the fact that scientific explanations should be based on empirical evidence rather than on ideological dogmas, I do not see the statement that mental development of people in traditional societies suffers because of the lack of schooling to be any more racist or Eurocentric than the statement

---

[1] It is worthy of note that Cole never responded to this empirical criticism of his theoretical position either in his preface to Tulviste's (1991) publication (Cole, 1991) or in his subsequent publications (Cole, 1992, 1996; Cole & Cole, 1993, 2001).

[2] As Luria's students (Homskaya, 2001; Tulviste, 1999) testify, his cross-cultural data led to accusations of racism against Luria from the authorities of Stalin's oppressive regime. Tulviste (1999) indicated that, in his opinion, "this is similar to the present-day ideological critique that accuses researchers of eurocentrism" (p. 68).

that their health suffers because of the lack of medical care. The Vygotskian view of the role of schooling in the development of cognition is, on the contrary, probably the most antiracist and humanistic view of this matter because it proclaims that all humans have an equal potential for cognitive development and appeals for social changes that will make it possible for them to fully realize this potential.

Shortcomings of the Traditional System of School Instruction

Although, as discussed, even 1 or 2 years of schooling are sufficient to make it possible for people to solve simple syllogistic problems, many American adolescents have been shown to experience serious difficulties when dealing with more complicated formal–logical problems (for overviews, see Cole & Cole, 1993, 2001). Cole (1990) interpreted these data as contradicting the view of Vygotsky and his followers that "'empirical' thinking is replaced by 'theoretical' thinking as a consequence of schooling" (p. 100). However, another interpretation of these data is possible, which makes them highly consistent with Vygotsky's view of the role of schooling in children's mental development.

As mentioned in chapter 1, Vygotsky emphasized that a development-generating effect of instruction would take place only if the process of instruction were organized in the proper way: "The only good kind of instruction is that which marches ahead of development and leads it; it must be aimed not so much at the ripe as at the ripening functions" (Vygotsky, 1934/1986, p. 188). As an example of instruction that did not lead development, he mentioned an instructional system that had been used in the former Soviet Union in the 1920s:

> For a time, our schools favored the "complex" system of instruction, which was believed to be adapted to the child's ways of thinking. In offering the child problems he was able to handle without help, this

> method failed to utilize the zone of proximal development and to lead
> the child to what he could not yet do. Instruction was oriented to the
> child's weakness rather than his strength, thus encouraging him to
> remain at the preschool stage of development. (Vygotsky, 1934/1986,
> p. 189)

Thus, the fact that traditional instruction does not result in fully developed formal–logical thought could be explained as an outcome of
shortcomings of traditional school instruction.

This explanation finds support in many studies and observations by
American researchers that have revealed serious deficiencies in American students' learning of math, science, reading, and writing. Having
summarized empirical data, Bruer (1993) wrote that

> most students have command of lower-level, rote skills, such as com-
> putation in math, recalling facts in science, decoding words in read-
> ing, and spelling, grammar, and punctuation in writing....Many
> if not most students have difficulty using what they know to in-
> terpret an experiment, comprehend a text, or persuade an audi-
> ence. They can't rise above the rote, factual level to think critically
> or creatively. They can't apply what they know flexibly and spon-
> taneously to solve ill-structured, ambiguous problems that require
> interpretation. (p. 5)

Proceeding from this data, Bruer (1993) concluded that "current cur-
ricula and teaching methods successfully impart facts and rote skills
to most students but fail to impart high-order reasoning and learning
skills" (p. 5).

To be sure, Bruer (1993) is partially right when explaining the deficiencies of American students' learning as a result of behaviorist ideas
that dominated (and, although to a less extent, continue to influence)
American system of school instruction. This reference to the negative
influence of behaviorist ideas, however, can explain the *severity* of the
deficiencies of American students' learning rather than providing the
major reason for these deficiencies. Indeed, Russian psychologists and

educators have observed similar (although in a less severe form) deficiencies of learning outcomes of Russian students, although behaviorism has never influenced the Russian system of school instruction (for overviews, see Davydov, 1986, 1972/1990; Elkonin, 1989; Talyzina, 2001). What, then, is the basic shortcoming of traditional systems of school instruction in the United States and Russia (as well as, probably, in other countries) that is responsible for the deficiencies of student learning just discussed?

The analysis by Russian and American researchers of the traditional systems of school instruction in their countries has revealed two typical learning outcomes of such instruction. The first typical outcome of traditional instruction is students' memorization of scientific conceptual knowledge (rules, concepts, definitions, or theorems), which, however, is not supported by their mastery of relevant procedural knowledge (that is, subject-domain strategies and skills; Bruer, 1993; Davydov, 1972/1990). The acquisition of verbal scientific knowledge has been shown not to lead to the students' use of this knowledge for solving subject-domain problems. Davydov (1972/1990) described the results of several studies with Russian students that illustrate this point. For example, having memorized the essential characteristics of mammals, birds, and fish, elementary school students, when classifying animals, proceeded from surface characteristics of the animals rather than from the memorized concepts (e.g., they associated the whale with the class of fish). In another study, sixth-graders, having memorized the concept of a right-angled triangle, did not recognize as such a right-angled triangle when it was presented to them with the right angle at the top (they called it "an acute-angled triangle"). Similar results have been obtained in studies with American school students. For example, in one study, children's conceptual number knowledge was not shown to ensure their ability to perform computational operations (Bruer, 1993).

The second typical learning outcome of traditional instruction is students' mastery of procedural knowledge (subject-domain strategies and skills) without their acquisition of the domain-relevant conceptual knowledge (Bruer, 1993; Davydov, 1972/1990; Talyzina, 1975/1981). In discussing the American traditional programs for teaching math, Bruer (1993) drew the following conclusion:

> Many students don't know why the math procedures they learn in school work. Students leave school having the computational skills to solve standard problems but lacking the higher-order mathematical understanding that would allow them to apply their skills widely in novel situations. Too often, math instruction produces students who can manipulate number symbols but who don't understand what the symbols mean. (p. 81)

Other studies and observations have also shown that pure procedural knowledge, whether learned in math or in any other subject domain, tends to remain meaningless and nontransferable (Bruer, 1993; Davydov, 1972/1990; Hiebert & Wearne, 1985; Talyzina, 1975/1981).

In summary, neither the acquisition of scientific concepts nor the mastery of procedural knowledge in itself should be viewed as a desirable outcome of school instruction. That is why contemporary American psychologists came up with the idea of "marrying concepts to procedures" (Bruer, 1993, p. 95), that is, combining these two kinds of knowledge in the course of teaching.

A similar idea was formulated by Russian neo-Vygotskians back in the 1930s (Leontiev, 1983) and has been elaborated by them in numerous studies since then (Davydov, 1986, 1972/1990; Galperin, 1957, 1969; Galperin, Zaporozhets, & Elkonin, 1963; Talyzina, 1975/1981). As discussed in chapter 2, the neo-Vygotskians renounced Vygotsky's notion of semiotic tools as mediators of human mental processes in favor of viewing the procedures that are relevant to these tools as such mediators. Proceeding from this general theoretical position, they have emphasized that scientific concepts serve as mediators of students' thinking and problem solving in different subject domains only if they are supported by students' mastery of relevant procedures that underlie these concepts. As Leontiev (1983) indicated, "In order for a child to develop the highest generalization (a concept), it is necessary to develop in him the system of psychological operations [procedures] that are relevant to this highest generalization" (p. 347). For example, the acquisition of Archimedes' law implies not only that students are able to repeat this law, but that they have also mastered the procedures for calculating the density of different objects and comparing these densities with the density of water. Similarly, the acquisition of the concept of perpendicular lines implies not only that students are able to repeat the definition of perpendicular lines, but that they have also mastered the procedures for identifying within a given pair of lines those attributes that are necessary and sufficient for associating (or not associating) this pair of lines with the concept of perpendicular lines.

Thus, the Russian neo-Vygotskians, as well as some American scholars, have attributed deficiencies in students' learning and development to the shortcomings of the traditional system of school instruction. From this perspective, Vygotsky (1978, 1934/1986) was right in viewing properly organized school instruction as the major avenue for mediated learning during the period of middle childhood, which leads to students' acquisition of scientific knowledge and the development of their formal–logical thought. Scientific knowledge, however, cannot be reduced to the verbal definitions of scientific concepts but should include procedural knowledge relevant to these concepts as well.

Theoretical Learning as the Avenue for the Acquisition of Scientific Knowledge and Cognitive Development

Having defined scientific knowledge (that is, a combination of scientific concepts and relevant procedures) as the content of properly organized school instruction, the neo-Vygotskians concerned themselves with answering another question: How should the process of learning be organized so that it will result in students' acquisition of scientific knowledge? To answer this question, Russian followers of Vygotsky compared two types of learning: empirical and theoretical (Davydov, 1986, 1972/1990; Galperin, 1985; Talyzina, 1975/1981).

Empirical learning is based on children's comparison of several different objects or events, picking out their common salient characteristics, and "discovering," on this basis, a "general concept" about this class of objects or events. This strategy may work if the common salient characteristics of objects or events reflect their significant, essential characteristics (for example, children can develop the concept of the color red in this way). However, this strategy will not work if the common characteristics of several representatives of a class of objects with which the child is dealing are not the common characteristics of all the objects of this class. This explains why the preschooler in the example given in the beginning of the chapter, having observed a needle, a pin, and a coin sinking, wrongly concluded that "all small objects sink." Small size is a common salient characteristic of a needle, a pin, and a coin, but it is not the common characteristic of all the objects that sink. Moreover, even if the common characteristics of several objects with which the child is dealing do reflect the common characteristics of all the objects of this class, they still may not reflect the essential characteristics of these objects. A tail and fins are common, but not essential, characteristics of fish. Therefore, the child's concept of fish "discovered" as the result of empirical learning would be a misconception.

Thus, empirical learning often leads to misconceptions. Given that both Russian and American school students have been shown to hold many such misconceptions (Davydov, 1972/1990; DiSessa, 1982), it is reasonable to assume that the traditional system of school instruction often promotes empirical learning. Indeed, as discussed in the previous section, under the traditional system of school instruction, students often are taught rote skills or verbal definitions of scientific concepts rather than true scientific knowledge (that is, combined conceptual and procedural knowledge in the given subject domain; Bruer, 1993; Davydov, 1972/1990). In both cases (whether students have mastered a rote skill or have learned the verbal definition of a scientific concept), the acquired knowledge cannot be flexibly applied for solving problems in the relevant subject domain: Rote skills are meaningless and nontransferable, and pure verbal knowledge is inert. That is why students, in fact, are forced to "discover" their own concepts and relevant procedures with which to deal with the subject domain problems.

This explains why the elementary school students in the earlier example, having memorized the concepts of mammals and fish, associated the whale with the class of fish when classifying animals. It could be reasonably assumed that, not being able to use the memorized definitions of these scientific concepts to solve the subject-domain problems, they involved themselves in the process of empirical learning. They compared "typical" fishes among themselves, picked out their common salient features, and "discovered" on this basis a concept of fish, which turned out to be wrong. Probably, this misconception involved the shape of a body, fins, tail, and living in the water as the essential characteristics that are necessary and sufficient for belonging to the class of fish. In the same way, they developed a wrong concept of mammals. Then, when asked to classify animals, they analyzed them using the developed misconceptions as the basis for analysis, which resulted in their associating the whale with the class of fish.

Similarly, mastery of rote meaningless skills also often leads to students' involving themselves in the process of empirical learning, which results in developing misconceptions. For example, having mastered computational operations at the level of rote skills, students have difficulty figuring out which of these operations should be applied in solving a given word problem. To overcome such difficulty, they

> look for a key word that reveals which operation to use. For example, "altogether" means add, "take away" means subtract, and "each" means multiply. Students pick an operation on the basis of the key word and apply it slavishly to every number in the problem, whether it makes sense or not. (Bruer, 1993, p. 102)

Thus, empirical learning reflects students' attempts to compensate for the deficiencies of the traditional system of school instruction by "discovering" for themselves the scientific knowledge that they have not been taught at school. These attempts, however, are mostly unsuccessful and lead to students' development of misconceptions rather than scientific concepts. In Vygotsky's terms, empirical learning results in students' development of spontaneous rather than scientific concepts.

What kind of learning would make it possible to overcome all the disadvantages of empirical learning? When answering this question, the neo-Vygotskians proceeded from Vygotsky's (1934/1986) theoretical views of mediation in general and of the acquisition of scientific concepts in particular. In contrast to Piaget's (1970, 1971a) and Dewey's (1902, 1938/1963) constructivist notions (discussed later), Vygotsky held that children should not and cannot be required to rediscover scientific knowledge already discovered by humankind. Indeed, human progress, in general, occurs when every new generation appropriates the essence of knowledge accumulated by previous generations.[3] Why, when dealing with particular students, should we require them to reinvent this knowledge? Therefore, according to Vygotsky, scientific concepts should be presented to school students in the form of precise verbal definitions rather than being "constructed" by

---

[3] As Bruner (1966) noted, "culture...is not discovered; it is passed on or forgotten" (p. 101).

185

students themselves (Vygotsky, 1934/1986, p. 148). Having elaborated this notion of Vygotsky with an emphasis on the importance of mastery by students of procedures that underlie scientific concepts, Russian neo-Vygotskians have developed the *theoretical learning* approach to instruction (Davydov, 1986, 1972/1990; Galperin, 1985; Talyzina, 1975/1981).

Under the theoretical learning approach, students are taught scientific knowledge (that is, subject-domain concepts and procedures) and then master and internalize this knowledge in the course of using it for solving subject-domain problems. What follows is a description of the use of theoretical learning for teaching 6-year-old children to write letters of the Russian alphabet (Pantina, 1957). At first glance, writing letters of an alphabet could hardly be associated with any kind of scientific knowledge, and, traditionally, writing skills are taught through drill and practice. This is why it is especially revealing to show how the theoretical learning approach works for teaching such "nonscientific" knowledge.

Any letter (or, in general, any contour) can be represented by a set of dots, each of which is placed in a position where a change occurs in the direction of the contour. Such a set of dots would represent the essence of the given contour, that is, its model. Pantina's (1957) instructional program was built around teaching students this scientific concept of a contour as well as a general procedure for analyzing any contour and constructing its model. The procedure involved the following steps (Fig. 6.1): (a) analyzing the letter to be copied to determine where the direction of the contour changes, (b) placing dots in those positions where a change occurs in the direction of the contour, and (c) reproducing the same system of dots in another place on the page (i.e., constructing the model of the letter). Then, the students had to connect the marked dots, that is, to write the required letter. Initially, the students were taught to perform all of these steps at the visual-motor level, but as they mastered the procedure, its major parts started

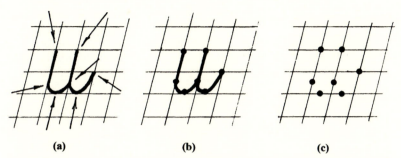

(a)   **(b)**   **(c)**

Figure 6.1. Steps of the theoretical learning procedure for teaching 6-year-old children to write letters of the Russian alphabet (adapted from Pantina, 1957).

to occur at the visual-imagery level. The students visually analyzed the letter to be copied, made a mental image of its model, and copied the letter promptly and surely.

The use of this program has shown that both the course and the outcomes of the students' learning were very different from what can be observed in a "traditional" classroom (Pantina, 1957). The students' learning proceeded quickly and with few errors. The mastered procedure was meaningful and broadly transferable; the students were able to use this procedure for copying any new contour, including letters of the Latin and Arabic alphabets, as well as unfamiliar pictures. Thus, the outcomes of the use of this program match the definition of scientific knowledge, which, as discussed in the previous section, should be the content of learning at school.

Similar outcomes (high level of mastery of acquired scientific knowledge, its broad transfer, and its meaningful use by students) have been shown to be the results of the use of other theoretical learning programs. These programs have been used for more than 40 years to teach students of different ages (from 5-year-old children through college students) a variety of subjects, including elementary mathematics, algebra, geometry, physics, chemistry, biology, language, and history (Aidarova, 1978; Davydov, 1986; Elkonin, 1976; Elkonin & Davydov, 1966; Galperin, 1977, 1985; Galperin & Talyzina, 1957/1961,

1972; Salmina & Sokhina, 1975; Venger, 1986; Zhurova, 1978; and many others).[4] Schmittau, an American researcher, studied Russian elementary school students after they had been taught mathematics for 3 years under the theoretical learning approach. She revealed that they

> evidenced mathematical understanding typically not found among U.S. high school and university students. . . . [She] found it refreshing to observe the degree to which . . . children . . . understood mathematics concepts at their most abstract level and were likewise able to generalize them to new and unfamiliar situations. (Schmittau, 1993, p. 35)

Russian Vygotskians' ideas of the differences between empirical and theoretical learning and of the advantage of theoretical learning have directly influenced the work of several American educational psychologists (Panofsky, John-Steiner, & Blackwell, 1992; Schmittau, 1993, 2003). Moreover, these ideas are very close to the ideas of some of non-Vygotskian-oriented American psychologists who have discussed different types of learning and transfer.

Thus, Bassok and Holyoak (1993) discussed bottom-up and top-down types of transfer. Bottom-up transfer is based on induction from examples: "By integrating information from multiple examples of a category, people can abstract the components shared by the examples. The features that remain relatively constant across examples are likely to be viewed as relevant" (p. 71). The disadvantage of this type of transfer, however, is that it "may lead to erroneous learning [misconceptions] if irrelevant features are constantly present in the examples" (Bassok & Holyoak, 1993, p. 72). In contrast to bottom-up transfer, top-down transfer occurs on the basis of students' knowledge of the

---

[4] For additional descriptions in English of the theoretical learning programs and the outcomes of their use, see Arievitch and Stetsenko, 2000; Haenen, 1996; Karpov, 1995; Kozulin, 1984, 1990, 1998; Schmittau, 2003; Stetsenko and Arievitch, 2002.

"pragmatic relevance," that is, the knowledge of domain rules, laws, and principles, and such knowledge "will foster more flexible transfer to novel but related problems" (Bassok & Holyoak, 1993, p. 72). If such knowledge is missing, "the teacher (or the text) should provide direct instruction focusing the student's attention on the goal-relevant aspects" (Bassok & Holyoak, 1993, p. 73).

Similar views are expressed by some other American scholars. Determan (1993), for example, emphasized the advantage of providing the general rule to the students at the beginning of the instructional cycle as opposed to expecting them to infer this rule from specific examples. Gagné (1966) expressed his position in this regard even more explicitly: "To expect a human being to engage in a trial-and-error procedure in discovering a concept appears to be a matter of asking him to behave like an ape" (p. 143). Referring to the study of Biederman and Shiffrar (1987), Anderson, Reder, and Simon (1995) concluded that "20 minutes of abstract instruction [that is, teaching general rules] brought novices up to the levels of experts who had years of practice" (p. 8). A similar differentiation between a "mere generalization" (that "only correlates observables via actuarial techniques") and a "law of nature" (that "explains its subject matter") is provided in the literature on the philosophy of science (Hanson, 1970, p. 235).

The advantages of the use of theoretical learning, however, are not limited to students' mastery of meaningful and broadly transferable scientific knowledge. An even more important outcome of the systematic use of theoretical learning is that it has been shown to facilitate students' cognitive development. One of the studies aimed at the analysis of the developmental outcomes of theoretical learning was performed with second- and fourth-grade students who attended a "traditional" school and second-grade students from an experimental school in which instruction was built on the theoretical learning approach (Davydov, 1986; Davydov, Pushkin, & Pushkina, 1972). The children were offered a series of problems. In each of the problems, a

Given Disposition   **Requested Disposition**

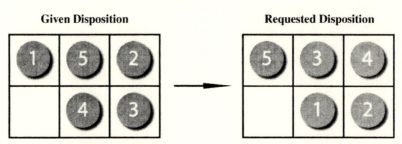

Figure 6.2. Example of the problems offered to students who attended "traditional" and "theoretical learning" schools. Adapted from Davydov et al. (1972).

child had to change the given disposition of five numbered chips on a six-cell grid into the requested disposition, using as few moves as possible (Fig. 6.2). The chips could be moved only horizontally or vertically (not diagonally), one chip at a time, onto the square that was unoccupied at that particular moment. The children were told that each of the problems could be solved with as few as eight moves. What they were not told, however, was that the optimal 8-move solutions of all the problems involved the same sequence of moves (Fig. 6.3).

The study revealed substantial differences between the "theoretical learning" students and the "traditional learning" students (both second- and fourth-graders) not only in their problem-solving success

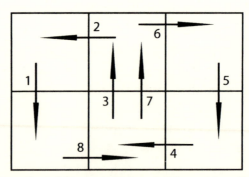

Figure 6.3. The optimal eight-move solution of all the problems that were offered to students who attended "traditional" and "theoretical learning" schools (see Fig. 6.2 for an example of the problems). Adapted from Davydov et al. (1972).

but, more important, in their problem-solving approaches. Seventy-five percent of the "theoretical learning" students immediately realized that the optimal solution of all the problems involved the same sequence of moves (see Fig. 6.3), and they correctly solved all the problems using this general principle. In contrast, only 20% of the second-graders and 30% of the fourth-graders who attended a "traditional" school found this general principle and used it to solve the problems.

This study, as well as some others (Maksimov, 1979; Zak, 1984), has shown that the systematic use of theoretical learning results in the development in children of a general "scientific" approach to problem solving. When encountering a new problem, children who have been taught under the theoretical learning approach try from the very beginning to find a general principle or a "theory," which they then use to solve the problem.[5] This developmental outcome of theoretical learning is anything but surprising. Indeed, the child engaged in theoretical learning

> starts to realize that essential characteristics of objects do not necessarily lie on the surface but should be uncovered. This is an important lesson for understanding scientific truth, where the lack of coincidence between empirical appearance and theoretical essence is the norm, and not an exception. (Kozulin, 1998, pp. 55–56)

Thus, the "theoretical" or "scientific" approach to problem solving, which children involved in theoretical learning are taught to implement when dealing with particular problems, becomes their general cognitive approach to solving any new problem.

Discussing adolescents' formal–logical thought, Inhelder and Piaget (1958) indicated that it involves the ability to operate at the level of theoretical possibilities, to formulate and test hypotheses, or,

---

[5] It is worthy of note that, as a rule, under traditional instruction, even adults demonstrate such an approach only when dealing with problems in their area of expertise (Chi, Feltovich, & Glaser, 1981; Novick, 1988).

in other words, to be engaged in a scientific analysis of data and events. Although it would be an exaggeration to claim that the "theoretical learning" second-graders in the study just discussed demonstrated fully developed formal–logical thought, their general approach to problem solving matched the preceding definition of formal–logical thought fairly well.

Does Guided Discovery Learning Lead to the Acquisition of Scientific Knowledge?

Whereas, as discussed in the previous section, Russian neo-Vygotskians and some American researchers advocate the advantages of theoretical learning, the idea of empirical learning (or discovery learning, as it has been called in American psychological literature) has had strong supporters among American educators and psychologists.

The discovery learning approach was popular among American educators in the 1960s and 1970s (for description and analysis, see Morine & Morine, 1973; Shulman & Keislar, 1966). The outcomes of the implementation of this approach in educational practice, however, turned out to be very consistent with the predictions of Russian Vygotskians described in the previous section: Concepts that students "discovered" were often misconceptions (e.g., Brown & Campione, 1990). Summarizing the findings from the research on discovery learning, Anderson et al. (1995) pointed out that "there is very little positive evidence for discovery learning and it is often inferior" (p. 13). Similarly, Mayer's (2004) analysis led him to write of "the failure of pure discovery as an effective instructional method" (p. 17).

Recently, however, the discovery learning ideas have been reanimated by some influential American and Canadian educational and cognitive psychologists (Brown & Campione, 1990, 1994; Brown, Campione, Reeve, Ferrara, & Palincsar, 1991; Chang-Wells & Wells,

1993; Cobb & McClain, 2002; Cobb, Wood, & Yackel, 1993; Cobb, Yackel, & Wood, 1992; Cognition and Technology Group at Vanderbilt, 1990, 1992, 1994; Scardamalia, Bereiter, & Lamon, 1994; Schoenfeld, 1985, 1992; Wells, 1999, 2002; Wells, Chang, & Maher, 1990). Although not advocating pure discovery learning because of its obvious shortcomings, they, at the same time, criticize didactic teaching as the major method of traditional school instruction. Therefore, they "have argued in favor of a middle ground between didactic teaching and un-trammeled discovery learning, that of 'guided discovery'" (Brown & Campione, 1994, p. 230).

The guided discovery approach is heavily based on construc-tivist ideas of learning influenced by certain works of Dewey (1902, 1938/1963) and Piaget's (1970, 1971a) writings. According to these ideas, scientific knowledge should not be taught to students but rather should be constructed by students themselves in the course of discus-sions, sharing their personal experiences, and carrying out some kind of research activity. A group of students involved in guided discovery is similar to a group of research collaborators solving a scientific prob-lem (Cobb et al., 1992), whereas the role of the teacher is to guide and to orchestrate students' discovery processes (Brown & Campione, 1994).

Thus, in contrast to the position of Vygotskians, the adherents of guided discovery view the mastery of scientific knowledge by students as the outcome of the elaboration and refinement of their spontaneous concepts. Some of them clearly contrast Vygotsky's emphasis on "the importance of formal definitions and of the teacher's explicit explana-tions" with their own emphasis on "inquiry mathematics," which is "interactively constituted in the classroom" (Cobb et al., 1993, p. 100).[6]

---

[6] Often, however, Vygotsky is viewed by American researchers as an advocate of con-structivism (see, for example, Geary, 1995; Windschhitl, 2002). Proceeding from the analysis I have offered, one can see that this view is simply wrong. A partial reason

Does guided discovery learning lead to the acquisition of scientific knowledge? To answer this question, it is necessary to test the validity of the theoretical contentions of the advocates of guided discovery learning and to analyze the learning outcomes of the use of their instructional procedures.

The *theoretical contentions* of the adherents of guided discovery learning are arguable. First, the criticism of traditional school instruction that guided discovery advocates use to substantiate their approach seems to miss the point. They hold that, under the traditional system of school instruction, students do not achieve mastery of scientific knowledge because this knowledge is taught by the teacher rather than being discovered by the students themselves. As argued earlier, the shortcoming of traditional education is not that students are taught scientific knowledge rather than being engaged in discovering this knowledge by themselves. These students, on the contrary, are actively engaged in unsuccessful attempts to discover scientific knowledge because it has not been taught to them. Thus, it is reasonable to expect that implementation of guided discovery learning at school will aggravate rather than overcome this shortcoming of traditional instruction.

Second, guided discovery advocates often draw an analogy between a group of students engaged in guided discovery and a group of scientists solving a scientific problem. This analogy has two weaknesses. First, the process of solving a scientific problem may take years; this is hardly acceptable in the case of school instruction. Second, research scientists possess methods of scientific research and analysis that were taught to them in special university courses or that they have developed during many years of research experience. School students

for this mistaken view is that many proponents of guided discovery learning refer in their writings to some of Vygotsky's concepts, especially to his concept of the zone of proximal development (for two of many examples, see Brown & Campione, 1994; Wells, 1999). As discussed in chapter 1, these references often reflect gross misunderstanding of Vygotsky's ideas.

are unlikely to possess these methods. Actually, as was shown earlier, the principal method of "scientific research" that they use in a situation in which they need to solve a problem in the absence of necessary scientific knowledge relates to considering common salient features of phenomena rather than their essential characteristics – a method that often results in misconceptions.

Third, the process of elaborating and refining spontaneous concepts into scientific concepts under guided discovery learning is inevitably a slow, step-by-step process. Even under the most favorable conditions, this process involves students operating with their original spontaneous concepts (often misconceptions) at the intermediate steps of learning. Probably, this is why many advocates of guided discovery enthusiastically support students' rights to make errors in the course of learning: "As long as you're in my class it is okay to make a mistake" (Cobb et al., 1993, p. 98). Some of them even claim that "we especially want students to recognize that there is no right or wrong side in most decisions" (Heller & Gordon, 1992, p. 10). A theoretical concern that can be raised in this respect is that such a "relaxed" attitude toward scientific knowledge that is conveyed to the students will hardly contribute to their understanding of the value of acquiring such knowledge.

Finally, although students' learning under the discussed approach is supposed to be guided by the teacher, there is still a danger that this learning will result in misconceptions. As Brown and Campione (1994) observed, guided discovery is difficult to orchestrate. The procedures of guided discovery involve many unguided students' activities when, for example, they are working as a research group on a project. As Chang-Wells and Wells (1993) indicated, "a great deal of the learning... takes place as students work together (more or less) collaboratively, without the involvement of the teacher" (p. 84). As was pointed out earlier, unguided learning activity often results in misconceptions. Moreover, some experimental data show that such activity of a group of peers

195

may even result in their rejection of the correct concept in favor of an incorrect concept that one of them has formulated (Tudge, 1992).

Thus, the theoretical assumptions of the guided discovery approach are arguable. Of much more importance to our discussion of this approach, however, is the analysis of the learning outcomes of the use of the guided discovery learning procedures.

The *learning outcomes* of the use of guided discovery learning as presented by its adherents seem to support the benefits of such learning. Their reports indicate that students under this approach acquire and transfer knowledge better, their planning and monitoring abilities improve, their critical thinking and argumentation skills develop, and their learning motivation is higher than under the traditional system of school instruction (Brown & Campione, 1994; Chang-Wells & Wells, 1993; Cobb et al., 1991; Cognition and Technology Group at Vanderbilt, 1994; Schoenfeld, 1992). However, as Anderson et al. (1995) pointed out, the problem with the evaluation by constructivists of the outcomes of their instructional methods "is a failure to specify precisely the competence being tested for and a reliance on subjective judgment instead" (p. 18). A striking example of constructivists' reliance on subjective judgment when assessing learning outcomes of their teaching methods is Ball's (1997) reflection (quoted in Windschhitl, 2002) on the outcomes of a student's learning of elementary math:

> Ball (1997)...describes how one young girl in her elementary mathematics class argued convincingly that 5/5 had to be more than 4/4. The girl presented a persuasive explanation, drawing two circular cookies, dividing them into four and five pieces, and showing that with 5/5 there was enough to pass out a piece to each of five friends, but with 4/4 one friend would not get any cookie. Ball reflected:
>
>> As I listened to Sheena, I knew that next year's teacher might not be charmed by Sheena's way of thinking about this. She might see Sheena as lacking mathematical skills. Was she? Sheena could

complete standard fraction worksheet items correctly, (e.g., shade ¾ of a rectangle) and she got the fraction items right on the end-of-year standardized test. Yet this nonstandard part of Sheena's thinking made me wonder...some aspects of her answer were right. But her nonstandard approach had actually changed the question. And her response to the original question was wrong. What should be the right answer for me here? To this day, that remains uncertain. (Windschhitl, 2002, pp. 149–150)

In my opinion, a prospective "next year's teacher" was absolutely right if he or she was not "charmed" with Sheena's "nonstandard" thinking; her thinking simply demonstrated that she had developed the wrong concept of a fraction. To return, however, to our discussion, it is astonishing to see how some contemporary constructivists are reluctant to admit a failure of their instructional programs even in cases in which such failure is obvious. This attitude is very similar to the attitude of the proponents of discovery learning in the 1960s who supported their ideas "by generalizing wildly from equivocal and even negative findings" (Ausubel, 1968, quoted in Anderson et al., 1995, p. 13).

To be sure, not all the constructivist instructional programs result in such an obvious failure as the one just discussed. What follows is my analysis of learning outcomes of two instructional programs, which are presented by advocates of guided discovery learning as proof of the advantages of this type of learning.

Heller and Gordon (1992), who worked within Brown and Campione's (1994) approach, described a guided discovery lesson aimed at students' mastery of the concept of an animal. A substantial part of the lesson was spent on a rather long discussion, during which the children were exchanging their spontaneous concepts of an animal. Then, one of the children opened a dictionary and read aloud the scientific definition of an animal. The authors claimed that the lesson was a success because of the students' engaging in the discussion, keeping the discussion focused, asking for clarification when needed, and eliciting comments from their classmates. Two points, however, should be emphasized in regard to this example. First, the children took the ready-made scientific concept of an animal from a dictionary rather than discovering this concept by themselves via the elaboration of their spontaneous concepts. Second, there is no indication that the children's learning led to their mastery of the procedural knowledge relevant to the concept of an animal. For the given case, the procedural knowledge should be the method of identifying within the given object those attributes that are necessary and sufficient for associating (or not associating) this object with the concept of an animal.

The second example deals with the outcomes of the use of the Computer Supported Intentional Learning Environments (CSILE) instructional program (Scardamalia et al., 1994; for a description, see also Bruer, 1993, pp. 250–256). Heavily based on the constructivist ideas of guided discovery learning, CSILE also involves a broad use of modern computer technology, including students' exchange of e-mail messages and their collaborative generation of a curriculum-related database. According to Bruer (1993), the major outcome of the CSILE program is that the students' writing improves. Particularly, "when giving handwritten answers to the question 'What have I learned from doing this unit?' the CSILE students write well-constructed essays which contain some mature text conventions, whereas typically elementary students rely on straightforward knowledge telling" (p. 253). Because "better learning and better reasoning... lead to better writing" (Bruer, 1993, p. 251), Bruer interpreted these data as proof of the success of the CSILE program.

To illustrate the benefits of the CSILE program, Bruer (1993) compared paragraphs from two "What I Learned About Primates" essays, one written by a CSILE student and the other by a non-CSILE student. I limit myself to quoting the three first and the three last sentences from each paragraph. The non-CSILE student wrote:

> I know most about gorillas so that's what I'll start with. There are different types of gorillas. For instance, the mountain gorilla has much nicer, shinier fur than the low-land gorilla.... The silverback – the leader has exclusive breeding rights. The baby will sleep in the same night nest with their mother until the mother has another baby which will usually not happen until the first baby is about 4 or 5. A night nest is a big nest made of all kinds of big plants. (Bruer, 1993, p. 254)

The CSILE student wrote:

> There is another primate which I want to talk about. I expressed great interest in learning about this one special gorilla. This gorilla's name is Koko.... I think that Koko is a warm and gentle gorilla who loves animals and people. I also want to say thank-you to Dr. Patterson who has taught Koko everything. I'm glad I did this project because I had fun doing it and I now feel that I know Koko myself. (Bruer, 1993, p. 254)

To support his view on the superiority of the paragraph by the CSILE student, Bruer (1993) points out that "independent judges consistently rate CSILE students' end-of-unit summaries higher than those of non-CSILE students on the quality of knowledge expressed and quality of organization and presentation" (pp. 253–254).

Bruer's evaluation of the quoted paragraphs seems arguable. First, the paragraphs do not make it possible to evaluate the students' procedural knowledge, that is, their ability to solve problems relevant to the discussed topic. Thus, the data presented can be used only for evaluation of their declarative knowledge. Second, even in regard to the quality of the students' declarative knowledge, Bruer's position is disputable. For the last 8 years, I have asked several hundreds of my graduate students (most of them have been highly experienced teachers) to evaluate the paragraphs quoted, and their responses have been consistently very different from Bruer's evaluation. They have indicated that, as opposed to the non-CSILE student's paragraph, the paragraph of the CSILE student was very egocentric, was immature, and did not match the topic of the essay. Whereas the non-CSILE student demonstrated his conceptual knowledge in the field by discussing the essential characteristics of gorillas, the CSILE student expressed her emotions in regard to Koko and presented some facts about this particular gorilla. Some of my graduate students even conjectured that the CSILE student was much younger than the non-CSILE student. Similar evaluations of the paragraphs were given by my colleagues (psychologists, linguists, and educators) at the Graduate School of Education and Psychology of Touro College.

Thus, the examples of the learning outcomes of guided discovery learning discussed, as well as the theoretical concerns expressed earlier in regard to this approach, make it doubtful that guided discovery leads to students' acquisition of scientific knowledge (although such learning may be of some value in other respects on which I am not commenting). Proceeding from the contention of Vygotsky and his Russian followers that the acquisition of scientific knowledge is the major determinant of the development of students' ability to operate at the level of formal–logical thought, it can reasonably be assumed that guided discovery is not advantageous for the development of formal–logical thought in students. Indeed, to the best of my knowledge, there is not any evidence in the works of guided discovery proponents that their programs have ever facilitated the development of students' formal–logical thought. In light of this discussion, the general statement of Anderson et al. (1995) that "constructivism advocates very inefficient learning and assessment procedures" (p. 1) seems well grounded.

As Prawat (1995) indicated, two previous reforms of American education built around constructivist principles had failed. On the basis of the preceding discussion, the guided discovery approach, which can be viewed as a part of the third wave of constructivist educational reform, also does not look promising. These failures can reasonably be attributed to the shortcomings of constructivism as a learning theory.

Why Is Learning at School Children's Leading Activity During the Period of Middle Childhood?

As discussed, children's ability to perform at the level of formal–logical thought is a direct outcome of schooling, but *how well* this ability is developed in students depends on how school instruction is organized. Traditional school instruction often does not lead to students' acquisition of scientific knowledge, which limits the developmental outcomes of such instruction. The constructivist guided discovery approach aggravates rather than overcomes this shortcoming of traditional school instruction. In contrast, the use of the neo-Vygotskian theoretical learning programs both leads to children's acquisition of scientific knowledge and facilitates the development of their formal–logical thought. Thus, the use of theoretical learning has provided strong empirical support to Vygotsky's (1934/1986) contention of the role of properly organized school instruction in the development of formal–logical thought in children.

As discussed in the next chapter, Vygotsky and his Russian followers view the development of formal–logical thought as a major prerequisite for children's transition to the next period of development, that is, the period of adolescence. Proceeding from this view, the neo-Vygotskians have characterized learning at school as the leading activity of children in industrialized societies during the period of middle childhood (Davydov, 1986, 1999; Elkonin, 1971/1972, 1989; Leontiev, 1959/1964; Zaporozhets, 1978/1997). Their analysis, however, is lacking in one important respect. As discussed in the previous chapters, the neo-Vygotskians define a certain activity as *leading* for a given age period because mediation within this activity leads to the development in children of both the new leading motive and new mental processes, which create the basis for children's transition to the next period, to the new leading activity. In regard to learning at school, the neo-Vygotskians have shown its role in the development of formal–logical thought but have never shown its role in the development of the new leading motive in children. To be sure, this omission weakens the neo-Vygotskian contention of learning at school as children's leading activity during the period of middle childhood.

7 The Period of Adolescence: Interactions with Peers as the Leading Activity of Adolescents

Rephrasing the words of Lerner and Villarruel (1996, p. 130), adolescence is a period about which much is known, but little has been explained. There is no shortage of descriptions of specific characteristics of cognition, personality, emotional life, and social behavior of adolescents. Adolescence is associated with the ability to think at the formal–logical level (Inhelder & Piaget, 1955/1958), which leads, in particular, to a qualitatively new level of moral reasoning (Kohlberg, 1981, 1984); with adolescents' search for personal identity (Erikson, 1968); with a the development of new sexual desires and sexual intercourse becoming the major motive of adolescent behavior (Freud, 1920/1965); with a substantially increased role of peer interactions in adolescents' lives (Brown, 1990); and with the period of "storm and stress" characterized by conflicts with parents, mood disruptions, and adolescents' risk behavior (see Arnett, 1999, for an overview). What is missing, however, is a holistic explanation of the reasons for the development of all these neo-formations. Whereas different theories (Erikson, 1968; Freud, 1920/1965; Inhelder & Piaget, 1955/1958) make it possible to explain some of the accomplishments and problems that are typical of the period of adolescence in industrialized societies, none of them

203

gives a holistic explanation of the reasons for all the neo-formations during this period. The neo-Vygotskian approach to the analysis of the period of adolescence is not an exception to this rule. From my point of view, however, this approach attempts to integrate the major points of other approaches to the problem of adolescent development and to suggest a more comprehensive solution to this problem than the alternative approaches.

Vygotsky's Analysis of the Period of Adolescence

The neo-Vygotskian approach to adolescence is an elaboration of Vygotsky's analysis of this period, which is presented in selected chapters of his book *Pedology of the Adolescent* (Vygotsky, 1984/1998, pp. 1–184) written in the beginning of the 1930s. It is remarkable that, in contrast to criticism of Vygotsky by some contemporary Western researchers for viewing children as passive recipients of social influences (see chapter 1 for examples of such criticism), he dedicated a whole chapter in the book to the analysis of adolescent interests (that is, motives) and started this chapter with the following statement:

> The key to the whole problem of the psychological development of the adolescent is the *problem of interests* during [this] age. All human psychological functions at each stage of development function not without a system, not automatically and not accidentally but within a certain system, directed by certain tendencies, trends, and interests established in the personality. . . . These driving forces of our behavior change at each age level, and their evolution is the base for change in behavior itself. (Vygotsky, 1984/1998, p. 3)

Discussing the change of adolescent motives, Vygotsky (1984/1998) found its roots in physiological maturation – especially in sexual maturation: "Sexual maturation means the appearance . . . of new needs and stimulations – this is what lies at the base of the whole change

204

in the system of interests in the adolescent" (Vygotsky, 1984/1998, p. 16). He stressed, however, that "development of interest in the true sense of the word is the content of the social-cultural development of the child to a much greater degree than of his biological formation" (Vygotsky, 1984/1998, p. 11). In the course of sociocultural development, "there is a reconstruction and formation of interests from the top, from the aspect of the maturing personality and the world view of the adolescent" (Vygotsky, 1984/1998, p. 23). Such "a reconstruction and formation of interests from the top" becomes possible, according to Vygotsky, because of adolescents' transition to formal–logical thought. As he noted, "an adolescent appears before us primarily as a thinking being" (Vygotsky, 1984/1998, p. 30).

As a result of adolescents' transition to formal–logical thought, "the whole content of [their] thinking is reformed and reconstructed" (Vygotsky, 1984/1998, p. 42). In particular, "a whole world with its past and future, nature, history, and human life opens before the adolescent" (Vygotsky, 1984/1998, p. 42). Also, formal–logical thought leads to the development of adolescents' ability for self-reflection: reflection on their feelings, abilities, competencies, and their place in the world, the existence of which they have just "discovered." This self-reflection results in the development by adolescents of "self-consciousness" (Vygotsky, 1984/1998, p. 182), that is, their "social-political world view . . . the views on life, people, and society are worked out, and one kind or another of social sympathies and antipathies are formed" (Vygotsky, 1984/1998, p. 45). As one can see, Vygotsky's notion of the development of self-consciousness as the major achievement of adolescence is very similar to Erikson's (1968) notion of identity formation as "a process 'located' *in the core of the individual* and yet also *in the core of his communal culture*" (p. 22).

Thus, Vygotsky (1984/1998) viewed adolescents' transition to the level of formal–logical thought as the main reason for the development of major neo-formations of this period. He emphasized that "development of thinking has a central, key, decisive significance for all the other functions and processes" during the period of adolescence (Vygotsky, 1984/1998, p. 81). This emphasis on the role of formal–logical thinking as instrumental in the development of adolescents is highly consistent with Piaget's ideas (Inhelder & Piaget, 1955/1958). Although the idea of the importance of formal–logical thought for adolescents' development has been supported by much empirical data (which is discussed later), Vygotsky's "cognitivist" approach to the analysis of adolescence is not free of serious shortcomings.

First, Vygotsky failed to explain the development of new motives in adolescents. As discussed, according to Vygotsky (1984/1998), the change of adolescents' motives is the result of a reconstruction of adolescents' sexual needs and desires, which takes place because of their new ability to operate at the level of formal–logical thought. He, however, never explained the mechanism of such a reconstruction. Moreover, this view of Vygotsky on the development of adolescents' motives contradicts some of his theoretical notions, which he expressed earlier in the same book.

In particular, Vygotsky (1984/1998, p. 13) correctly criticized other researchers for not distinguishing well enough between the development of a new motive of thinking processes and the development of thinking processes themselves. In his analysis of adolescence, however, he made the same error when not distinguishing between the development of adolescents' *motive* for self-reflection and the development of their *ability* to engage in self-reflection. Both neo-formations are explained by Vygotsky as direct outcomes of adolescents' transition to formal–logical thought.

Vygotsky (1984/1998) also criticized those authors who "are inclined toward the conclusion that together with the formation of habits, new conditioned reflexes and new mechanisms of behavior, new interests and new driving motives are created" (p. 5). He stressed that, when a new need arises, "the system of . . . thinking operations that must lead to a satisfaction of this need has not been created and formed" (p. 9). Thus, according to Vygotsky's general theoretical position, the *motive* to do something develops earlier than the *ability* to do it. He, however, undermined this theoretical position in his analysis of adolescence. Indeed, because, according to Vygotsky's notion, the development of both the *motive* and the *ability* to engage in self-reflection is the result of adolescents' transition to formal–logical thought, this notion leads to a logical assumption that the motive and the ability for self-reflection develop simultaneously.

The *second shortcoming* of Vygotsky's "cognitivist" approach to the analysis of adolescence is that adolescents' transition to formal–logical thought by itself is not sufficient to explain such an achievement of this period as self-consciousness (or, in Erikson's terms, personal identity). As Vygotsky (1984/1998) himself noted, "self-consciousness is social consciousness transferred within" (p. 182). In other words, "the transfer inward of external social relations between people is the basis for the structure of the personality" (Vygotsky, 1984/1998, p. 170). Thus, adolescents' self-consciousness develops in the course of their active participation in social life. Vygotsky, however, never elaborated this contention. His analysis of the role of society in adolescents' development remained limited to the discussion of how schooling leads to adolescents' transition to formal–logical thought (Vygotsky, 1934/1986).

Thus, Vygotsky (1984/1998) attempted to present a holistic model of adolescent development, which integrated maturational, cognitive, social, and motivational aspects of this development. However, his assumption of the major role of formal–logical thought in transformation of adolescents' sexual needs into their new motives remained unsubstantiated and is highly disputable. Also, Vygotsky's analysis of social factors in adolescents' development was reduced to stressing the role of schooling as leading to the development of adolescents' ability to perform at the formal–logical level.

207

The Neo-Vygotskian Analysis of Adolescence

One of the earliest empirical confirmations of Vygotsky's (1984/1998) idea of the role of cognitive development in the development of adolescent personality was provided by Luria's (1974/1976) classical cross-cultural study, which he performed in the early 1930s in Asian Republics of the former Soviet Union. As discussed in chapter 6, one of the findings of this study was that, in contrast to educated adults, their illiterate neighbors were not able to perform at the level of formal–logical thought. Cognitive abilities, however, were not the only domain that Luria and his team studied; the ability of educated and illiterate adults for self-reflection was studied as well. In the course of an informal discussion, the researcher asked a subject "how he evaluated his own character, in what way he differed from other people, and what positive traits and shortcomings he could discern in himself" (Luria, 1974/1976, p. 146).

As the study demonstrated, the majority of educated subjects described themselves in terms of psychological traits. In contrast, the majority of their illiterate neighbors either did not grasp the question at all or described themselves in terms of external material circumstances and everyday situations. What follows, is a self-evaluation of a barely literate 18-year-old woman:

> After a lengthy conversation about people's characteristics and their individual differences, the following question was asked: *What shortcomings are you aware of in yourself, and what would you like to change about yourself?*
> "Everything's all right with me. I myself don't have any shortcomings, but if others do, I point them out.... As for me, I have only one dress and two robes, and those are all my shortcomings." ...
> *No, that's not what I'm asking you about. Tell me what kind of a person you are now and what you would like to be. Aren't there any differences?*

208

"I would like to be good, but now I'm bad; I have few clothes, so I can't go to other villages like this." . . .
And what does "be good" mean?
"To have more clothes." (Luria, 1974/1976, p. 148)

Thus, the inability of illiterate subjects to engage in formal–logical thought was shown to be associated with their low level of self-reflection.

These data are highly consistent with both Vygotsky's (1984/1998) and the neo-Vygotskians' (Bozhovich, 1968, 1995) views of the importance of formal–logical thought for the development of adolescents' self-consciousness. Bozhovich (1995), for example, argued that the most important contribution of formal–logical thought to the formation of adolescent personality is that it "results in the development of self-reflection – the ability to 'think about thinking,' as well as in [adolescents'] understanding of their own mental processes and all the characteristics of their personality" (p. 234).

In contrast to Vygotsky, however, his Russian followers view the ability for formal–logical thought as a *contributor to*, rather than the *major determinant of*, the development of adolescents' self-consciousness. They strongly disagree with Vygotsky's disregard in his analysis of adolescence of his own ideas of the dominant role of social mediation as the major determinant of development. In their analysis of adolescent development, the neo-Vygotskians have proceeded from Vygotsky's (1984/1998) general theoretical contention that "self-consciousness is social consciousness transferred within" (p. 182; Bozhovich, 1968, 1995; Dubrovina, 1987; Elkonin, 1971/1972, 1989; Elkonin & Dragunova, 1967). Therefore, the major goal of their research and observations has been to study how social mediation determines the development of adolescent personality.

Having analyzed adolescents' values and moral norms, the neo-Vygotskians have found that they reflect values and moral norms of adults in their society (Bozhovich, 1968, 1995; Dubrovina, 1987; Elkonin, 1989; Elkonin & Dragunova, 1967). Although some of these values and moral norms (or, using Vygotsky's words, "social consciousness") may be adopted by adolescents from such sources as books, movies, and so on, the most important sources of social consciousness for adolescents are significant adults. In particular, as Dubrovina's (1987) study has shown, communication with authoritative parents "promotes the acquisition [by adolescents] of adult social experience and knowledge, which substantially influences the development of their self-consciousness" (p. 106).

The transformation of social consciousness into self-consciousness, however, is not the process of a passive adoption by adolescents of social values and norms. The neo-Vygotskians hold that, like other psychological tools, these components of social consciousness can be mastered and internalized only in the course of their application for solving relevant problems (see chapter 2 for the neo-Vygotskian contention of the acquisition of psychological tools). Because social values and norms regulate relationships among members of the society, the mastery and internalization of these components of social consciousness take place in the course of their use by adolescents in the context of interpersonal interactions – especially in the context of interactions with peers (Bozhovich, 1968, 1995; Dubrovina, 1987; Elkonin, 1971/1972, 1989; Elkonin & Dragunova, 1967). Interactions within a peer group require that adolescents meet the group standards for their behavior, which leads to the development of "motives propelling adolescents to do self-reflection and to compare themselves with others" (Bozhovich, 1995, p. 234). Using social norms and values adopted from parents as standards for the behavior of their peers, as well as reflecting on their peers' use of social norms and values as standards for their own behavior, adolescents test, master, and internalize these social norms and values. This leads to the development of adolescents' self-consciousness (or, in Erikson's terms, personal identity). Thus, the neo-Vygotskians view interactions with peers as instrumental in the development of self-consciousness as the major achievement of adolescence, which has led some of them to define these interactions as *the leading activity* of adolescents (Elkonin, 1971/1972, 1989).[1]

The most important experimental findings, which support the neo-Vygotskian analysis of the role of interactions with peers in the development of adolescents' self-reflection were obtained in studies by Gurkina (1950, quoted in Bozhovich, 1968) and Dubrovina (1987). In both studies, 13- to 16-year-old adolescents were asked to do self-evaluations as well as to evaluate their peers. The studies documented that the quality of adolescents' evaluations of their peers were consistently higher than the quality of their self-evaluations. It is worthy of note that the same pattern was found in Luria's (1974/1976) study discussed earlier: Illiterate adults, who did not describe themselves in terms of psychological traits, might use these terms when asked to evaluate their neighbors. These data are highly consistent with the neo-Vygotskian contention that an experience in the use of social norms and values as standards for evaluation of peers creates the zone of proximal development of the mastery of these norms and values and their use as tools for self-reflection (Bozhovich, 1968).

Proceeding from the contention that interactions with peers is adolescents' leading activity, with mastery and internalization of adult norms and values emerging within this activity, the neo-Vygotskians have suggested an explanation of some of the problems that are often associated with this period of life (Elkonin, 1989; Elkonin & Dragunova, 1967). Their observations have shown that, as adolescents master and internalize adult norms and values and start to use them as tools for self-reflection, they come to expect others, not only peers,

---

[1] It is interesting in this respect to draw an analogy between preschoolers' sociodramatic play and adolescents' interactions with peers. Both activities, at first glance, look like the emancipation of children from the world of adults. As a matter of fact, however, they both serve the purpose of children's mastery (of course, at different levels) of adult norms and values.

to treat them in accordance with these norms and values, that is, as grown-ups rather than as children. In particular, adolescents seek more independence from parents in making their everyday-life choices and decisions. If parents do not meet these expectations of adolescents, it may lead to conflicts between them. Thus, parent–adolescent conflicts, rather than being an inevitable outcome of pubertal changes, are the result of parents' inability or unwillingness to modify their relationships with adolescents to meet adolescents' new needs and expectations.

Another problem associated with adolescents' transition to interactions with peers as their new leading activity is that learning at school becomes of secondary importance for them, which often leads to their poor progress in learning (Elkonin, 1989; Elkonin & Dragunova, 1967; Markova, 1975). Therefore, the neo-Vygotskians suggest that, to meet adolescents' new needs, their learning at school should involve more collaborative problem solving. This suggestion, however, has nothing to do with the ideas of guided discovery learning, which were discussed in the previous chapter. The neo-Vygotskians hold that adolescent learning, like any other form of school learning, should be built around the ideas of *theoretical learning*, that is, students should be taught scientific knowledge. Therefore, the purpose of their collaborative problem solving should be mastery and internalization of acquired scientific knowledge rather than discovery of this knowledge. In this way, "the students' desire to engage in interpersonal contact becomes fully realized, but it is employed as a means for achieving the goals of learning" (Kozulin, 1998, p. 57).

In conclusion, in contrast to Vygotsky's "cognitivist" view of adolescence, the neo-Vygotskians stress the role of social mediation as the major determinant of adolescent development. Their studies and observations have made it possible to differentiate between two major agents of social mediation in adolescence: significant adults and peers. Whereas significant adults are the major sources of social consciousness for adolescents, interactions with peers make it possible for adolescents to master and internalize social consciousness, that is, to develop self-consciousness (or personal identity).

There is, however, another important difference in analysis of adolescence between Vygotsky and the neo-Vygotskians: In line with their general disregard of the role of maturation in child development, Russian followers of Vygotsky have abandoned his view of adolescent development as rooted in pubertal changes (Bozhovich, 1968, 1995; Elkonin, 1989; Elkonin & Dragunova, 1967). This position of the neo-Vygotskians has been supported by their empirical findings that there are no direct relationships between pubertal changes and the development of adolescent self-consciousness (Elkonin & Dragunova, 1967) as well as by empirical data of some of Western researchers discussed in the next section. However, the neo-Vygotskians' disregard of the role of pubertal changes in adolescent development creates a theoretical problem for their analysis of this period, which is discussed in the concluding section.

Western Studies of Cognitive and Sociocultural Factors in Adolescent Development

Western studies have provided much empirical support for the neo-Vygotskian analysis of the role of cognitive and sociocultural factors in adolescent development. In this section, I discuss findings in three fields of adolescence research in Western psychology: development of moral reasoning, identity formation, and adolescent "storm and stress."[2]

---

[2] These fields of research represent the major traditions of studying adolescence in Western psychology rather than three independent aspects of adolescent development. Indeed, "if being moral is central to your deepest sense of who you are," morality becomes a natural component of personal identity (Moshman 1999, p. 66). Also, as has already been discussed and is explored in more detail later, adolescents' storm and stress is often an outcome of their stressful search for personal identity.

DEVELOPMENT OF MORAL REASONING

Major empirical data on the role of cognitive factors in the development of adolescent morality have been obtained in studies performed within Kohlberg's (1981, 1984) theory of moral reasoning. As these studies have demonstrated, there is a correspondence between children's stages of cognitive development as defined by Piaget and their levels of moral reasoning in Kohlbergian terms (Walker, 1980, 1986; Walker & Richards, 1979). Before children start to transit to the stage of formal–logical thought, their moral reasoning is, as a rule, "preconventional," that is, it proceeds from self-interest perspectives. For "preconventional" children, "good" behavior is behavior that leads to rewards or serves the person's interests, whereas "bad" behavior is that which results in punishment or does not serve the person's interests. Children's transition to formal–logical thought results in their advancement to the "conventional" level of moral reasoning: It now proceeds from "social conventions," that is, from social expectations, norms, and rules rather than from self-interest perspectives. "Good" behavior is now associated with following social expectations, norms, and rules, whereas "bad" behavior is associated with breaking these expectations, norms, and rules. Further development of formal–logical thought may result in a person's advancement to the "postconventional" level of moral reasoning, that is, to understanding that social rules and laws are not "carved in stone" and that they should be changed by the society (and even broken by an individual) if they come to contradict certain human rights and values.

As discussed in the previous chapter, Vygotsky's (1934/1986) view of schooling as instrumental in the development of formal–logical thought has been confirmed by much empirical data. Proceeding from such data, as well as from the data described earlier of a correspondence between children's ability for formal–logical thought and their levels of moral reasoning, one can assume that schooling is essential for the development of adolescents' moral reasoning.

Indeed, as several studies have demonstrated, there is a significant correlation between educational level and the level of moral reasoning (Colby, Kohlberg, Gibbs, & Lieberman, 1983; Haan, Weiss, & Johnson, 1982; Pratt, Golding, & Hunter, 1983; Rest & Narvaez, 1991). In particular, a follow-up study of high school graduates has shown that those graduates who went to college continued to advance in moral reasoning, whereas those who did not started to reveal a decline in moral reasoning several years after their high school graduation (Rest & Narvaez, 1991). Another empirical finding that is highly consistent with the assumption of the role of schooling in the development of cognitive foundation for moral reasoning was reported by Tietjen and Walker (1985). Their cross-cultural study demonstrated that moral reasoning by ordinary members of a Papua New Guinea society who did not enjoy a high level of schooling most often remained at the "preconventional" level and never reached the "postconventional" level.[3]

Formal–logical thought is not, however, the only factor in the development of moral reasoning. Children's active engagement in the social life of their community also promotes their moral reasoning. It has been shown, in particular, that socially active Israeli kibbutz adolescents demonstrate more advanced levels of moral reasoning than their American and Turkish peers (Snarey, Reimer, & Kohlberg, 1985). The role of active engagement in social life in promoting moral reasoning has also been demonstrated in the cross-cultural study by Tietjen and Walker (1985). In contrast to ordinary members of a Papua New

---

[3] To be sure, these data should not lead to the conclusion that, as a rule, people in preliterate societies are less "moral" than educated people in industrialized societies. Although some studies have revealed a moderate positive relationship between a person's level of moral reasoning and his or her moral behavior (see Blasi, 1980; Harris, Mussen, & Rutherford, 1976), there are other factors that determine whether people will follow moral rules in real-life situations. In particular, "if morality is not important to you, then you are less likely to apply moral reasoning in your daily life and act on the basis of moral judgments" (Moshman, 1999, p. 66).

Guinea society whose typical level of moral reasoning was, as indicated, "preconventional," those people who carried important social responsibilities in this society tended to reason at the "conventional" level.

What aspects of adolescents' social lives are most important for the development of their moral reasoning? The prevailing answer to this question in Western psychology has been that of Piaget (1932/1965), who stressed the role of interactions with peers and disregarded the role of interactions with parents in adolescents' moral development. Indeed, research has demonstrated that the development of adolescents' moral reasoning is promoted by peer discussions on moral issues (Berkowitz & Gibbs, 1983; Walker, Henning, & Krettenauer, 2000). Research has also demonstrated, however, that, contrary to Piaget's theoretical views, the encouragement by parents of moral discussions in the family promotes adolescents' moral reasoning as well (Walker, Henning, & Krettenauer, 2000; Walker & Taylor, 1991).

Especially important for this analysis are the findings that, to be beneficial for the development of adolescents' moral reasoning, their interactions with peers and parents have to be *two different types of interactions* (Walker et al., 2000). In the case of parent–child discussions, parents should provide their child with advanced models of moral reasoning within, using Vygotsky's term, the zone of proximal development of the adolescent's moral reasoning. In contrast, in the case of peer discussions of moral issues, their moral reasoning benefits most by their just sharing information and opinions while reasoning at relatively comparable levels.[4] Another important finding is that "there was a tendency for children to evidence a higher level of moral reasoning in the family session than in the interview" (Walker

---

[4] These findings were obtained with 11- to 15-year-old children. In contrast, 21-year-old college students were shown to benefit the most by participating in moral discussions with peers whose moral reasoning was higher (but not much higher) than their own (Berkowitz & Gibbs, 1983).

& Taylor, 1991, p. 279). As Walker and Taylor (1991) interpreted this finding,

> this is illustrative of Vygotsky's (1978) notion of the "zone of proximal development": the difference between the level of actual development and the level of proximal development. In this case, children's level of actual development was indicated by their independent reasoning about moral dilemmas in the interview, whereas their level of potential development was indicated by their performance in the family session, a somewhat instructional social context where parents were providing support for the child's acquisition of new moral concepts. (p. 279)

In conclusion, the findings discussed here are highly consistent with the neo-Vygotskian assumption that the major role of adults in the development of adolescent personality is to provide adolescents with social consciousness, whereas interactions with peers (at least during precollege years) serve the purpose of mastery and internalization by adolescents of this social consciousness.

IDENTITY FORMATION

Although Erikson's (1968) notion of identity has not been clearly defined, "identity is generally seen as related to the self" (Moshman, 1999, p. 67).[5] "The self," in turn, is described in American literature in terms of "self-concept, self-image, self-esteem, self-worth, self-evaluation, self-perception, self-representations, self-schemas, self-affects, self-efficacy, and self-monitoring, to name but a few" (Harter, 1999, p. 3). As Wylie (1979, 1989) has argued, "the plethora of terminology and contradictory definitions, both conceptual and operational, have rendered much of the literature uninterpretable" (quoted in Harter, 1999, p. 3). There are, however, well-established facts about

---

[5] Erikson (1968) himself wrote that "identity in its vaguest sense suggests, of course, much of what has been called the self by a variety of workers" (p. 208).

the development of the self, one of which is that adolescents' self-descriptions, which reflect the self, are qualitatively different from self-descriptions of younger children (Damon & Hart, 1988; Harter, 1999). In particular, whereas at the beginning of the period of middle childhood children describe themselves in concrete terms with emphasis on specific competencies, young adolescents start to describe themselves in more abstract terms of psychological traits.

What factors are responsible for the development of adolescents' selves, which is reflected in the advanced level of their self-descriptions? Many researchers, especially those working within the Piagetian approach, held that "the self is, first and foremost, a *cognitive construction*" (Harter, 1999, p. 8). From this perspective, adolescents' ability to describe themselves in abstract terms of psychological traits was considered to be a direct outcome of their transition to formal–logical thought. Recent empirical findings, however, have led most Western researchers to conclude that, although adolescents' emerging ability for formal–logical thought is a prerequisite for the development of abstractions about the self, it does not automatically lead to the development of such abstractions (for reviews, see Harter, 1999; Moshman, 1999). As a result, they have rejected purely cognitivist explanations of the development of the self in favor of the notion that "both cognitive and social processes contribute to this proliferation of selves" (Harter, 1999, p. 62).

Discussing social factors in the development of the self, Western researchers differentiate, although not always explicitly, between two kinds of social factors, that is, between adolescents' interactions with parents and peers. Summarizing empirical studies and observations on the role of adolescent–parent interactions in development of the self, Harter (1999) wrote:

> Thus, the personal self develops in the crucible of interpersonal relationships with caregivers. One outcome is that the child adopts

> the opinions that significant others are perceived to hold toward the self, reflected appraisals that will define one's sense of self as a person. Through an *internalization* process, the child comes to own these evaluations as his/her personal judgments about the self.... In addition to the incorporation of the opinions of significant others, children come to internalize the standards and values of those who are important to them, including the values of the larger society. (pp. 12–13)

It has been shown, in particular, that political, religious, moral, and occupational values of adolescents are very similar to those of their parents (Brown, 1990; Steinberg, 1990). According to findings of Damon and Hart (1988), expectations that parents have for their child "almost certainly affect the child's understanding of self. If parents demand academic achievement from a child, that child will evaluate the self, at least at times, in terms of school grades, intelligence, interest in school subjects, and so on" (p. 170).

The data on the major role of adoption and internalization of parents' values and standards in the development of adolescents' selves seem to contradict a popular view of adolescents as rebelling against parental values and standards. Indeed, adolescence is associated with increased frequency of parent–adolescent conflicts (reasons for this situation are discussed in the next section). Analysis of experimental findings and observations of contemporary researchers, however, lead to the following conclusion:

> Even amidst relatively high conflicts, parents and adolescents tend to report that overall their relationships are good, that they share a wide range of core values, and that they retain a considerable amount of mutual affection and attachment. The conflicts tend to be over apparently mundane issues such as personal appearance, dating, curfews, and the like.... Even if they disagree on these issues, they tend to agree on more serious issues such as the value of honesty and the importance of education. (Arnett, 1999, p. 320)

Even if adolescents disagree with parents on more serious issues, "quite often adolescent who rebel against parental values and norms come back in adult years to parental values and imitate the parental ways of life" (Wolman, 1998, p. 57).

The second social factor in the development of adolescents' selves relates to their interactions with peers. As Brown (1990) indicated, for decades, adolescent peer culture was viewed by Western researchers as "a unified, monolithic culture opposed to adult society" (p. 172). Empirical data, however, have demonstrated that this view is simply wrong. Even in choosing their peers, "adolescents typically gravitate toward those who exhibit attitudes and values consistent with those maintained by the parents" (Guerney & Arthur, 1983, quoted in Lerner & Villarruel, 1996, p. 132), and their values and attitudes are more similar to those of their parents than of their friends (Kandel & Lesser, 1972). As many studies have reported, "peers usually *reinforce* rather than contradict parental values" (Brown, 1990, p. 174).[6] Proceeding from these data, as well as from the data on the major role of adoption and internalization of parental values and standards in the development of adolescents' selves, the conclusion that peer interaction "lends support in the search for identity" (Wolman, 1998, p. 78) is anything but surprising.

How do peer interactions contribute to adolescent search for identity? Discussing this question, Western psychologists stress the importance of adolescents' "exploration or reaffirmation of their values and aspirations" (Brown, 1990, p. 180) for their identity formation. Even within interactions with parents, adolescents, rather than passively adopting parental values and norms, tend to explore them by challenging them and expressing their own opinions (Grotevant &

---

[6] Discussing exceptions to this rule, Brown (1990) wrote:

> In cases where peer group norms are in obvious opposition to prevailing adult norms, such as in delinquent gangs, researchers have found that adolescents are not so much being pulled away from adults by the deviant crowd as driven to this crowd by parents' ineffective child-rearing practices. (p. 174)

Cooper, 1998), although, as discussed, they, as a rule, end up with adopting and internalizing these norms and values.[7] Parent–adolescent interactions, however, are "asymmetric," that is, they involve "individuals who differ in knowledge, authority, and/or power," and, therefore, these interactions often do not leave much room for adolescents to express their disagreements or opinions (Moshman, 1999, p. 39). In contrast, "symmetric" peer interactions, in which "one is particularly likely to face challenges to one's perspective, and encounter alternative perspectives" (Moshman, 1999, p. 39), are a natural context to explore and reaffirm parental values, which leads to mastery and internalization of these values by adolescents as their " 'own' . . . personal choices" (Harter, 1999, p. 79).

As one can see, these findings of Western researchers are highly consistent with the neo-Vygotskian analysis of the complimentary roles of adolescents' interactions with adults and peers in the development of their identities: Interactions with parents lead to the adoption of social values and norms by adolescents, whereas interactions with peers are instrumental in adolescents' mastery and internalization of these norms and values. However, the *mechanism* of mastery and internalization of social norms and values within peer interactions is still not clear. As discussed, the neo-Vygotskian studies seemed to document that the quality of adolescents' evaluations of their peers was consistently higher than the quality of their self-evaluations. These data provide strong empirical support for the neo-Vygotskian contention that adolescents' experience in the use of social norms and values as standards

---

[7] Wolman (1998) made an insightful observation:

> The 16-, 17-, 18-, and 19-year-old hippies, punks, or members of any of the other youth cults believed that they, and only they, were in a position to create a new type of culture. Actually, however, in a vast majority of the cases, the attitudes and actions of the "rebels" were a replica of the hedonistic and egotistic philosophies of their parents. (p. 89)

for evaluation of peers creates the zone of proximal development of the mastery of these norms and values and their use as tools for self-reflection. Not all findings of Western researchers, however, are consistent with these neo-Vygotskian data. Having reviewed Western studies aimed at the comparison of how subjects describe themselves and other people, Damon and Hart (1988) found that, whereas some studies "suggest that descriptions of others should more frequently include psychological characteristics" (p. 184), other studies "suggest a tendency for children to think of the self in more psychological terms than when thinking about the other" (p. 185). Damon and Hart (1988) themselves performed a study that revealed "no consistent trend for children to use higher-level reasoning for describing the self, or the friend, or the parent" (p. 187) and led the researchers to the conclusion that self-understanding and other-understanding develop synchronously and "constantly inform one another" (p. viii). To be sure, more empirical studies to address this issue are needed.

ADOLESCENT "STORM AND STRESS"

A popular view of adolescence as the universal and inevitable period of "storm and stress," which is characterized by conflicts with parents, mood disruptions, and adolescent risk behavior, is heavily rooted in nativist explanations of this period suggested by Hall (1904) and Anna Freud (1958, 1968, 1969) (see Arnett, 1999; Petersen, 1988). Empirical data and observations, however, have come to contradict such a nativist view of adolescent storm and stress. First, starting with Mead's (1928/1973) classical observations in Samoa, many cross-cultural observations have demonstrated that adolescents in preindustrial societies do not experience storm and stress at all, or experience it to a substantially lesser degree than their Western peers (for an overview, see Schlegel & Barry, 1991). Second, the nativist explanation of adolescent storm and stress has been challenged by empirical data suggesting very minor, if any, contribution of pubertal changes to adolescent storm and stress. As Larson and Richards (1994) summarized their data, as well as data of other researchers, "contrary to folk wisdom, we found little relationship between pubertal stage and negative emotion or variability in emotion" (p. 86).[8] Similarly, Petersen (1988) concluded her overview with the following statement: "Research linking pubertal change and psychological status has thus found little evidence for pervasive pubertal effects on psychological difficulties" (p. 594). Although Arnett's (1999) view on the discussed issue is less categorical, his review of empirical data has also led to the conclusion that "the hormonal contribution to adolescent mood disruptions appears to be small and tends to exist only in interaction with other factors" (p. 322).

Having rejected nativist explanations of storm and stress, contemporary American researchers have provided alternative explanations of this phenomenon. *The first factor* that they have emphasized as a major contributor to storm and stress is adolescents' newly developed cognitive abilities. The ability to perform at the formal–logical level allows adolescents "to see beneath the surface of situations and envision hidden and more long-lasting threats to their well-being. As a consequence, adolescents are often troubled by nuances and implications of daily life that do not enter the minds of preadolescents" (Larson & Richards, 1994, p. 86). Adolescents' self-reflection often results in their realization of discrepancies between what they would like to be and what they perceive themselves to be, which also contributes to their depressive mood (Harter, 1999). Thus, the ability to do formal–logical thought is partially responsible for adolescent mood disruption.

---

[8] Larson and Richards (1994) indicated, however, that physiological maturation may contribute to storm and stress indirectly by negatively influencing social interactions of adolescents. For example, "both daughters' and fathers' moods during their shared time dropped as a function of puberty.... Discomfort, censored feelings, uneasiness over a daughter's interest in and attractiveness to teenage boys create a barrier of denial and noncommunication" (Larson & Richards, 1994, p. 174).

Because adolescents often become engaged in risk behavior "in an effort to allay inner anxiety, to overcome feelings of inadequacy and inferiority, and to cope with depression" (Wolman, 1998, p. 69), it can be concluded that formal–logical thought is responsible, although partially and indirectly, for adolescent risk behavior as well.

Formal–logical thought also results in adolescents' starting to question parental regulation. Young adolescents "begin to see some of their parents' rules as capricious and arbitrary. They realize that there is no God-given reason why they need to be in by 9 or 10 pm" (Larson & Richards, 1994, p. 140). Adolescents' tendency to question and resist parental regulation often leads to conflicts with parents (for data and analysis, see Arnett, 1999; Larson & Richards, 1994; Petersen, 1988; Wolman, 1998).

The *second major contributor* to storm and stress relates to sociocultural factors. As far back as the 1920s, Mead (1928/1973) attributed, at least partially, the lack of storm and stress among Samoan adolescents to the fact that adolescents in preindustrial societies did not face many conflicting choices and decisions. A similar position is held by contemporary researchers, who suggest that:

> adolescence is more stressful when individuals are confronted by a large number of choices, as they frequently are in Western cultures. In non-Western societies, in which roles are frequently more clearly defined and choices are more limited, the transition to adulthood appears to be much smoother. For example, if the firstborn child is expected to take over the family business and assume care of the aging parents, it is not necessary for him to explore a variety of social roles to find a suitable adult identity. The important decisions have already been made for him. (Gardiner & Kosmitzki, 2002, p. 144)

Because, as discussed, engagement in risk behavior is often a consequence of the adolescent's stressful search for personal identity, a large number of choices imposed on adolescents by modern society can be seen as partially responsible for adolescent risk behavior. Other sociocultural factors that contribute to adolescent mood disruption and risk behavior are poor school performance, troubled peer relationships, family problems, and parents' inability to serve as adequate role models (for analysis and overviews, see Arnett, 1999; Brown, 1990; Larson & Richards, 1994; Wolman, 1998).

As discussed, conflicts with parents typical for this period are partially due to adolescents' newly developed capacity of formal–logical thinking, which results in their starting to question parental regulation. As also mentioned, adolescent–parent conflicts often tend to be over minor issues. Larson and Richards (1994) provided an example of a girl who

> got very upset because her mother woke her up at 1 pm, when she hadn't gotten home from a field trip the night before until 2:30 am. She felt she was old enough to be able to sleep when she wanted. But most mothers do not experience parallel changes in their view of their jurisdiction; therefore large differences can open up between mothers and adolescents regarding who has say over many matters, and conflict increases. (pp. 139–140)

Thus, giving more freedom to adolescents in making their own choices over minor issues could substantially reduce the frequency of their conflicts with parents. Even when dealing with more serious issues, a parent saying, "I'm older than you are and your elder, so do what I say" does not seem to be an effective strategy (Larson & Richards, 1994, p. 140). Rather than that, to both reach an acceptable solution and avoid excessive conflicts with adolescents, parents should reason with them on disputable issues, which is now possible because of their children's new formal–logical abilities (Larson & Richards, 1994). On the basis of the discussion above, it would be reasonable to suggest that conflicts between adolescents and their parents are heavily determined by parent–adolescent styles of interaction, that is, they are

225

anything but inevitable.[9] Indeed, "there are many parents and adolescents between whom there is little conflict" (Arnett, 1999, p. 320).

In conclusion, the rejection of nativist explanations of storm and stress in favor of a sociocognitive explanation of this phenomenon has led American researchers to substantially revise their view of storm and stress as a universal and inevitable characteristic of adolescence. As Arnett (1999) indicated, "storm and stress in adolescence is not something written indelibly into the human life course" (p. 324). Even in industrialized "stressful" societies, "none of the indicators identify a majority of adolescents with difficulties" (Petersen, 1988, p. 592).

Why Are Interactions With Peers the Leading Activity of Adolescents?

As discussed, the neo-Vygotskian analysis of adolescence is highly consistent with recent ideas and findings of Western researchers. Both the neo-Vygoskians and Western researchers view the development of adolescents' self-consciousness, that is, their personal identity, as the major achievement of this period. They also have suggested similar explanations of this achievement, as well as of the problems associated with this period, as outcomes of both adolescents' emerging abilities for formal–logical thought and their social interactions.

Discussing adolescents' social interactions, Western researchers, like the neo-Vygotskians, differentiate between two kinds of interactions: interactions with parents and interactions with peers.

---

[9] An interesting, at least partial, explanation of the popular view of inevitability of stormy parent–adolescent relationships was suggested by Wolman (1998):

> Psychoanalytic studies stress the stormy relationship between adolescents and their parents because these studies are related to what psychoanalysts and other psychotherapists deal with in their clinical practice. In my own psychotherapeutic experience in hospitals and private practice I did not see anyone but rebellious, maladjusted adolescents and their maladjusted parents. Small wonder that psychoanalytic studies report the same experience. (p. 26)

Although not always explicitly, some Western researchers assign different roles to parent–adolescent and peer–adolescent interactions in identity formation. Within interactions with parents, adolescents adopt social norms and values, whereas within interactions with peers they master, explore, and internalize these norms and values as their "'own' ... personal choices" (Harter, 1999, p. 79), which leads to their identity formation. Thus, interactions with peers are viewed as instrumental in identity formation, which makes the neo-Vygotskian characterization of these interactions as adolescents' leading activity highly consistent with the ideas and findings of some Western researchers.

There is, however, a substantial flaw in the neo-Vygotskians' contention of interactions with peers as adolescents' leading activity. The neo-Vygotskians have not answered the question, What motive propels adolescents to become engaged in interactions with peers?

A possible answer to this question can be drawn from Vygotsky's (1984/1998) idea of sexual maturation as lying "at the base of the whole change in the system of interests in the adolescent" (p. 16). Similarly, discussing biological changes associated with children's transition to adolescence, Cole (1992) wrote:

> The most revolutionary of the changes that will occur is the development of the entirely new potential for individuals to engage in biological reproduction (Katchadourian, 1989). These biological changes have profound social implications for the simple reason that reproduction cannot be accomplished by a single human being. As their reproductive organs reach maturity, boys and girls begin to engage in new forms of social behavior because they begin to find the opposite sex attractive. (p. 107)[10]

---

[10] A possible objection to this statement is that, initially, adolescents become involved in interactions with same-sex peers. Studies have demonstrated, however, that a key function of such same-sex peer groups "is to provide a context for the transition to sexual relationships" (Cole & Cole, 2001, p. 626).

Incorporation of these "maturationist" views into the previous analysis of adolescence makes it possible to present this analysis as follows. Sexual motives propel young adolescents to become engaged in interactions with peers. Like any other kind of interpersonal interaction, interactions with peers require that adolescents meet social standards for their behavior. Taking advantage of their new cognitive abilities, adolescents use social norms and values adopted from parents as standards for the behavior of their peers and reflect on their peers' use of social norms and values as standards for their own behavior. As a result, adolescents test, master, and internalize these social norms and values, which leads to their identity formation.

Thus, adoption of the assumption that it is sexual motives that propel adolescents to become engaged in interactions with peers as their new leading activity enriches rather than undermines the previous analysis of adolescent development as determined by only sociocognitive factors. This assumption, however, is not consistent with general disregard by the neo-Vygotskians of the role of maturation in child development, which is discussed in more detail in the concluding chapter.

Conclusion The Neo-Vygotskian Approach to Child Development: Accomplishments and Shortcomings

Russian followers of Vygotsky have elaborated his theoretical ideas into a logical and internally consistent *activity theory* of child development, which integrates cognitive, motivational, and social aspects of child development with an emphasis on the role of children's activity in their development. To highlight the innovative features of the neo-Vygotskian activity theory, it is worthwhile to compare this theory with the theories of child development of Vygotsky and Piaget, even though such a comparison will involve some repetition of already-discussed issues.

In Piaget's (1936/1952) theory, the major determinant of children's cognitive development is their independent activity aimed at the exploration of the external world, which leads to the formation of children's mental procedures (schemas). This explanation of the determinant of child development stresses the role of children as active contributors to their cognitive development but undermines the role of social environment in child development. In contrast to Piaget, Vygotsky (1978, 1981a, 1934/1986) stressed the role of social environment in child development. In his theory, adult mediation (that is, supplying children with new psychological tools and the organization of the process of their acquisition and mastery of these tools) is considered the major determinant of children's development. Vygotsky, however, defined psychological tools as semiotic tools rather than as mental procedures. Also, he was not consistent in his views on the role of children's activity in their development, sometimes describing mediation as the process of assimilation by children of semiotic tools presented to them by adults in the course of interpersonal communication.

Similar to Piaget, the neo-Vygotskians stress the role of children's activity in their development. They, however, have also adopted Vygotsky's idea of mediation as the major determinant of child development (Elkonin, 1971/1972, 1989; Leontiev, 1959/1964, 1975/1978; Zaporozhets, 1978/1997; Zaporozhets & Elkonin, 1964/1971). In neo-Vygotskian activity theory, mediation takes place within specially organized children's activities rather than in the context of child–adult interpersonal communication, and it involves children's mastery of new mental procedures rather than just semiotic tools. This synthesis of the notions of children's activity and mediation in the activity theory of child development is an important innovation of the neo-Vygotskians.

Another strong feature of activity theory is the incorporation of motivational factors into the model of child development. In Piaget's (1936/1952) theory, the role of motives in children's development is, for the most part, disregarded. His basic assumption is that children are born as active explorers of their environment, with their explorations during different age periods driven by curiosity rooted in the inherited need to seek new stimulation. In contrast to Piaget, Vygotsky (1984/1998) did stress the role of formation of new motives in children's development, but he did not explain the mechanism of the formation of new motives.

Viewing children's activity as the context for social mediation, the neo-Vygotskians have paid special attention to the problem of development in children of new motives as prerequisites for children's engagement in new activities (Elkonin, 1971/1972, 1989; Leontiev, 1959/1964, 1975/1978, 1972/1981; Zaporozhets, 1978/1997; Zaporozhets & Elkonin, 1964/1971). The neo-Vygotskians view the development of a new motive in a child as an outcome of adult mediation, which leads to the conversion of the goal of one of the actions within the child's current activity into the child's new motive.

Proceeding from these contentions, the neo-Vygotskians suggested an innovative model of children's stage-by-stage development (Elkonin, 1971/1972, 1989; Leontiev, 1959/1964, 1975/1978; Zaporozhets, 1978/1997; Zaporozhets & Elkonin, 1964/1971). In this model, each period in children's development is characterized by the leading activity, that is, the activity that plays the major role in children's development during the given age period in the given culture. This activity is driven by the children's leading motive, that is, the most important one in the hierarchy of the children's motives in this age period. The children's present mental processes serve this activity, but they are not sufficient for the children's independent performance of this activity. Therefore, this activity is performed as joint child–adult activity, in which adults serve as mediators of this activity. As an outcome of mediation in the context of children's leading activity, the goal of one of the actions within this activity converts into a motive, which becomes the children's new leading motive, propelling them to become engaged in the new activity. Another outcome of mediation is the children's acquisition and mastery of new psychological tools, which results in the development of new mental processes. Not only does the mastery of these mental processes make it possible for the children to perform this activity independently, but these mental processes outgrow the children's current leading activity. These outcomes of mediation in the context of the children's leading activity create the basis for their transition to the new leading activity, which is specific to their next age period.

Thus, the neo-Vygotskian approach can be presented as a creative synthesis and elaboration of the strong points of Vygotsky's and Piaget's theories with a successful avoidance of these theories' shortcomings. The major advantage of this approach is that it has made it possible to explain children's transitions from one period of development to the next, which, as discussed, all the alternative theories of child development fail to do.

To be sure, the sequence of leading activities as described by Russian neo-Vygotskians is not "carved in stone." *First*, as they emphasize, children's leading activities are determined by their social environment (Leontiev, 1959/1964). The leading activities described in this book are those that are specific for children in industrialized societies. In contrast, in preliterate societies, sociodramatic play is not the leading activity during the period of early childhood (Elkonin, 1978), and learning in educational settings is not the leading activity during the period of middle childhood. This does not mean, however, that the development of children in preliterate societies is not determined by mediation in the context of their age- and culturally specific activities. For example, cross-cultural observations presented by Schieffelin and Ochs (1986) document that language acquisition by toddlers in some nonindustrialized societies takes place within activities other than object-centered joint activity with adults, which is defined by the neo-Vygotskians as the leading activity for children of this age group in industrialized societies. However, adults in these nonindustrialized societies also mediate children's language acquisition in the context of their culturally specific activities: "Even before a child's first words, social order organizes the communicative interactions in which infants participate" (Schieffelin & Ochs, 1986, p. 7).

Second, even in industrialized societies, children may not be engaged in a certain activity which, from the point of view of Russian neo-Vygotskians, is leading for the given period of development. It is important, however, that if this is the case, it is associated with serious shortcomings in children's further development. For example, as discussed, serious deficiencies of self-regulation of American elementary school children can be explained as an outcome of their nonengagement in sociodramatic play during the period of early childhood.

Thus, the leading activities described by Russian neo-Vygotskians seem to be the most beneficial for children's development in industrialized societies. It is possible, however, that psychologists and educators may suggest another activity that could be even more beneficial for children's development than, for example, sociodramatic play. If this activity is also shown to "ripen" within the preceding leading activity of children and to result in their transition to the next period of development, it could be suggested that this activity "replace" sociodramatic play as the leading activity during the period of early childhood. Then, the efforts of adults and society in general should be directed to promote and mediate this new type of leading activity rather than promoting and mediating children's sociodramatic play.

As I tried to demonstrate, although some of the neo-Vygotskians' particular notions still remain at the level of theoretical speculation, their analysis of periods in child development has found strong empirical support in the studies of contemporary Western scholars. One of the neo-Vygotskians' general theoretical contentions, however, seems to be hardly acceptable to the majority of Western researchers: As repeatedly indicated in the text, the neo-Vygotskians hold that heredity plays a minimal, if any, role in child development. Special analysis of this neo-Vygotskian contention is provided in the following section.

Does Heredity Determine Development?

The neo-Vygotskian disregard for the role of heredity in children's development is rooted in Vygotsky's contention that both mental processes and the laws of their development are qualitatively different in animals and humans (Vygotsky & Luria, 1930/1993). Animals are born with low mental processes, the development of which is genetically predetermined. In contrast, although human children are also born with low mental processes, their development relates to the formation of higher mental processes, which are determined by social mediation. Vygotsky, therefore, would strongly disagree with those contemporary Western researchers for whom "the mouse has become a valuable resource for modeling the critical processes regulating learning and memory in humans" (Wehner & Balogh, 2003, p. 103).

Despite his emphasis on the qualitative difference between the determinants of animal and human development, however, Vygotsky acknowledged the role of genotype in human development. He argued that:

> The growing of the normal child into civilization usually represents a single merging with processes of his organic maturation. Both planes of development – the natural and the cultural – coincide and merge. Both orders of change mutually penetrate each other and form in essence a single order of social-biological formation of the child's personality. (Vygotsky, 1983/1997, pp. 19–20)

For example, as indicated in chapter 7, Vygotsky (1984/1998) held that the change of adolescents' motives is rooted in their genetically predetermined sexual maturation.

Proceeding from Vygotsky's analysis of human development as a process determined by social mediation, the neo-Vygotskians, at the same time, have taken a more extreme stand than Vygotsky himself in regard to the role of genotype in human development. According to the neo-Vygotskians, genetically predetermined maturation is just a prerequisite for development, which does not determine either general characteristics of, or individual differences in, children's development (Leontiev, 1959/1964; Zaporozhets, 1978/1997; Zaporozhets & Elkonin, 1964/1971).

The disregard by Russian neo-Vygotskians of the contribution of genotype to individual differences in development has been supported, in particular, by their memory studies discussed in chapter 1. For example, as Luria's (1936) study with identical and fraternal twins demonstrated, differences in heredity were indeed responsible for differences in children's lower mental processes, such as visual recognition. However, differences in children's higher mental processes, such as memorization mediated by mnemonics, were shown not to be related to differences in children's heredity. Findings by neuropsychologists and neurobiologists (Greenough & Black, 1992; Luria, 1962; Shore, 1996) that the development of brain structures is strongly influenced by children's activity also seem to be consistent with the neo-Vygotskian disregard of the role of genotype in child development. Indeed, because children's involvement in different activities is the result of social mediation, these findings indicate that maturation itself is partially determined by social mediation.[1]

There are, however, just the opposite findings regarding the role of genotype in children's development. Most of these findings have been collected in studies aimed at the comparison of intellectual

---

[1] To be sure, this statement will evoke objections from contemporary nativists, who hold that a child's, just like an animal's, engagement in a certain activity is predetermined by heredity. Rowe (2003), for example, wrote:

> The beaver drastically modifies its environment, cutting down trees and building dams. Yet this environment-modifying behavior is instinctive. Among people, individual differences in characteristics lead them to seek out and prefer different environments. A child with good chess skills gravitates toward the chess club; one with natural assertiveness and strength toward team sports. (p. 71)

I believe, that I have already brought up sufficient empirical evidence in the text that, without proper mediation, a child will not become engaged either in object-centered activity, or in sociodramatic play, or in any other activity discussed in this book. Also, with reference to Rowe's (2003) example, "one with natural assertiveness and strength" may "gravitate" not only toward team sports, but toward criminal gangs as well (which happened, by the way, with many Russian sportsmen after the collapse of the Soviet Union) depending on moral norms and values mastered as a result of social mediation.

development of genetically related and unrelated individuals with the use of standardized intelligence tests (for overviews, see Loehlin, Willerman, & Horn, 1988; Plomin, DeFries, & Fulker, 1988; Scarr, 1992). Although data obtained in these studies varied, the general tendency was rather consistent: The correlation of IQ test scores of genetically related individuals was much higher than that of genetically unrelated individuals irrespective of whether these individuals had been sharing the same environment. For example, as Scarr's (1992) summary of several studies indicates, the correlation of IQ test scores of identical twins was .86 if they had been reared together and .76 if they had been reared apart, whereas for fraternal twins reared together this correlation was .55, and for adopted children reared together it was .00.

As Plomin (1989) has correctly noted, these data make "it difficult to escape the conclusion that heredity importantly influences individual differences in IQ scores" (p. 106). Another question, however, can be raised in relation to these data: What do intelligence tests actually measure? Twice in the history of psychology, in 1921 and 1986, prominent psychologists were asked to give their views on the nature of intelligence, and their definitions of intelligence turned out to be surprisingly different (Sternberg & Detterman, 1986). Many contemporary proponents of the notion of genetically predetermined intelligence, however, concordantly associate intelligence with an individual's speed of information processing (see Eysenck, 1985; Jensen, 1982, 1998; Luciano et al., 2003; Posthuma, de Geus, & Boomsma, 2003).

The idea that differences in intelligence relate to inherited differences in individuals' speed of information processing is rooted in Galton's (1883) suggestion that reaction time can serve as a measure of intelligence (Eysenck, 1985). This idea was further elaborated in works of Jensen (1982, 1998) and Eysenck (1985) and has received additional empirical support in more recent studies (for overviews, see Luciano et al., 2003; Posthuma et al., 2003). In particular, many studies have reported a significant correlation between an individual's IQ score and such behavioral and electrophysiological measures of speed of information processing as choice reaction time, inspection time, and electroencephalographic characteristics. Individual differences in speed of information processing, in turn, are explained within this theoretical paradigm as an outcome of innate neurophysiological differences among people. Thus, as the proponents of this theoretical paradigm themselves admit, this paradigm is

> in some way "reductionist," and this line of thinking can clearly be extended in an even more analytic fashion to detailed statements about the role of transmitter substances and other biochemical agents.... Such a detailed extension to, say, the relationship between glutathionperoxidase and IQ...is obviously very much in accord with the general philosophy underlying the new paradigm. (Eysenck, 1985, p. 134)

Thus, the proponents of this theoretical paradigm reduce intelligence to speed of information processing as determined by neurophysiological or even biochemical factors, whereas the neo-Vygotskians stress the role of adult mediation in children's mental development. These positions, however, are not mutually exclusive.

In his writings, Haywood (Haywood, 1989; Haywood et al., 1992) suggested a sharp distinction between *intelligence* and *cognition* (these terms are often used interchangeably by other researchers). This distinction is similar to Cattell's (1980) distinction between "fluid" and "crystallized" intelligence (Haywood et al., 1992). In Haywood's terms, intelligence, as measured by intelligence tests, is genetically predetermined, difficult to modify, and relates to individual speed of information processing. In contrast, cognition, the development of which is the focus of Vygotskian and neo-Vygotskian studies, is not genetically predetermined, is highly modifiable, and relates to children's mastery of cognitive and metacognitive tools of learning and problem solving.

Proceeding from this distinction between intelligence and cognition, it is mediation but not innate speed of information processing that determines children's cognitive development. Indeed, irrespective of children's speed of information processing, to develop their memory, an adult has to mediate their mastery of memory aids; to promote their self-regulation, an adult has to mediate their mastery of verbal means of communication; to promote children's reading comprehension, an adult has to mediate their mastery of such strategies as questioning, summarizing, clarifying, and predicting; and to make it possible for children to predict the behavior of different objects in water, an adult has to mediate their mastery of Archimedes' law. What innate speed of information processing does influence is the speed of mastery of new cognitive and metacognitive tools by children, which may result in individual differences in IQ scores. As Jensen (1982) noted,

> *other things being equal* [emphasis mine], individuals with greater speed of information processing acquire more cognitively integrated knowledge and skills per unit of time that they interact with the environment. Seemingly small individual differences in speed of information processing, amounting to only a few milliseconds per bit of information, when multiplied by months or years of interaction with the environment can account in part for the relatively large differences observed between individuals in vocabulary, general information, and the other developed cognitive skills assessed by IQ tests. (p. 99)

It is important to stress, however, that, as Jensen himself indicated, speed of information processing will influence the development of children's cognition "other things being equal." Indeed, for example, as discussed in chapter 6, the use of theoretical learning has been shown to result not only in much better learning outcomes, but also in much faster mastery of scientific knowledge by children than occurs with alternative approaches to instruction. Thus, not only outcomes of children's learning but their speed of learning is crucially determined by adult mediation.

Proceeding from this discussion, the neo-Vygotskians are correct in stressing mediation as the major *determinant* of cognitive development and learning but are wrong in their disregard of heredity as a *factor* that may influence cognitive development and learning. Probably, the same analysis can be applied to noncognitive aspects of child development as well. For example, as discussed in chapter 7, it may be maturation of sexual motives that propels young adolescents to become engaged in interactions with peers; however, it is adolescents' use of social norms and values, adopted from parents, in the course of peer interactions that results in their identity formation. Similarly, it seems indisputable that genetic factors significantly contribute to individual differences in temperament (Ebstein, Benjamin, & Belmaker, 2003), which result in different responsiveness of infants and toddlers to new experiences (Kagan & Snidman, 1991). However, as discussed in chapters 3 and 4, it is parental mediation that determines children's development during these age periods.

Thus, it seems advisable to include maturational factors in the neo-Vygotskian model of child development. This suggestion, however, has nothing to do with the ideas of "adding nature to nurture" and of calculating the proportional contribution of heredity and environment to children's development, to which many contemporary scholars are inclined (see, e.g., Scarr, 1992). Rather, it seems more promising to analyze how maturational factors contribute to children's leading activity in each period of life (for example, how children's temperaments influence their participation in emotional interactions with caregivers during the first year of life, or how children's differences in speed of information processing influence their learning at school). Such an analysis would enrich the neo-Vygotskian model of child development with maturational factors without losing its emphasis on the role of mediation in the context of children's joint activity with adults and peers as the major determinant of their development.

References

Aidarova, L. I. (1978). *Psikhologicheskie problemy obucheniya mladshikh shkol-nikov russkomu yazyku* [Psychological problems of teaching Russian language to elementary-school pupils]. Moscow: Prosveschenie.

Ainsworth, M. D. S. (1992). A consideration of social referencing in the context of attachment theory and research. In S. Feinman (Ed.), *Social referencing and the social construction of reality in infancy* (pp. 349–367). New York: Plenum Press.

Anderson, J. R., Reder, L. M., & Simon, H. A. (1995). *Applications and misapplications of cognitive psychology to mathematics education.* Retrieved June 12, 1996, from http://www.psy.cmu.edu/~mm4b/misapplied.html

Arievitch, I. M., & Stetsenko, A. (2000). The quality of cultural tools and cognitive development: Galperin's perspective and its implications. *Human Development, 43,* 69–92.

Arnett, J. J. (1999). Adolescent storm and stress, reconsidered. *American Psychologist, 54*(5), 317–326.

Baldwin, A. L. (1967). *Theories of child development.* New York: Wiley.

Bassok, M., & Holyoak, K. J. (1993). Pragmatic knowledge and conceptual structure: Determinants of transfer between quantitative domains. In D. K. Detterman & R. J. Sternberg (Eds.), *Transfer on trial: Intelligence, cognition, and instruction* (pp. 68–98). Norwood, NJ: Ablex.

Beizer, L., & Howes, C. (1992). Mothers and toddlers: Partners in early symbolic play: Illustrative study #1. In C. Howes, O. Unger, & C. C. Matheson

(Eds.), *The collaborative construction of pretend: Social pretend play functions* (pp. 25–44). Albany: State University of New York Press.

Belsky, J., & Most, R. K. (1981). From exploration to play: A cross-sectional study of infant free play behavior. *Developmental Psychology, 17,* 630–639.

Bering, J. M., Bjorklund, D. F., & Ragan, P. (2000). Deferred imitation of object-related actions in human-reared juvenile chimpanzees and orangutans. *Developmental Psychobiology, 36,* 218–232.

Berk, L. E., & Landau, S. (1993). Private speech of learning disabled and normally achieving children in classroom academic and laboratory contexts. *Child Development, 64,* 556–571.

Berk, L. E., & Spuhl, S. T. (1995). Maternal interaction, private speech, and task performance in preschool children. *Early Childhood Research Quarterly, 10,* 145–169.

Berk, L. E., & Winsler, A. (1995). *Scaffolding children's learning: Vygotsky and early childhood education.* Washington, DC: NAEYC.

Berkowitz, M. W., & Gibbs, J. C. (1983). Measuring the developmental features of moral discussion. *Merrill-Palmer Quarterly, 29*(4), 399–410.

Biederman, I., & Shiffrar, M. (1987). Sexing day-old chicks: A case study and expert systems analysis of a difficult perceptual learning task. *Journal of Experimental Psychology: Learning, Memory, and Cognition, 13,* 640–645.

Bijou, S. W. (1976). *Child development: The basic stage of early childhood.* Englewood Cliffs, NJ: Prentice Hall.

Bijou, S. W. (1992). Behavior analysis. In R. Vasta (Ed.), *Six theories of child development: Revised formulations and current issues* (pp. 61–83). London: Jessica Kingsley.

Bivens, J. A., & Berk, L. E. (1990). A longitudinal study of the development of elementary school children's private speech. *Merrill-Palmer Quarterly, 36,* 443–463.

Bjorklund, D. F. (1997). In search of a metatheory for cognitive development (or, Piaget is dead and I don't feel so good myself). *Child Development, 68* (1), 144–148.

Blair, C. (2002). School readiness: Integrating cognition and emotion in a neurobiological conceptualization of children's functioning at school entry. *American Psychologist, 57*(2), 111–127.

Blasi, A. (1980). Bringing moral cognition and moral action: A critical review of the literature. *Psychological Bulletin, 88*(1), 1–45.

Bodrova, E., & Leong, D. J. (1996). *Tools of the mind: The Vygotskian approach to early childhood education.* Englewood Cliffs, NJ: Prentice Hall.

Boesch, C., & Tomasello, M. (1998). Chimpanzee and human nature. *Current Anthropology, 39*(5), 591–614.

REFERENCES

Bondioli, A. (2001). The adult as a tutor in fostering children's symbolic play. In A. Göncö & E. Klein (Eds.), *Children in play, story, and school* (pp. 107–131). New York: Guilford Press.

Borkowski, J. G., & Kurtz, B. E. (1987). Metacognition and executive control. In J. G. Borkowski & J. D. Day (Eds.), *Cognition in special children* (pp. 123–152). Norwood, NJ: Ablex.

Bowlby, J. (1951). *Maternal care and mental health*. Geneva: World Health Organization.

Bowlby, J. (1982). *Attachment and loss: Vol. 1. Attachment*. New York: Basic Books. (Original work published 1969)

Boysen, S. T., & Himes, G. T. (1999). Current issues and emerging theories in animal cognition. *Annual Review of Psychology, 50*, 683–705.

Bozhovich, L. I. (1948). Psikhologocheskie voprosy gotovnosti rebenka k shkolnomu obucheniu [Psychological issues of children's readiness for school]. In A. N. Leontiev & A. V. Zaporozhets (Eds.), *Voprosy psikhologii rebenka doshkolnogo vozrasta* (pp. 122–131). Moscow: Izdatelstvo APN RSFSR.

Bozhovich, L. I. (1968). *Lichnost i ee formirovanie v detskom vozraste* [Personality and its development in childhood]. Moscow: Prosveschenie.

Bozhovich, L. I. (1995). *Problemy formirovaniya lichnosti* [Problems of the development of personality]. Moscow-Voronezh: Modek.

Bretherton, I. (1984). Representing the social world in symbolic play: Reality and fantasy. In I. Bretherton (Ed.), *Symbolic play: The development of social understanding* (pp. 3–41). Orlando, FL: Academic Press.

Brown, A. L. (1987). Metacognition, executive control, self-regulation, and other more mysterious mechanisms. In F. E. Weinert & R. H. Kluwe (Eds.), *Metacognition, motivation, and understanding* (pp. 64–116). Hillsdale, NJ: Erlbaum.

Brown, A. L., Bransford, J. D., Ferrara, R. A., & Campione, J. C. (1983). Learning, remembering, and understanding. In J. H. Flavell & E. M. Markman (Eds.), *Handbook of child psychology. Volume III: Cognitive development* (pp. 77–116). New York: Wiley.

Brown, A. L., & Campione, J. C. (1990). Communities of learning and thinking: Or a context by any other name. *Contributions to Human Development, 21*, 108–126.

Brown, A. L., & Campione, J. C. (1994). Guided discovery in a community of learners. In K. McGilly (Ed.), *Classroom lessons: Integrating cognitive theory and classroom practice* (pp. 229–270). Cambridge, MA: MIT Press.

Brown, A. L., Campione, J. C., Reeve, R. A., Ferrara, R. A., & Palincsar, A. S. (1991). Interactive learning and individual understanding: The case of reading and mathematics. In L. T. Landsman (Ed.), *Culture, schooling, and psychological development* (pp. 136–170). Hillsdale, NJ: Erlbaum.

Brown, A. L., & DeLoache, J. S. (1978). Skills, plans, and self-regulation. In R. S. Siegler (Ed.), *Children thinking: What develops* (pp. 3–35). Hillsdale, NJ: Erlbaum.

Brown, B. B (1990). Peer groups and peer cultures. In S. S. Feldman & G. R. Elliott (Eds.), *At the threshold: The developing adolescent* (pp. 171–196). Cambridge, MA: Harvard University Press.

Bruer, J. T. (1993). *Schools for thought: A science of learning in the classroom.* Cambridge, MA: MIT Press.

Bruner, J. S. (1966). Some elements of discovery. In L. S. Shulman & E. R. Keislar (Eds.), *Learning by discovery: A critical appraisal* (pp. 101–113). Chicago: Rand McNally.

Bruner, J. S. (1973). *Beyond the information given: Studies in the psychology of knowing.* New York: Norton.

Bruner, J. S. (1975a). The ontogenesis of speech acts. *Journal of Child Language, 2,* 1–19.

Bruner, J. S. (1975b). From communication to language. *Cognition, 3,* 255–287.

Bruner, J. S. (1985). Vygotsky: A historical and conceptual perspective. In J. V. Wertsch (Ed.), *Culture, communication, and cognition: Vygotskian perspective* (pp. 21–34). Cambridge: Cambridge University Press.

Bruner, J. S. (1995). From joint attention to the meeting of minds: An introduction. In C. Moore & P. Dunham (Eds.), *Joint attention: Its origins and role in development* (pp. 1–14). Hillsdale, NJ: Erlbaum.

Bruner, J. S., & Koslowski, B. (1972). Visually preadapted constituents of manipulatory action. *Perception, 1*(1), 3–14.

Bugrimenko, E., & Smirnova, E. (1994). Paradoxes of children's play in Vygotsky's theory. In G. Cupchick & J. Laszlo (Eds.), *Emerging visions of the aesthetic process* (pp. 286–299). Cambridge: Cambridge University Press.

Bühler, K. (1930). *Ocherk dukhovnogo razvitija rebenka* [Outline of the mental development of the child]. Moscow: GUPI. (Original work published 1918)

Burns, S. M., & Brainerd, C. J. (1979). Effects of constructive and dramatic play on perspective taking in very young children. *Developmental Psychology, 15*(5), 512–521.

Byrne, R. W., & Russon, A. E. (1998). Learning by imitation: A hierarchical approach. *Behavioral and Brain Sciences, 21,* 667–721.

Campos, J., & Stenberg, C. (1981). Perception, appraisal, and emotion: The onset of social referencing. In M. Lamb & L. Sherrod (Eds.), *Infant social cognition: Empirical and theoretical considerations* (pp. 273–314). Hillsdale, NJ: Erlbaum.

Carlton, M. P., & Winsler, A. (1999). School readiness: The need for a paradigm shift. *School Psychology Review, 28*(3), 338–352.

Case, R. (1985). *Intellectual development: A systematic reinterpretation*. New York: Academic Press.

Cattell, R. B. (1980). The heritability of fluid, g-sub(f), and crystallized, g-sub(c), intelligence, estimated by a least squares use of the MAVA method. *British Journal of Educational Psychology, 50,* 253–265.

Chaiklin, S. (2003). The zone of proximal development in Vygotsky's analysis of learning and instruction. In A. Kozulin, B. Gindis, V. S. Ageyev, & S. M. Miller (Eds.), *Vygotsky's educational theory in cultural context* (pp. 39–64). Cambridge: Cambridge University Press.

Chang-Wells, G. L. M., & Wells, G. (1993). Dynamics of discourse: Literacy and the construction of knowledge. In E. A. Forman, N. Minick, & C. A. Stone (Eds.), *Contexts for learning: Sociocultural dynamics in children's development* (pp. 58–90). New York: Oxford University Press.

Cheah, C. S. L., Nelson, L. J., & Rubin, K. H. (2001). Noncosial play as a risk factor in social and emotional development. In A. Göncö & E. Klein (Eds.), *Children in play, story, and school* (pp. 39–71). New York: Guilford Press.

Chi, M. T. H., Feltovich, P. J., & Glaser, R. (1981). Categorization and representation of physics problems by experts and novices. *Cognitive Science, 5,* 121–152.

Clayton, V. P., & Birren, J. E. (1980). The development of wisdom across the life span: A reexamination of an ancient topic. In P. B. Baltes & O. G. Brim, Jr. (Eds.), *Life-span development and behavior* (pp. 103–135). New York: Academic Press.

Cobb, P., & McClain, K. (2002). Supporting students' learning of significant mathematical ideas. In G. Wells & G. Claxton (Eds.), *Learning for life in the 21st century: Sociocultural perspectives on the future of education* (pp. 154–166). Malden, MA: Blackwell.

Cobb, P., Wood, T., & Yackel, E. (1993). Discourse, mathematical thinking, and classroom practice. In E. A. Forman, N. Minick, & C. A. Stone (Eds.), *Contexts for learning: Sociocultural dynamics in children's development* (pp. 91–120). New York: Oxford University Press.

Cobb, P., Wood, T., Yackel, E., Nicholls, J., Wheatley, G., Trigatti, B., & Perlwitz, M. (1991). Assessment of a problem-centered second grade mathematics project. *Journal for Research in Mathematics Education, 22,* 3–29.

REFERENCES

Cobb, P., Yackel, E., & Wood, T. (1992). A constructivist alternative to the representational view of mind in mathematics education. *Journal for Research in Mathematics Education, 23*, 2–33.

Cognition and Technology Group at Vanderbilt. (1990). Anchored instruction and its relationship to situated cognition. *Educational Researcher, 19*(6), 2–10.

Cognition and Technology Group at Vanderbilt. (1992). The Jasper experiment: An exploration of issues in learning and instructional design. *Educational Technology Research and Development, 40*, 65–80.

Cognition and Technology Group at Vanderbilt. (1994). From visual word problems to learning communities: Changing conceptions of cognitive research. In K. McGilly (Ed.), *Classroom lessons: Integrating cognitive theory and classroom practice* (pp. 157–200). Cambridge, MA: MIT Press.

Colby, A., Kohlberg, L., Gibbs, J., & Lieberman, M. (1983). A longitudinal study of moral judgment. *Monographs of the Society for Research in Child Development, Serial No 200, 48* (1–2).

Cole, M. (1976). Foreword. In A. R. Luria, *Cognitive development: Its cultural and social foundations* (pp. xi–xvi). Cambridge, MA: Harvard University Press.

Cole, M. (1990). Cognitive development and formal schooling: The evidence from cross-cultural research. In L. C. Moll (Ed.), *Vygotsky and education: Instructional implications and applications of sociohistorical psychology* (pp. 89–110). Cambridge: Cambridge University Press.

Cole, M. (1991). Preface. In P. Tulviste, *The cultural-historical development of verbal thinking* (pp. IX–X). Commack, NY: Nova Science.

Cole, M. (1992). Culture in development. In M. H. Bornstein & M. E. Lamb (Eds.), *Developmenmtal psychology* (pp. 731–789). Hillsdale, NJ: Erlbaum.

Cole, M. (1996). *Cultural psychology: A once and future discipline.* Cambridge, MA: Belknap Press of Harvard University Press.

Cole, M., & Cole, S. R. (1993). *The development of children* (2nd ed.). New York: Freeman.

Cole, M., & Cole, S. R. (2001). *The development of children* (4th ed.). New York: Worth.

Cole, M., Gay, J., Glick, J. A., & Sharp, D. W. (1971). *The cultural context of learning and thinking: An exploration in experimental anthropology.* New York: Basic Books.

Cole, M., & Scribner, S. (1974). *Culture and thought: A psychological introduction.* New York: Wiley.

Connolly, J. A., & Doyle, A. B. (1984). Relation of social fantasy play to social competence in preschoolers. *Developmental Psychology, 20*(5), 797–806.

REFERENCES

Connolly, K., & Dalgleish, M. (1993). Individual patterns of tool use by infants. In A. F. Kalverboer, B. Hopkins, & R. Geuze (Eds.), *Motor development in early and later childhood: Longitudinal approaches* (pp. 174–204). Cambridge: Cambridge University Press.

Cosmides, L., & Tooby, J. (1987). From evolution to behavior: Evolutionary psychology as the missing link. In J. Dupre (Ed.), *The latest on the best essays on evolution and optimality* (pp. 277–306). Cambridge, MA: MIT Press.

Cosmides, L., & Tooby, J. (1994). Origins of domain-specificity: The evolution of functional organization. In L. A. Hirschfeld & S. A. Gelman (Eds.), *Mapping the mind: Domain specificity in cognition and culture* (pp. 85–116). Cambridge: Cambridge University Press.

Cowles, J. T. (1937). Food-tokens as incentives for learning by chimpanzees. *Comparative Psychology Monographs, 14.*

Damon, W., & Hart, D. (1988). *Self-understanding in childhood and adolescence.* Cambridge: Cambridge University Press.

Davydov, V. V. (1986). *Problemy razvivayuschego obucheniya* [Problems of development-generating learning]. Moscow: Pedagogika.

Davydov, V. V. (1990). *Types of generalization in instruction.* Reston, VA: National Council of Teachers of Mathematics. (Original work published 1972)

Davydov, V. V. (1999). What is real learning activity? In M. Hedegaard & J. Lompscher (Eds.), *Learning activity and development* (pp. 123–138). Aarhus, Denmark: Aarhus University Press.

Davydov, V. V., Pushkin, V. N., & Pushkina, A. G. (1972). Zavisimost razvitiya myshleniya mladshikh shkolnikov ot kharaktera obucheniya [Dependence of the development of elementary-school students' thinking on the type of instruction]. *Voprosy Psikhologii, 6,* 124–132.

Detterman, D. K. (1993). The case for the prosecution: Transfer as an epiphenomenon. In D. K. Detterman & R. J. Sternberg (Eds.), *Transfer on trial: Intelligence, cognition, and instruction* (pp. 1–24). Norwood, NJ: Ablex.

Dewey, J. (1902). *The child and the curriculum.* Chicago: University of Chicago Press.

Dewey, J. (1963). *Experience and education.* New York: Collier Books. (Original work published 1938)

DiSessa, A. A. (1982). Unlearning Aristotelian physics: A study of knowledge-based learning. *Cognitive Science, 6,* 37–75.

Doise, W. (1988). On the social development of the intellect. In K. Richardson & S. Sheldon (Eds.), *Cognitive development to adolescence: A reader* (pp. 199–218). Hillsdale, NJ: Erlbaum.

Donaldson, M. (1978). *Children's minds.* London: Fontana.

247

REFERENCES

Dubrovina, I. V. (1987). *Formirovanie lichnosti v perekhodnyi period ot podrost-covogo k iunoshkeskomu vozrastu* [Development of personality during the transitional period from adolescence to adulthood]. Moscow: Pedagogika.

Dunn, J., & Dale, N. (1984). I a daddy: 2-year-olds' collaboration in joint pretend with sibling and with mother. In I. Bretherton (Ed.), *Symbolic play: The development of social understanding* (pp. 131–158). Orlando, FL: Academic Press.

Dunn, J., & Wooding, C. (1977). Play in the home and its implications for learning. In B. Tizard & D. Harvey (Eds.), *Biology of play* (pp. 45–58). London: Heinemann.

Dush, D. M, Hirt, M. L., & Schroeder, H. E. (1989). Self-statement modification in the treatment of child behavior disorders: A meta-analysis. *Psychological Bulletin, 106*(1), 97–106.

Dyachenko, O. M. (1980). Formirovanie deistvii prostranstvennogo mod-elirovaniya v protsesse oznakomleniya doshkolnikov s detskoi khudozh-estvennoi literaturoi [Formation of the actions of spatial modeling in the course of preschool children's becoming acquainted with children's literature]. In L. A. Venger (Ed.), *Problemy formirovaniya poznavatelnykh spocob-nostei v doshkolnom vozraste* (pp. 47–55). Moscow: Izdatelstvo NIIOP APN SSSR.

Dyachenko, O. M. (1986). Formirovanie sposobnosti k naglyadnomu mod-elirovaniyu pri oznakomlenii s detskoi khudozhestvennoi literaturoi [Formation of graphic modeling in the course of becoming acquainted with children's literature]. In L. A. Venger (Ed.), *Razvitie poznavatelnykh sposob-nostei v protsesse doshkolnogo vospitaniya* (pp. 94–113). Moscow: Pedagogika.

Ebstein, R. P., Benjamin, J., & Belmaker, R. H. (2003). Behavioral genet-ics, genomics, and personality. In R. Plomin, J. C. Defries, I. W. Craig, & P. McGuffin (Eds.), *Behavioral genetics in the postgenomic era* (pp. 365–388). Washington, DC: American Psychological Association.

Elagina, M. G. (1974). Vliyanie potrebnosti practicheskigo sotrudnichestva so vzroslymi na razvitie aktivnoy rechi u detei rannego vozrasta [The in-fluence of the need in practical collaboration with adults on the devel-opment of active speech in children in early age]. In M. I. Lisina (Ed.), *Obschenie i ego vliyanie na razvitie psikhiki doshkolnika* (pp. 114–128). Moscow: Pedagogika.

Elagina, M. G. (1977). Vliyanie nekotorykh osobennostei obscheniya na vozniknovenie aktivnoi rechi v rannem bozraste [The influence of some characteristics of communication on the emergence of active speech in early childhood]. *Voprosy Psikhologii, 2*, 135–142.

REFERENCES

Elias, C. L., & Berk, L. E. (2002). Self-regulation in young children: Is there a role for sociodramatic play? *Early Childhood Research Quarterly, 17*(2), 216–238.

Elkind, D. (1987). *Miseducation: Preschoolers at risk.* New York: Knopf.

Elkind, D. (1990). Too much, too soon. In E. Klugman & S. Smilansky (Eds.), *Children's play and learning: Perspectives and policy implications* (pp. 3–17). New York: Teachers College Press.

Elkonin, D. B. (1948). Psikhologicheskie voprocy doshkolnoy igri [Psychological issues of preschool play]. In A. N. Leontiev & A. V. Zaporozhets (Eds.), *Voprosy psikhologii rebenka doshkolnogo vozrasta* (pp. 16–33). Moscow: Izdatelstvo APN RSFSR.

Elkonin, D. B. (1956). Nekotorye voprosy psikhologii usvoeniya gramoty [Some psychological issues of learning literacy]. *Voprosy Psikhologii, 5,* 28–37.

Elkonin, D. B. (1960). *Detskaya psikhologiya* [Child psychology]. Moscow: Uchpedgiz.

Elkonin, D. B. (1972). Toward the problem of stages in the mental development of the child. *Soviet Psychology, 10,* 225–251. (Original work published 1971)

Elkonin, D. B. (1976). *Kak uchit detei chitat* [How to teach children to read]. Moscow: Znanie.

Elkonin, D. B. (1978). *Psikhologiya igry* [Psychology of play]. Moscow: Pedagogika.

Elkonin, D. B. (1989). *Izbrannye psikhologicheskie trudy* [Selected psychological works]. Moscow: Pedagogika.

Elkonin, D. B., & Davydov, V. V. (Eds.). (1966). *Vozrastnye vozmozhnosti usvoeniya znanii* [Age-dependent potentialities of acquiring knowledge]. Moscow: Prosveschenie.

Elkonin, D. B., & Dragunova, T. V. (Eds.). (1967). *Vozrastnye i individualnye osobennosti mladshikh podrostkov* [Age-dependent and individual characteristics of young adolescents]. Moscow: Prosveschenie.

Elkonin, D. B., & Venger, A. L. (Eds.). (1988). *Osobennosti psikhicheskogo razvitiya detei 6–7-letnego vozrasta* [Characteristics of mental development of six- to seven-year-old children]. Moscow: Pedagogika.

Emde, R. N. (1992). Social referencing research: Uncertainty, self, and the search for meaning. In S. Feinman (Ed.), *Social referencing and the social construction of reality in infancy* (pp. 79–94). New York: Plenum Press.

Erikson, E. H. (1963). *Childhood and society.* New York: Norton.

Erikson, E. H. (1968). *Identity, youth, and crisis.* New York: Norton.

REFERENCES

Ervin, R. A., Bankert, C. L., & DuPaul, G. J. (1996). Treatment of attention-deficit/hyperactivity disorder. In M. A. Reinecke & F. M. Dattilio (Eds.), *Cognitive therapy with children and adolescents: A casebook for clinical practice* (pp. 38–61). New York: Guilford Press.

Eysenck, H. J. (1985). Revolution in the theory and measurement of intelligence. *Psychological Assessment, 1*(1–2), 99–158.

Fantuzzo, J., & McWayne, C. (2002). The relationship between peer-play interactions in the family context and dimensions of school readiness for low-income preschool children. *Journal of Educational Psychology, 94*(1), 79–87.

Fein, G. (1975). A trasformational analysis of pretending. *Developmental Psychology, 1*(3), 291–296.

Fein, G. G. (1981). Pretend play in childhood: An integrative review. *Child Development, 52*, 1095–1118.

Feinman, S., & Lewis, M. (1983). Social referencing at ten months: A second-order effect on infants' responses to strangers. *Child Development, 54*, 878–887.

Feinman, S. (Ed.). (1992). Social referencing and the social construction of reality in infancy. New York: Plenum Press.

Feinman, S., Roberts, D., Hsieh, K. F., Sawyer, D., & Swanson, D. (1992). A critical review of social referencing in infancy. In S. Feinman (Ed.), *Social referencing and the social construction of reality in infancy* (pp. 15–54). New York: Plenum Press.

Feitelson, D. (1977). Cross-cultural studies of representational play. In B. Tizard & D. Harvey (Eds.), *Biology of play* (pp. 6–14). London: Heinemann Medical Books.

Fenson, L. (1984). Developmental trends for action and speech in pretend play. In I. Bretherton (Ed.), *Symbolic play: The development of social understanding* (pp. 249–270). Orlando, FL: Academic Press.

Fiese, B. (1990). Playful relationships: A contextual analysis of mother–toddler interaction and symbolic play. *Child Development, 61*, 1648–1656.

Figurin, N. L., & Denisova, M. P. (1949). *Etapy razvitiya povediniya detei v vozraste ot rozhdeniya do odnogo goda* [The stages of development of children's behavior from birth to one year]. Moscow: Medgiz.

Filippova, E. V. (1976). O psikhologicheskikh mekhanizmakh perekhoda k operatsionalnoi stadii razvitiya intellekta u detei doshkolnogo vozrasta [The psychological mechanism of transition to the operational stage of intellectual development in preschool children]. *Voprosy Psikhologii, 1*, 82–92.

REFERENCES

Fisher, E. P. (1992). The impact of play on development: A meta-analysis. *Play and Culture, 5*(2), 159–181.

Flavell, J. H. (1976). Metacognitive aspects of problem solving. In L. B. Resnick (Ed.), *The nature of intelligence* (pp. 231–235). Hillsdale, NJ: Erlbaum.

Fradkina, F. I. (1946). *Psikhologiya igry v rannem detstve* [Psychology of play in early childhood]. Unpublished doctoral dissertation, Leningrad, Russia.

Fradkina, F. I. (1955). Vozniknovenie rechi u rebenka [The emergence of children's speech]. *Uchenye Zapiski LGPI, 12*, 396–402.

Fraiberg, S. H. (1974). Blind infants and their mothers: An examination of the sign system. In M. Lewis & L. A. Rosenblum (Eds.), *The effect of the infant on its caregiver* (pp. 215–232). New York: John Wiley.

Frankel, K. A., & Bates, J. E. (1990). Mother–toddler problem solving: Antecedents in attachment, home behavior, and temperament. *Child Development, 61*, 810–819.

Frauenglass, M. H., & Diaz, R. M. (1985). Self-regulatory functions of children's private speech: A critical analysis of recent challenges to Vygotsky's theory. *Developmental Psychology, 21*, 357–364.

Freud, A. (1927). *Vvedenie v tekhniku detskogo psikhoanaliza* [Introduction to the technique of child psychoanalysis]. Odessa: Poligraf.

Freud, A. (1958). Adolescence. *Psychoanalytic Study of the Child, 15*, 255–278.

Freud, A. (1968). Adolescence. In A. E. Winder & D. Angus (Eds.), *Adolescene: Contemporary studies* (pp. 13–24). New York: American Book.

Freud, A. (1969). Adolescence as a developmental disturbance. In G. Caplan & S. Lebovici (Eds.), *Adolescence: Psychosocial perspectives* (pp. 5–10). New York: Basic Books.

Freud, S. (1954). *Collected works*. London: Hogarth Press.

Freud, S. (1955). Beyond the pleasure principle. In J. Strachey (Ed.), *The standard edition of the complete psychological works of Sigmund Freud*. London: Hogarth Press. (Original work published 1920)

Freud, S. (1964). An outline of psychoanalysis. In J. Strachey (Ed.), *The standard edition of the complete psychological works of Sigmund Freud*. London: Hogarth Press. (Original work published 1940)

Freud, S. (1965). *A general introduction to psychoanalysis*. New York: Washington Square Press. (Original work published 1920)

Gagné, R. M. (1966). Varieties of learning and the concept of discovery. In L. S. Shulman & E. R. Keislar (Eds.), *Learning by discovery: A critical appraisal* (pp. 135–150). Chicago: Rand McNally.

Galperin, P. Ya. (1937). *Psikhologicheskoe razlichie orudii cheloveca i vspomogatelnykh sredstv u zhivotnykh I ego znachenie* [Psychological difference between

REFERENCES

tools of humans and auxiliary means of animals, and its significance]. Unpublished doctoral dissertation, Kharkov, Russia.

Galperin, P. Ya. (1957). Umstvennoe deistviye kak osnova formirovaniya mysli i obraza [Mental act as the basis for formation of thought and image]. *Voprosy Psikhologii, 6,* 58–69.

Galperin, P. Ya. (1966). K ucheniyu ob interiorizacii [On the concept of internalization]. *Voprosy Psikhologii, 6,* 25–32.

Galperin, P. Ya. (1969). Stages in the development of mental acts. In M. Cole & I. Maltzman (Eds.), *A handbook of contemporary Soviet psychology* (pp. 34–61). New York: Basic Books.

Galperin, P. Ya. (Ed.). (1977). *Upravlyaemoe formirovanie psikhicheskikh protsessov* [Guided formation of the mental processes]. Moscow: Izdatelstvo MGU.

Galperin, P. Ya. (1985). *Metody obucheniya i umstvennoe razvitie rebenka* [Methods of instruction and the child's mental development]. Moscow: Izdatelstvo MGU.

Galperin, P. Ya., & Elkonin, D. B. (1967). Posleslovie: Zh. Piazhe k analizu teorii o razvitii detskogo myshleniya [Afterword: Analysis of Piaget's theory of the development of child's thinking]. In J. Flavell, *Geneticheskaya psikhologiya Zhana Piazhe* (pp. 596–621). Moscow: Prosvecshenie.

Galperin, P. Ya., & Talyzina, N. F. (1961). Formation of elementary geometrical concepts and their dependence on directed participation by the pupils. In N. O'Connor (Ed.), *Recent Soviet psychology* (pp. 247–272). New York: Liveright. (Original work published 1957)

Galperin, P. Ya., & Talyzina, N. F. (Eds.). (1972). *Upravlenie poznavatelnoi deyatelnostyu uchaschikhsya* [Guidance of cognitive activity of students]. Moscow: Izdatelstvo MGU.

Galperin, P. Ya., Zaporozhets, A. V., & Elkonin, D. B. (1963). Problemy formirovaniya znanii i umenii u shkolnikov i novye metody obucheniya v shkole [The problems of formation of knowledge and skills in schoolchildren and the new methods of instruction at school]. *Voprosy Psikhologii, 5,* 61–72.

Galton, F. (1883). Inquires into human faculty and its development. London: Macmillan.

Gardiner, H. W., & Kosmitzki, C. (2002). *Lives across cultures: Cross-cultural human development.* Boston: Allyn & Bacon.

Gauvain, M. (2001). *The social context of cognitive development.* New York: Guilford Press.

REFERENCES

Geary, D. C. (1995). Reflections of evolution and culture in children's cognition: Implications for mathematical development and instruction. *American Psychologist, 50*(1), 24–37.

Gesell, A. (1933). Maturation and the patterning of behavior. In C. Murchison (Ed.), *A handbook of child psychology* (pp. 209–235). Worcester, MA: Clark University Press.

Glaubman, R., Kashi, G., & Koresh, R. (2001). Facilitating the narrative quality of sociodramatic play. In A. Göncö & E. Klein (Eds.), *Children in play, story, and school* (pp. 132–157). New York: Guilford Press.

Göncü, A. (1993). Development of intersubjectivity in the dyadic play of preschoolers. *Early Childhood Research Quarterly, 8,* 99–116.

Goodall, J. (1986). *The chimpanzees of Gombe: Patterns of behavior.* Cambridge, MA: Belknap Press of Harvard University Press.

Greenough, W. T., & Black, J. E. (1992). Induction of brain structure by experience: Substrates for cognitive development. In M. R. Gunnar & C. A. Nelson (Eds.), *Developmental behavioral neuroscience* (pp. 155–200). Hillsdale, NJ: Erlbaum.

Gregor, T. (1977). *Mehinaku: The drama of daily life in a Brazilian Indian village.* Chicago: University of Chicago Press.

Griffing, P. (1980). The relationship between socioeconomic status and sociodaramatic play among black kindergarten children. *Genetic Psychology Monographs, 101*(1), 3–34.

Grotevant, H. D., & Cooper, C. R. (1998). Individuality and connectedness in adolescent development: Review and prospects for research on identity, relationships, and context. In E. E. A. Skoe & A. L. von der Lippe (Eds.), *Personality development in adolescence: A cross national and life span perspective* (pp. 3–37). New York: Routledge.

Guddemi, M., & Jambor, T. (Eds.). (1993). *A right to play.* Little Rock, AR: Southern Early Childhood Association.

Haan, N., Weiss, R., & Johnson, V. (1982). The role of logic in moral reasoning and development. *Developmental Psychology, 18,* 245–256.

Haenen, J. (1996). *Piotr Gal'perin: Psychologist in Vygotsky's footsteps.* Commack, NY: Nova Science.

Haight, W. L., & Miller, P. J. (1993). *Pretending at home: Early development in a sociocultural context.* Albany: State University of New York Press.

Hall, G. S. (1904). *Adolescence.* New York: Appleton-Century-Grofts.

Hanson, N. R. (1970). A picture theory of theory meaning. In R. G. Colodny (Ed.), *The nature and function of scientific theories* (pp. 233–273). Pittsburgh: University of Pittsburgh Press.

REFERENCES

Harlow, H. F. (1959). Love in infant monkeys. *Scientific American, 200*(6), 68–74.

Harlow, H. F. (1961). The development of affectional patterns in infant monkeys. In B. M. Foss (Ed.), *Determinants of infant behavior, Vol. 1* (pp. 75–88). New York: Wiley.

Harlow, H. F., & Harlow, M. K. (1966). Learning to love. *American Scientist, 54,* 244–272.

Harris, P. L., & Kavanaugh, R. D. (1993). *Young children's understanding of pretence. Monograph of the Society for Research in Child Development, 58M, Serial No. 231.*

Harris, S., Mussen, P. H., & Rutherford, E. (1976). Some cognitive, behavioral, and personality correlates of maturity of moral judgment. *Journal of Genetic Psychology, 128,* 123–135.

Harter, S. (1999). *The construction of the self: A developmental perspective.* New York: Guilford Press.

Haywood, H. C. (1989). Multidimensional treatment of mental retardation. *Psychology in Mental Retardation and Developmental Disabilities, 15*(1), 1–10.

Haywood, H. C., & Tzuriel, D. (Eds.). (1992). *Interactive assessment.* New York: Springer-Verlag.

Haywood, H. C., Tzuriel, D., & Vaught, S. (1992). Psychoeducational assessment from a transactional perspective. In H. C. Haywood & D. Tzuriel (Eds.), *Interactive assessment* (pp. 38–63). New York: Springer-Verlag.

Heller, J. I., & Gordon, A. (1992). Lifelong learning. *Educator, 6*(1), 4–19.

Hetherington, E. M., & McIntyre, C. W. (1975). Developmental psychology. *Annual Review of Psychology, 26,* 97–136.

Hiebert, J., & Wearne, D. (1985). A model of students' decimal computation procedures. *Cognition and Instruction, 2,* 175–205.

Homskaya, E. D. (2001). *Alexander Romanovich Luria: A scientific biography.* New York: Kluwer Academic/Plenum.

Huttenlocher, J., & Higgins, E. T. (1978). Issues in the study of symbolic development. In W. A. Collins (Ed.), *Minnesota Symposia on Child Psychology, Vol. 11* (pp. 98–140). Hillsdale, NJ: Erlbaum.

Inhelder, B., & Piaget, J. (1958). *The growth of logical thinking from childhood to adolescence: An essay on the construction of formal operational structures.* New York: Basic Books. (Original work published 1955)

Inoue-Nakamura, N., & Matsuzawa, T. (1997). Development of stone tool use by wild chimpanzees *(Pan troglodytes). Journal of Comparative Psychology, 111*(2), 159–173.

REFERENCES

Istomona, Z. M. (1948). Razvitie proizvolnoi pamayti u detei v doshkolnom vozraste [The development of voluntary memory in preschoolers]. In A. N. Leontiev & A. V. Zaporozhets (Eds.), *Voprosy psikhologii rebenka doshkolnogo vozrasta* (pp. 65–80). Moscow: Izdatelstvo APN RSFSR.

Jamieson, J. R. (1995). Visible thought: Deaf children's use of signed and spoken private speech. *Sign Language Studies, 86,* 63–80.

Jennings, K., Harmon, R., Morgan, G., Gaiter, J., & Yarrow, L. (1979). Exploratory play as an index of mastery motivation: Relationships to persistence, cognitive functioning, and environmental measures. *Developmental Psychology, 15*(4), 386–394.

Jensen, A. R. (1982). Reaction time and psychometric *g*. In H. J. Eysenck (Ed.), *A model for intelligence* (pp. 93–132). New York: Springer-Verlag.

Jensen, A. R. (1998). *The g factor: The science of mental ability.* New York: Praeger.

Johnson, J. E., Christie, J. F., & Yawkey, T. D. (1987). *Play and early childhood development.* Glenview, IL: Scott, Foresman.

Johnston, T. D. (1994). Genes, development, and the "innate" structure of the mind. *Behavioral and Brain Sciences, 17,* 721–722.

Kagan, J., & Snidman, N. (1991). Temperamental factors in human development. *American Psychologist, 46*(8), 856–862.

Kandel, D. B., & Lesser, G. S. (1972). *Youth in two worlds: United States and Denmark.* San Francisco: Jossey-Bass.

Karmiloff-Smith, A. (1993). Self-organization and cognitive change. In M. H. Johnson (Ed.), *Brain development and cognition: A reader* (pp. 592–618). Malden, MA: Blackwell.

Karpov, Y. V. (1995). L. S. Vygotsky as the founder of a new approach to instruction. *School Psychology International, 16,* 131–142.

Karpova, S. N., & Lysyuk, L. G. (1986). *Igra i nravstvennoe razvitie doshkolnikov* [Play and moral development of preschoolers]. Moscow: Izdatelstvo MGU.

Kaverina, E. K. (1950). *O razvitii rechi detei pervykh dvukh let zhizni* [On the development of child's speech in the first two years of life]. Moscow: Medgiz.

Kistyakovskaya, M. U. (1970). *Razvitie dvizheniay u detei pervogo goda zhizni* [The development of motor skills in infants]. Moscow: Pedagogika.

Kluwe, R. H. (1987). Executive decisions and regulation of problem solving behavior. In F. E. Weinert & R. H. Kluwe (Eds.), *Metacognition, motivation, and understanding* (pp. 31–63). Hillsdale, NJ: Erlbaum.

Kohlberg, L. (1981). *The philosophy of moral development.* San Francisco: Harper & Row.

Kohlberg, L. (1984). *The psychology of moral development*. San Francisco: Harper & Row.

Köhler, W. (1930). *Issledovanie intellecta chelovekoobraznykh obezian* [The study of apes' intellegence]. Moscow: Izdatelstvo Kommunisticheskoy Academii.

Kozulin, A. (1984). *Psychology in Utopia: Toward a social history of Soviet psychology*. Cambridge, MA: MIT Press.

Kozulin, A. (1986). The concept of activity in Soviet psychology: Vygotsky, his disciples and critics. *American Psychologist, 41*(3), 264–274.

Kozulin, A. (1990). *Vygotsky's psychology: A biography of ideas*. Cambridge, MA: Harvard University Press.

Kozulin, A. (1998). *Psychological tools: A sociocultrural approach to education*. Cambridge, MA: Harvard University Press.

Kravtsov, G. G., & Kravtsova, E. E. (1987). *Shestiletniy rebenok: Psikhologicheskaya gotovnoct k shkole* [Six-year-old child: Psychological school readiness]. Moscow: Znanie.

Kuczaj, S. A., II, Borys, R. H., & Jones, M. (1989). On the interaction of language and thought: Some thoughts on developmental data. In A. Gellatly, D. Rogers, & J. A. Sloboda (Eds.), *Cognition and the social world* (pp. 168–189). New York: Oxford University Press.

Kuhn, D. (1992). Cognitive development. In M. H. Bornstein & M. E. Lamb (Eds.), *Developmenmtal psychology* (pp. 211–273). Hillsdale, NJ: Erlbaum.

Ladygina-Kohts, N. N. (1935). *Ditya shimpanze I ditya cheloveka* [The child of an ape and the child of a human]. Moscow: Izdatelstvo Muzeya Darvina.

Lancy, D. F. (2002). Cultural constrains on children's play. In J. L. Roopnarine (Ed.), *Conceptual, social-cognitive, and contextual issues in the fields of play* (pp. 53–60). Westport, CT: Ablex.

La Paro, K. M., & Pianta, R. C. (2000). Predicting children's competence in the early school years: A meta-analytic review. *Review of Educational Research, 70*(4), 443–484.

Larson, R., & Richards, M. H. (1994). *Divergent realities: The emotional lives of mothers, fathers, and adolescents*. New York: Basic Books.

Lekhtman-Abramovich, R. Ya., & Fradkina, F. I. (1949). *Etapy razvitiya igry i deistviy s predmetami v rannem vozraste* [Stages of development of play and manipulation of objects in early childhood]. Moscow: Medgiz.

Leonard, L. (1998). *Children with specific language impairment*. Cambridge, MA: MIT Press.

Leontiev, A. N. (1931). *Razvitie pamyati: Eksperimentalnoe issledovanie vysshikh psikhologicheskikh funktsii* [Memory development: Experimental study of higher mental processes]. Moscow: GUPI.

REFERENCES

Leontiev, A. N. (1959). *Problemy razvitiya psikhiki* [Problems of mental development]. Moscow: Izdatelstvo APN RSFSR.

Leontiev, A. N. (1964). *Problems of mental development.* Washington, DC: US Joint Publication Research Service. (Original work published 1959)

Leontiev, A. N. (1978). *Activity, consciousness, and personality.* Englewood Cliffs, NJ: Prentice Hall. (Original work published 1975)

Leontiev, A. N. (1981). The problem of activity in psychology. In J. V. Wertsch (Ed.), *The concept of activity in Soviet psychology* (pp. 37–71). Armonk, NY: Sharpe. (Original work published 1972)

Leontiev, A. N. (1983). Ovladenie uchaschimisya nauchnymi poniatiyami kak problema pedagogicheskoi psikhologii [Mastering scientific concepts by students as a problem of educational psychology]. In A. N. Leontiev, *Izbrannye psikhologicheskie proizvedeniya, Tom 1* (pp. 324–347). Moscow: Pedagogika.

Leontiev, A. N., & Luria, A. R. (1968). The psychological ideas of L. S. Vygotskii. In B. B. Wolman (Ed.), *Historical roots of contemporary psychology* (pp. 338–367). New York: Harper & Row.

Lerner, R. M., & Villarruel, F. A. (1996). Adolescence. In E. DeCorte & F. E. Weinert (Eds.), *International encyclopedia of developmental and instructional psychology* (pp. 130–136). New York: Elsevier Science.

Levin, D. (1998). Play with violence: Understanding and responding effectively. In D. P. Fromberg & D. Bergen (Eds.), *Play from birth to twelve and beyond: Contexts, perspectives, and meanings* (348–356). New York: Garland.

Lidz, C., & Elliott, J. G. (Eds.). (2000). *Dynamic assessment: Prevailing models and applications.* New York: Elsevier Science.

Lisina, M. I. (1974). Vliyanie obscheniya so vzroslym na razvitie rebenka pervogo polugodiya zhizni [The influence of communication with adults on the development of children during the first six months of life]. In A. V. Zaporozhets & M. I. Lisina (Eds.), *Razvitie obscheniya u doshkolnikov* (pp. 65–112). Moscow: Pedagogika.

Lisina, M. I. (Ed.). (1985). *Obschenie i rech: Razvitie rechi u detei v obschenii so vzroslymi* [Communication and speech: The development of children's speech in the course of communication with adults]. Moscow: Pedagogika.

Lisina, M. I. (1986). *Problemy ontogeneza obscheniya* [Problems of the ontogenesis of communication]. Moscow: Pedagogika.

Loehlin, J. C., Willerman, L., & Horn, J. M. (1988). Human behavior genetics. *Annual Review of Psychology, 39,* 101–133.

Luciano, M., Wright, M. J., Smith, G. A., Geffen, G. M., Geffen, L. B., & Martin, N. G. (2003). Genetic covariance between processing speed and

IQ. In R. Plomin, J. C. Defries, I. W. Craig, & P. McGuffin (Eds.), *Behavioral genetics in the postgenomic era* (pp. 163–181). Washington, DC: American Psychological Association.

Lukov, G. D. (1937). *Ob osoznanii rebenkom rechi v protsese igry* [To child's realization of language in the course of play]. Unpublished doctoral dissertation, Leningrad, Russia.

Luria, A. R. (1936). The development of mental functions in twins. *Character and Personality, 5,* 35–47.

Luria, A. R. (1961). *The role of speech in the regulation of normal and abnormal behavior.* Oxford, England: Pergamon Press.

Luria, A. R. (1962). *Vysshie korkovye funktsii cheloveka i ikh narusheniya pri lokalnykh porazheniyakh mozga* [Higher cortical functions in man and their disorganization under local damages of the brain]. Moscow: Izdatelstvo MGU.

Luria, A. R. (1976). *Cognitive development: Its cultural and social foundations.* Cambridge, MA: Harvard University Press. (Original work published 1974)

Luria, A. R. (1979). *The making of mind: A personal account of Soviet psychology.* Cambridge, MA: Harvard University Press.

Luria, A. R., & Yudovich, F. Ya. (1956). *Rech i razvitie psikhicheskikh protsessov u rebenka* [Speech and the development of child's mental processes]. Moscow: Izdatelstvo APN RSFSR.

Lyamina, G. M. (1960). Razvitie ponimamiya rechi u detei vtorogo goda zhizni [The development of understanding of speech by 2-year-old children]. *Voprosy Psikhologii, 3,* 106–121.

Main, M. (1983). Exploration, play, and cognitive functioning related to infant-mother attachment. *Infant Behavior and Development, 6,* 167–174.

Maksimov, L. K. (1979). Zavisimost razvitiya matematicheskogo myshleniya shkolnikov ot kharaktera obucheniya [Dependence of the development of students' mathematical reasoning on the instructional methods]. *Voprosy Psikhologii, 2,* 57–65.

Manuilenko, Z. V. (1948). Razvitie proizvolnogo povedeniya u detei goshkolnogo vozrasta [The development of voluntary behavior in preschoolers]. *Izvestiya APN RSFSR, 14,* 43–51.

Markova, A. K. (1975). *Psikhologiya obucheniya podrostka* [Psychology of adolescent learning]. Moscow: Znanie.

Marshall, H. R. (1961). Relations between home experiences and children's use of language in play interactions with peers. *Psychological Monographs, 75*(5), no. 509.

REFERENCES

Matas, L., Arend, R., & Sroufe, L. A. (1978). Continuity of adaptation in the second year: The relationship between quality of attachment and later competence. *Child Development, 49,* 547–556.

Matsuzawa, T., Biro, D., Humle, T., Inoue-Nakamura, N., Tonooka, R., & Yamakoshi, G. (2001). Emergence of culture in wild chimpanzees: Education by master-apprenticeship. In T. Matsuzawa (Ed.), *Primate origins of human cognition and behavior* (pp. 557–574). New York: Springer-Verlag.

Mayer, R. E. (2004). Should there be a three-strikes rule against pure discovery learning? *American Psychologist, 59*(1), 14–19.

McCune-Nicolich, L. (1977). Beyond sensorimotor intelligence: Assessment of symbolic maturity through analysis of pretend play. *Merrill-Palmer Quarterly, 33*(2), 89–99.

McGrew, W. C. (1992). *Chimpanzee material culture: Implications for human evolution.* Cambridge: Cambridge University Press.

Mead, M. (1930). *Growing up in New Guinea.* Oxford, England: Morrow.

Mead, M. (1973). *Coming of age in Samoa: A psychological study of primitive youth.* New York: American Museum of Natural History. (Original work published 1928)

Meichenbaum, D. H., & Goodman, J. (1971). Training impulsive children to talk to themselves: A means of developing self-control. *Journal of Abnormal Psychology, 77*(2), 115–126.

Meins, E. (1997). *Security of attachment and the social development of cognition.* East Sussex: Psychology Press.

Mikhailenko, N. Ya. (1975). *Formirovanie syuzhetno-rolevoi igry v rannem vozraste* [The development of role play during the second and third years of life]. Unpublished doctoral dissertation, Leningrad, Russia.

Miller, P., & Garvey, C. (1984). Mother–baby role play: Its origins in social support. In I. Bretherton (Ed.), *Symbolic play: The development of social understanding* (pp. 101–130). Orlando, FL: Academic Press.

Morine, H., & Morine, G. (1973). *Discovery: A challenge to teachers.* Englewood Cliffs, NJ: Prentice Hall.

Moshman, D. (1999). *Adolescent psychological development: Rationality, morality, and identity.* Mahwah, NJ: Erlbaum.

Moss, E. (1992). The socioaffective context of joint cognitive activity. In L. T. Winegar & J. Valsiner (Eds.), *Children's development within social context: Vol. 2, Research and Methodology* (pp. 117–154). Hillsdale, NJ: Erlbaum.

Muir, D., & Field, J. (1979). Newborn infants orient to sounds. *Child Development, 50,* 431–436.

Nagell, K., Olguin, K., & Tomasello, M. (1993). Process of social learning in tool use of chimpanzees (*Pan troglodytes*) and human children (*Homo sapiens*), *Journal of Comparative Psychology, 107*, 174–186.

Nedospasova, V. A. (1972). *Psikhologicheskii mekhanizm preodoleniya "tcentratcii" v mishlenii detei doshkolnogo vozrasta* [The psychological mechanism for overcoming "centration" in preschoolers' thinking]. Unpublished doctoral dissertation, Moscow, Russia.

Newson, J. (1979). The growth of shared understanding between infant and caregiver. In M. Bullowa (Ed.), *Before speech: The beginning of interpersonal communication* (pp. 207–222). Cambridge: Cambridge University Press.

Ninio, A., & Bruner, J. S. (1978). The achievements and antecedents of labelling. *Journal of Child Language, 5*, 1–15.

Normandeau, S., & Guay, F. (1998). Preschool behavior and first-grade school achievement: The mediational role of cognitive self-control. *Journal of Educational Psychology, 90*, 111–121.

Novick, L. R. (1988). Analogical transfer, problem similarity, and expertise. *Journal of Experimental Psychology: Learning, Memory, and Cognition, 14*, 510–520.

O'Connell, B., & Bretherton, I. (1984). Toddler's play, alone and with mother: The role of maternal guidance. In I. Bretherton (Ed.), *Symbolic play: The development of social understanding* (pp. 337–368). Orlando, FL: Academic Press.

O'Reilly, A. W., & Bornstein, M. N. (1993). Caregiver-child interaction in play. In M. N. Bornstein & A. Watson O'Reilly (Eds.), *The role of play in the development of thought* (pp. 55–66). San Francisco: Jossey-Bass.

Olson, S. L., Bayles, K., & Bates, J. E. (1986). Mother–child interaction and children's speech progress: A longitudinal study of the first two years. *Merrill-Palmer Quarterly, 32*, 1–20.

Ormrod, J. E. (1995). *Human learning*. Englewood Cliffs, NJ: Prentice Hall.

Palincsar, A. S., & Brown, A. L. (1984). Reciprocal teaching of comprehension-fostering and comprehension-monitoring activities. *Cognition and Instruction, 1*, 117–175.

Palincsar, A. S., Brown, A. L., & Campione, J. C. (1993). First-grade dialogues for knowledge acquisition and use. In E. A. Forman, N. Minick, & C. A. Stone (Eds.), *Contexts for learning: Sociocultural dynamics in children's development* (pp. 43–57). New York: Oxford University Press.

Palkes, H., Stewart, M., & Kahana, B. (1968). Porteus maze performance of hyperactive boys after training in self-directed verbal commands. *Child Development, 39*(3), 817–826.

REFERENCES

Panofsky, C. P., John-Steiner, V., & Blackwell, P. J. (1992). The development of scientific concepts and discourse. In L. C. Moll (Ed.), *Vygotsky and education: Instructional implications of sociohistorical psychology* (pp. 251–270). Cambridge: Cambridge University Press.

Pantina, N. S. (1957). Formirovanie dvigatelnogo navyka pisma v zavisimosti ot tipa orientirovki v zadanii [Formation of writing skills depending on the type of task orientation]. *Voprosy Psikhologii, 4*, 117–132.

Parritz, R. H., Mangelsdorf, S., & Gunnar, M. R. (1992). Control, social referencing, and the infant's appraisal of threat. In S. Feinman (Ed.), *Social referencing and the social construction of reality in infancy* (pp. 209–228). New York: Plenum Press.

Pascual-Leone, J. (1970). A mathematical model for transition in Piaget's developmental stages. *Acta Psycholologica, 32*, 301–345.

Petersen, A. C. (1988). Adolescent development. *Annual Review of Psychology, 39*, 583–607.

Piaget, J. (1952). *The origins of intelligence in children*. New York: International University Press. (Original work published 1936)

Piaget, J. (1955). *The child's construction of reality*. London: Routledge and Kegan Paul.

Piaget, J. (1959). *The language and thought of the child*. London: Routledge and Kegan Paul. (Original work published 1923)

Piaget, J. (1962). *Play, dreams, and imitation in childhood*. New York: Norton. (Original work published 1945)

Piaget, J. (1965). *The moral judgment of the child*. New York: Free Press. (Original work published 1932)

Piaget, J. (1970). *Science of education and psychology of the child*. New York: Oxford University Press.

Piaget, J. (1971a). *Biology and knowledge*. Edinburgh, Scotland: Edinburgh Press.

Piaget, J. (1971b). The theory of stages in cognitive development. In D. R. Green, M. P. Ford, & G. B. Flamer (Eds.), *Measurement and Piaget* (pp. 1–11). New York: McGraw-Hill.

Piaget, J., Gellerier, G., & Langer, J. (1988). Extracts from Piaget's theory. In K. Richardson & S. Sheldon (Eds.), *Cognitive development to adolescence: A reader* (pp. 3–18). Hillsdale, NJ: Erlbaum. (Original work published 1970)

Plomin, R. (1989). Environment and genes: Determinants of behavior. *American Psychologist, 44*(2), 105–111.

Plomin, R., DeFries, J. C., & Fulker, D. W. (1988). *Nature and nurture during infancy and early childhood*. Cambridge: Cambridge University Press.

Popova, M. I. (1968). Osobennosti rechevykh proayavlenini detei pervogo polugodiya vtorogo goda zhizni [Characteristics of children's speech during the first half of the second year of life]. *Voprosy Psikhologii, 4,* 116–122.

Posthuma, D., de Geus, E. J. C., & Boomsma, D. I. (2003). Genetic contributions to anatomical, behavioral, and neurophysiological indices of cognition. In R. Plomin, J. C. Defries, I. W. Craig, & P. McGuffin (Eds.), *Behavioral genetics in the postgenomic era* (pp. 141–161). Washington, DC: American Psychological Association.

Pratt, M. W., Golding, G., & Hunter, W. J. (1983). Aging as ripening: Character and consistency of moral judgment in young, mature, and older adults. *Human Development, 26,* 277–288.

Prawat, R. S. (1995). Misreading Dewey: Reform, projects, and the language game. *Educational Researcher, 24* (7), 13–22.

Provenzo, E. F., Jr. (1998). Electronically mediated playscapes. In D. P. Fromberg & D. Bergen (Eds.), *Play from birth to twelve and beyond: Contexts, perspectives, and meanings* (513–518). New York: Garland.

Pyle, R. P. (2002). Best practices in assessing kindergarten readiness. *California School Psychologist, 7,* 63–73.

Rest, J. R., & Narvaez, D. (1991). The college experience and moral development. In W. M. Kurtines & J. L. Gewitz (Eds.), *Handbook of moral behavior and development* (Vol. 2, pp. 229–245). Hillsdale, NJ: Erlbaum.

Richardson, K. (1998). *Models of cognitive development.* East Sussex: Psychology Press.

Rogoff, B., Malkin, C., & Gilbride, K. (1984). Interaction with babies as guidance in development. In B. Rogoff & J. V. Wertsch (Eds.), *Children's learning in the "zone of proximal development"* (pp. 31–44). San Francisco: Jossey-Bass.

Rogoff, B., Mistry, J., Radziszewska, B., & Germond, J. (1992). Infants' instrumental social interaction with adults. In S. Feinman (Ed.), *Social referencing and the social construction of reality in infancy* (pp. 327–348). New York: Plenum Press.

Rosen, C. E. (1974). The effects of sociodramatic play on problem-solving behavior among culturally disadvantaged preschool children. *Child Development, 45,* 920–927.

Rowe, D. C. (2003). Assessing genotype-environment interactions and correlations in the postgenomic era. In R. Plomin, J. C. Defries, I. W. Craig, & P. McGuffin (Eds.), *Behavioral genetics in the postgenomic era* (pp. 71–86). Washington, DC: American Psychological Association.

Rozengard-Pupko, G. L. (1948). *Rech i razvitie vospriyatiya v rannem vozraste* [Language and the development of perception in early age]. Moscow: Izdatelstvo AMN SSSR.

Rozengard-Pupko, G. L. (1963). *Formirovanie rechi u detei rannego vozrasta* [The development of speech in young children]. Moscow: Izdatelstvo APN RSFSR.

Rubin, K. H., Fein, G. G., & Vandenberg, B. (1983). Play. In E. M. Hetherington (Ed.), *Handbook of child psychology, Vol. 4: Socialization, personality, and social development* (pp. 693–774). New York: Wiley.

Russon, A. E. (1999). Orangutans' imitation of tool use: A cognitive interpretation. In S. T. Parker, R. W. Mitchell, & H. L. Miles (Eds.), *The mentalities of gorillas and orangutans* (pp. 117–146). Cambridge: Cambridge University Press.

Salmina, N. G., & Sokhina, V. P. (1975). *Obuchenie matematike v nachalnoi shkole* [Teaching mathematics in elementary school]. Moscow: Pedagogika.

Saltz, E., Dixon, D., & Johnson, J. (1977). Training disadvantaged preschoolers on various fantasy activities: Effects on cognitive functioning and impulse control. *Child Development, 48*(2), 367–380.

Scardamalia, M., Bereiter, C., & Lamon, M. (1994). The CSILE project: Trying to bring the classroom into World 3. In K. McGilly (Ed.), *Classroom lessons: Integrating cognitive theory and classroom practice* (pp. 202–228). Cambridge, MA: MIT Press.

Scarr, S. (1992). Developmental theories for the 1990s: Development and individual differences. *Child Development, 63*, 1–19.

Schaffer, H. R., & Emerson, P. E. (1964). The development of social attachments in infancy. *Monographs of the Society for Research in Child Development, 29*, 1–77.

Schieffelin, B. B., & Ochs, E. (1986). *Language socialization across cultures.* Cambridge: Cambridge University Press.

Schlegel, A., & Barry, H., III. (1991). *Adolescence: An anthropological inquiry.* New York: Free Press.

Schmittau, J. (1993). Vygotskian scientific concepts: Implications for mathematics education. *Focus on Learning Problems in Mathematics, 15*(2&3), 29–39.

Schmittau, J. (2003). Cultural-historical theory and mathematics education. In A. Kozulin, B. Gindis, V. S. Ageev, & S. Miller (Eds.), *Vygotsky's educational theory in cultural context* (pp. 225–245). Cambridge: Cambridge University Press.

Schoenfeld, A. H. (1985). *Mathematical problem solving*. New York: Academic Press.

Schoenfeld, A. H. (1992). Learning to think mathematically: Problem solving, metacognition, and sense making in mathematics. In P. H. Grouws (Ed.), *Handbook of research on mathematics teaching: A project of the National Council of Teachers of Mathematics* (pp. 334–370). New York: Macmillan.

Scribner, S. (1975). Recall of classical syllogisms: A cross-cultural investigation of error in logical problems. In R. J. Falmagne (Ed.), *Reasoning: Representation and process in children and adults* (pp. 153–173). Hillsdale, NJ: Erlbaum.

Scribner, S. (1977). Modes of thinking and ways of speaking: Culture and logic reconsidered. In P. N. Johnson-Laird & P. C. Wason (Eds.), *Thinking: Readings in cognitive science* (pp. 483–500). Cambridge: Cambridge University Press.

Scribner, S., & Cole, M. (1973). The cognitive consequences of formal and informal education. *Science, 182*, 553–559.

Scribner, S., & Cole, M. (1981). *The psychology of literacy*. Cambridge, MA: Harvard University Press.

Sears, R. R., Maccoby, E. E., & Levin, H. (1957). *Patterns of child rearing*. New York: Harper & Row.

Segall, M. H., Dasen, P. R., Berry, J. W., & Poortinga, Y. H. (1999). *Human behavior in global perspective: An introduction to cross-cultural psychology*. Boston: Allyn & Bacon. (Original work published 1990)

Sharp, D., Cole, M., & Lave, C. (1979). Education and cognitive development: The evidence from experimental research. *Monographs of the Society for Research in Child Development, 44*(1–2, ser. no. 178).

Shore, A. N. (1996). The experience-dependent maturation of a regulatory system in the orbital prefrontal cortex and the origin of developmental psychopathology. *Development and Psychopathology, 8*(1), 59–87.

Shulman, L. S., & Keislar, E. R. (Eds.). (1966). *Learning by discovery: A critical appraisal*. Chicago: Rand McNally.

Siegler, R. S. (1991). *Children's thinking*. Englewood Cliffs, NJ: Prentice Hall.

Sigman, M., & Sena, R. (1993). Pretend play in high-risk and developmentally delayed children. In M. N. Bornstein & A. Watson O'Reilly (Eds.), *The role of play in the development of thought* (pp. 29–42). San Francisco: Jossey-Bass.

Sinclair, H. (1970). The transition from sensory-motor behavior to symbolic activity. *Interchange, 1*, 119–126.

Skinner, B. F. (1953). *Science and human nehavior*. New York: Appleton-Century-Crofts.

Slade, A. (1987). A longitudinal study of maternal involvement and symbolic play during the toddler period. *Child Development, 58*, 367–375.

Slavina, L. S. (1948). O razvitii motivov igrovoi deayatelnosti v doshkolnom vozraste [On the development of play motives at preschool age]. *Izvestiya APN RSFSR, 14,* 11–29.

Smilansky, S., & Shefatya, L. (1990). *Facilitating play: A medium for promoting cognitive, socio-emotional, and academic development in young children.* Gaithersburg, MD: Psychosocial & Educational Publications.

Smolucha, F. (1992). The relevance of Vygotsky's theory of creative imagination for contemporary research on play. *Creativity Research Journal, 5*(1), 69–76.

Smolucha, L., & Smolucha, F. (1998). The social origins of mind: Post-Piagetian perspectives on pretend play. In O. N. Saracho & B. Spodek (Eds.), *Multiple perspectives on play in early childhood education* (pp. 34–58). Albany: State University of New York Press.

Snarey, J. R., Reimer, J., & Kohlberg, L. (1985). Development of social-moral reasoning among Kibbutz adolescents: A longitudinal cross-cultural study. *Developmental Psychology, 21*(1), 3–17.

Snow, C., de Blauw, A., & van Roosmalen, G. (1979). Talking and playing with babies: The role of ideologies of child-rearing, In M. Bullowa (Ed.), *Before speech: The beginning of interpersonal communication* (pp. 269–288). Cambridge: Cambridge University Press.

Sokoliansky, I. A. (1962). *Obuchenie slepoglukhonemykh detei* [Teaching blind-and-deaf children]. Moscow: Prosveschenie.

Sokolova, N. D. (1973). *Osobennosti rukovodstva igroi umstvenno otstalykh detei* [Characteristics of guidance of play of mentally retarded preschoolers]. Unpublished doctoral dissertation, Moscow, Russia.

Spitz, R. A. (1945). Hospitalism: An inquiry into the genesis of psychiatric conditions in early childhood. *Psychoanalytic Study of the Child, 1,* 53–74.

Spitz, R. A. (1946). Hospitalism: A follow-up report on investigation described in Volume 1, 1945. *Psychoanalytic Study of the Child, 2,* 113–117.

Steinberg, L. (1990). Autonomy, conflict, and harmony in the family relationship. In S. Feldman & G. Elliot (Eds.), *At the threshold: The developing adolescent* (pp. 255–276). Cambridge, MA: Harvard University Press.

Sternberg, R. J., & Detterman, D. K. (Eds.). (1986). *What is intelligence? Contemporary viewpoints on its nature and definition.* Norwood, NJ: Ablex.

Stetsenko, A., & Arievitch, I. (2002). Teaching, learning, and development: A post-Vygotskian perspective. In G. Wells & G. Claxton (Eds.), *Learning for life in the 21st century: Sociocultural perspectives on the future of education* (pp. 84–96). Malden, MA: Blackwell.

Sumita, K., Kitahara-Frisch, J., & Norikoshi, K. (1985). The acquisition of stone-tool use in captive chimpanzees. *Primates, 26,* 168–181.

Sylva, K., Roy, C., & Painter, M. (1980). *Childwatching at playground and nursery school.* Ypsilanti, MI: High/Scope.

Takeshita, H., & van Hooff, J. A. R. A. M. (2001). Tool use by chimpanzees (*Pan troglodytes*) of the Arnhem zoo community. In T. Matsuzawa (Ed.), *Primate origins of human cognition and behavior* (pp. 519–536). New York: Springer-Verlag.

Talyzina, N. F. (1981). *The psychology of learning.* Moscow: Progress. (Original work published 1975)

Talyzina, N. F. (2001). *Pedagogicheskaya psikhologiya* [Pedagogical psychology]. Moscow: Academia.

Tamis-LeMonda, C. S., & Bornstein, M. H. (1991). Individual variation, correspondence, stability, and change in mother and toddler play. *Infant Behavior and Development, 14,* 143–162.

Tamis-LeMonda, C. S., & Bornstein, M. H. (1993). Play and its relations to other mental functions in the child. In M. N. Bornstein & A. Watson O'Reilly (Eds.), *The role of play in the development of thought* (pp. 17–27). San Francisco: Jossey-Bass.

Tamis-LeMonda, C. S., Bornstein, M. H., Cyphers, L., Toda, S., & Ogino, M. (1992). Language and play at one year: A comparison of toddlers and mothers in the United States and Japan. *International Journal of Behavioral Development, 15*(1), 19–42.

Thorndike, E. L. (1914*). Educational psychology.* New York: Teachers College Press.

Tietjen, A. M., & Walker, L. J. (1985). Moral reasoning and leadership among men in a Papua New Guinea society. *Developmental Psychology, 21*(6), 982–992.

Tizard, B. (1977). Play: The child's way of learning? In B. Tizard & D. Harvey (Eds.), *Biology of play* (199–208). London: Heinemann.

Tolman, E. C., & Honzik, C. H. (1930). Introduction and removal of reward, and maze performance in rats. *University of California Publications in Psychology, 4,* 257–275.

Tomasello, M. (1999). *The cultural origins of human cognition.* Cambridge, MA: Harvard University Press.

Tomasello, M., Davis-Dasilva, M., Camak, L., & Bard, K. A. (1987). Observational learning of tool-use by young chimpanzees. *Journal of Human Evolution, 2,* 175–183.

Tomasello, M., & Farrar, J. (1986). Joint attention and early language. *Child Development, 57,* 1454–1463.

REFERENCES

Tomasello, M., Savage-Rumbaugh, S., & Kruger, A. C. (1993). Imitative learning of actions on objects by children, chimpanzees, and enculturated chimpanzees. *Child Development, 64*, 1688–1705.

Tomasello, M., Striano, T., & Rochat, P. (1999). Do young children use objects as symbols? *British Journal of Developmental Psychology, 17*(4), 563–584.

Tomasello, M., & Todd, J. (1983). Joint attention and lexical acquisition style. *First Language, 4*, 197–212.

Trevarthen, C. (1979). Communication and cooperation in early infancy: A description of primary intersubjectivity. In M. Bullowa (Ed.), *Before speech: The beginning of interpersonal communication* (pp. 321–347). Cambridge: Cambridge University Press.

Trevarthen, C. (1980). Instincts for human understanding and for cultural cooperation: Their development in infancy. In M. von Cranach, K. Foppa, W. Lepenies, & D. Ploog (Eds.), *Human ethology* (pp. 530–571). Cambridge: Cambridge University Press.

Trevarthen, C. (1988). Universal co-operative motives: How infants begin to know the language and culture of their parents. In G. Jahoda & I. M. Lewis (Eds.), *Acquiring culture: Cross cultural studies in child development* (pp. 37–90). London: Groom Helm.

Tudge, J. (1992). Vygotsky, the zone of proximal development, and peer collaboration: Implications for classroom practice. In L. C. Moll (Ed.), *Vygotsky and education: Instructional implications and applications of sociohistorical psychology* (pp. 155–172). Cambridge: Cambridge University Press.

Tulviste, P. (1991). *The cultural-historical development of verbal thinking*. Commack, NY: Nova Science.

Tulviste, P. (1999). Activity as an explanatory principle in cultural psychology. In S. Chaiklin, M. Hedegaard, & U. J. Jensen (Eds.), *Activity theory and social practice: Cultural-historical approaches* (pp. 66–78). Aarhus, Denmark: Aarhus University Press.

Unger, O., & Howes, C. (1988). Mother-child interactions and symbolic play between toddlers and their adolescent or mentally retarded mothers. *Occupational Therapy Journal of Research, 8*, 237–249.

Usova, A. P. (1976). *Rol igry v vospitanii detei* [The role of play in children's upbringing]. Moscow: Pedagogika.

van der Veer, R., & van Ijzendoom, M. H. (1988). Early childhood attachment and later problem solving: A Vygotskian perspective. In J. Valsiner (Ed.), *Child development within culturally structured environments, Vol. 1* (pp. 215–246). Norwood, NJ: Ablex.

Vauclair, J. (1993). Tool use, hand cooperation and the development of object manipulation in human and non-human primates. In A. F.

Kalverboer, B. Hopkins, & R. Geuze (Eds.), Motor development in early and later childhood: Longitudinal approaches (pp. 205–216). Cambridge: Cambridge University Press.

Venger, L. A. (Ed.). (1986). *Razvitie poznavatelnykh sposobnostei v protsesse doshkolnogo vospitaniya* [Development of cognitive abilities in the course of preschool education]. Moscow: Pedagogika.

Venger, L. A. & Kholmovskaya, V. V. (Eds.). (1978). *Diagnostika umstvennogo razvitiya doshkolnikov* [Evaluation of mental development of preschoolers]. Moscow: Pedagogika.

Vygotsky, L. S. (1930). Predislovie [Preface]. In W. Köhler, *Issledovanie intellecta chelovekoobraznykh obezian* (pp. I–XXIX). Moscow: Izdatelstvo Kommunisticheskoy Academii.

Vygotsky, L. S. (1956). *Izbrannye psikhologicheskie issledovaniya* [Selected psychological works]. Moscow: Izdatelstvo APN PSFSR.

Vygotsky, L. S. (1976). Play and its role in the mental development of the child. In J. S. Bruner, A. Jolly, & K. Sylva. (Eds.), *Play: Its role in development and evolution* (pp. 537–554). New York: Basic Books. (Original work published 1966)

Vygotsky, L. S. (1978). M. Cole, V. John-Steiner, S. Scribner, & E. Souberman (Eds.), *Mind in society: The development of higher psychological processes.* Cambridge, MA: Harvard University Press.

Vygotsky, L. S. (1981a). The genesis of higher mental functions. In J. V. Wertsch (Ed.), *The concept of activity in Soviet psychology* (pp. 144–188). Armonk, NY: Sharpe.

Vygotsky, L. S. (1981b). The instrumental method in psychology. In J. V. Wertsch (Ed.), *The concept of activity in Soviet Psychology* (pp. 134–143). Armonk, NY: Sharpe.

Vygotsky, L. S. (1984). *Sobranie sochineniy, Tom 4: Detskaya psikhologiya* [The collected works, Vol. 4: Child Psychology]. Moscow: Pedagogika.

Vygotsky, L. S. (1986). *Thought and language.* Cambridge, MA: MIT Press. (Original work published 1934)

Vygotsky, L. S. (1987). R. W. Rieber (Ed.), *The collected works of L. S. Vygotsky: Vol. 1: Problems of general psychology.* New York: Plenum. (Original work published 1982)

Vygotsky, L. S. (1997). *The collected works of L. S. Vygotsky: Vol. 4: The history of the development of higher mental functions*, R. W. Rieber (Ed.). New York: Plenum. (Original work published 1983)

Vygotsky, L. S. (1998). *The collected works of L. S. Vygotsky, Vol. 5: Child psychology*, R. W. Rieber (Ed.). New York: Plenum. (Original work published 1984)

REFERENCES

Vygotsky, L. S., & Luria, A. R. (1993). *Etudy po istorii povedeniya* [Problems of history of behavior]. Moscow: Pedagogika. (Original work published 1930)

Wachs, T. D. (1993). Multidimentional correlates of individual variability in play and exploration. In M. N. Bornstein & A. Watson O'Reilly (Eds.), *The role of play in the development of thought* (pp. 43–53). San Francisco: Jossey-Bass.

Walden, T. A., & Baxter, A. (1989). The effect of context and age on social referencing. *Child Development, 60*, 1511–1518.

Walker, L. J. (1980). Cognitive and perspective-taking prerequisites for moral development. *Child Development, 51*(1), 131–139.

Walker, L. J. (1986). Experiential and cognitive sources of moral development in adulthood. *Human Development, 29*(2), 113–124.

Walker, L. J., & Richards, B. S. (1979). Stimulating transitions in moral reasoning as a function of stage of cognitive development. *Developmental Psychology, 15*(2), 95–103.

Walker, L. J., Henning, K. H., & Krettenauer, T. (2000). Parent and peer contexts for children's moral reasoning development. *Child Development, 71*(4), 1033–1048.

Walker, L. J., & Taylor, J. H. (1991). Family interactions and the development of moral reasoning. *Child Development, 62*(2), 264–283.

Warren, S. F., Yoder, P. J., Gazdag, G. E., Kim, K., & Jones, H. (1993). Facilitating prelinguistic communication skills in young children with developmental delay. *Journal of Speech & Hearing Research, 36*(1), 83–97.

Watson, J. B. (1925). *Behaviorism.* New York: Norton.

Wehner, J. M., & Balogh, S. A. (2003). Genetic studies of learning and memory in mouse models. In R. Plomin, J. C. Defries, I. W. Craig, & P. McGuffin (Eds.), *Behavioral genetics in the postgenomic era* (pp. 103–121). Washington, DC: American Psychological Association.

Wells, G. (1985). *Language development in the preschool years.* Cambridge: Cambridge University Press.

Wells, G. (1999). *Dialogic inquiry: Towards a sociocultural practice and theory of education.* New York: Cambridge University Press.

Wells, G. (2002). Inquiry as an orientation for learning, teaching and teacher education. In G. Wells & G. Claxton (Eds.), *Learning for life in the 21st century: Sociocultural perspectives on the future of education* (pp. 197–210). Malden, MA: Blackwell.

Wells, G., Chang, G. L., & Maher, A. (1990). Creating classroom communities of literate thinkers. In S. Sharan (Ed.), *Cooperative learning: Theory and research* (pp. 95–121). New York: Praeger.

REFERENCES

Welteroth, S. (2002). Increasing play competence for very young children: How two early head start home visitors conceptualize and actualize their roles. In J. L. Roopnarine (Ed.), *Conceptual, social-cognitive, and contextual issues in the fields of play* (pp. 183–207). Westport, CT: Ablex.

Wertsch, J. V. (1998). *Mind in action.* New York: Oxford University Press.

Wertsch, J. V., & Tulviste, P. (1992). L. S. Vygotsky and contemporary developmental psychology. *Developmental Psychology, 28*(4), 548–557.

Whiten, A. (1998). Imitation of the sequential structure of actions by chimpanzees (*Pan troglodytes*). *Journal of Comparative Psychology, 112*(3), 270–281.

Whiten, A., & Ham, R. (1992). On the nature and evolution of imitation in the animal kingdom: Reappraisal of a century of research. *Advances in the Study of Behavior, 21,* 239–283.

Windschhitl, M. (2002). Framing constructivism in practice as the negotiation of dilemmas: An analysis of the conceptual, pedagogical, cultural, and political challenges facing teachers. *Review of Educational Research, 72*(2), 131–175.

Winnicott, D. W. (1982). *Playing and reality.* New York: Tavistock.

Wolfe, J. B. (1936). Effectiveness of token rewards for chimpanzees. *Comparative Psychology Monographs, 12.*

Wolman, B. B. (1998). *Adolescence: Biological and psychological perspectives.* Westport, CT: Greenwood.

Yoder, P. (1992). Communication intervention with children who have disabilities. *Kennedy Center News, 21,* 1–2.

Youngblade, L. M., & Dunn, J. (1995). Individual differences in children's play with mother and siblings: Links to relationships and understanding of other people's feelings and beliefs. *Child Development, 66,* 1472–1492.

Zak, A. Z. (1984). *Razvitie teoreticheskogo myshleniya u mladshikh shkolnikov* [Development of theoretical thought in elementary school children]. Moscow: Pedagogika.

Zaporozhets, A. V. (1986a). Razvitie proizvolnykh dvizheniy [Development of voluntary actions]. In A. V. Zaporozhets, *Izbrannye psikhologicheskie trudy, Tom 2* (pp. 5–233). Moscow: Pedagogika.

Zaporozhets, A. V. (1986b). Deystvie i intellekt [Action and intelligence]. In A. V. Zaporozhets, *Izbrannye psikhologicheskie trudy, Tom 1* (pp. 177–190). Moscow: Pedagogika.

Zaporozhets, A. V. (1986c). Razvitie myshleniya [The development of thinking]. In A. V. Zaporozhets, *Izbrannye psikhologicheskie trudy, Tom 1* (pp. 200–215). Moscow: Pedagogika.

REFERENCES

Zaporozhets, A. V. (1997). Principal problems in the ontogeny of the mind. *Journal of Russian and East European Psychology, 35*(1), 53–94. (Original work published 1978)

Zaporozhets, A. V., & Elkonin, D. B. (Eds.). (1971). *The psychology of preschool children*. Cambridge, MA: MIT Press. (Original work published 1964)

Zaporozhets, A. V., & Lisina, M. I. (Eds.). (1974). *Razvitie obscheniya u doshkolnikov* [The development of communication in preschoolers]. Moscow: Pedagogika.

Zarbatany, L., & Lamb, M. E. (1985). Social referencing as a function of information source: Mothers versus strangers. *Infant Behavior and Development, 8*, 25–33.

Zeigarnik, B. V. (1986). *Patopsikhologiya* [Clinical psychology]. Moscow: Izdatelstvo MGU.

Zhurova, L. E. (1978). *Obuchenie gramote* v detskom sadu [Teaching reading and writing at the kindergarten]. Moscow: Pedagogika.

Author Index

AUTHOR INDEX

AUTHOR INDEX

Subject Index

actions, 54, 63, 70. *See also* conversion of
    actions into activities;
    object-centered actions

activity
    child–adult joint, 62, 63, 70, 73, 74,
      127, 231, 239
    child independent exploratory, 5, 6,
      19, 229
    difference between animal and
      human, 15–17, 45–46, 52–55,
      63–68
    leading, 71–73, 75–76, 231–233,
      239
    See also adolescence, peer interactions
      as leading activity in; conversion
      of actions into activities;
      emotional interactions of
      infants and caregivers as leading
      activity in infancy; learning at
      school as leading activity in
      middle childhood; object-
      centered activity as leading in
      toddlerhood; sociodramatic play
      as leading activity in early
      childhood

activity theory
    as an elaboration of Vygotsky's theory,
      12–13, 71–76, 229–233

disregard of the role of heredity in, 14,
    26–28, 76, 213, 228, 233–235,
    238–239

adolescence
    and self-consciousness. *See* identity
      formation and self-consciousness
    and identity formation. *See* identity
      formation
    and mediation. *See* mediation in
      adolescence
    and moral development. *See*
      adolescent moral development
    and motives. *See* adolescent motives
    neo-Vygotskian analysis of, 204,
      208–213, 217, 221–222,
      226–227
    peer interactions as leading activity in,
      210–212, 227–228
    and puberty, 204, 206, 213, 222–223,
      227–228, 239
    and "the self." *See* identity formation
      and "the self"
    and "storm and stress." *See* adolescent
      "storm and stress"
    Vygotsky's view of, 204–207,
      212–213
    Western approaches to analysis of,
      203–204, 205, 206, 213–227

SUBJECT INDEX